UNDERSTANDING AND HELPING FAMILIES

A Cognitive-Behavioral Approach

UNDERSTANDING AND HELPING FAMILIES

A Cognitive-Behavioral Approach

Andrew I. Schwebel
Ohio State University

Mark A. Fine
University of Dayton

LEA LAWRENCE ERLBAUM ASSOCIATES, PUBLISHERS
1994   Hillsdale, New Jersey   Hove and London

Lawrence Erlbaum Associates, Inc., Publishers
365 Broadway
Hillsdale, New Jersey 07642

Library of Congress Cataloging-in-Publication Data

Schwebel, Andrew I.
  Understanding and helping families : a cognitive-behavioral
approach / Andrew I. Schwebel, Mark A. Fine.
      p.   cm.
  Includes bibliographical references and index.
  ISBN 0-8058-1225-3 (cloth). — ISBN 0-8058-1449-3 (pbk.)
  1. Family psychotherapy. 2. Cognitive therapy. 3. Family—
Psychological aspects. I. Fine, Mark A. II. Title.
RC488.5.S384 1994
616.89′156—dc20   93-32023
                                                          CIP

Books published by Lawrence Erlbaum Associates are printed on acid-free
paper, and their bindings are chosen for strength and durability.

Printed in the United States of America
10 9 8 7 6 5 4 3 2 1

CONTENTS

v

PREFACE

Social scientists have made great progress over the past few decades in developing models and theories to explain how individuals both shape and respond to the environment in which they live. Family scientists and proponents of the cognitive-behavioral models of psychology are two of the groups of individuals who have played major roles in moving the social sciences forward, especially in recent years.

Our goal in writing this volume was to combine insights from the systems views of the family unit with insights from the perspective of psychology. Not coincidentally, the writings of family scientists as well as those of the proponents of the cognitive-behavioral models in psychology were the two sources from which we drew most heavily. The product we sought was a fresh perspective that would enable readers to understand in new ways both the functioning of the individual in the family unit and the functioning of the family unit itself.

In pursuing this outcome, we had several audiences in mind. The fact that we are both teaching faculty members motivated us to present the material in ways that would make the volume useful as a text in a college or university classroom. Further, as professionals who consult outside the academic setting, we wanted to describe our theory and approach in ways that were developed enough to be useful to practitioners, family educators, and researchers and, at the same time, concrete enough to be of value to students and laypersons.

As you will see from reading the first chapter of the text, we bridge the chasm that has existed in the literature between individual psychology and the family systems perspective. We accomplish this by exploring the reciprocal nature of the relationship between the individual and his or her family. We suggest how readers can gain new insights into the individual, through an appreciation of his or her family, and enhanced understandings of the family, through an appreciation of the cognitions held by the individual.

Another challenge we addressed was to develop a cognitive-behavioral approach to the family that had wide generalizability and which, therefore, could be broadly applied in understanding individuals' behaviors, regardless of their personalities or roles in the family unit. To accomplish this, we developed a theory (and related applications) that functions much like computer software programs. That is, the theory and the software stand ready to perform the jobs their users want done but do not operate until their users supply the specific data that are relevant to the case or questions at hand.

Put another way, the cognitive-behavioral theory of the family presented in this volume enables readers to "get a handle" on the uncountable number of cognitions a person holds about family life and how these cognitions affect that individual's functioning within the family unit. The theory does this by defining a set of concepts that can be used to organize family-related cognitions and by specifying both how these concepts function and how they are related to each other. Once users of this cognitive-behavioral theory of the family "plug in" the relevant data about a particular person (e.g., themselves, their clients, or their students), they will gain new understandings about that individual's functioning. Users will also be able to understand the functioning of that particular person's family unit in new ways.

We sought to develop a cognitive-behavioral theory of the family (and associated applications) that could serve as a starting point for those interested in understanding and helping families. The approach we took in this effort was intended more to be heuristic in nature than to be exhaustive. From the outset, we believed that if we could successfully develop such a theory, others could build their own unique ideas upon what we presented, either in their research studies, in their classroom or professional work, or in their understanding of their own family.

By utilizing the theory we present, we hope that readers will gain new insights. We hope that readers, in turn, whether they are faculty members, family educators, or researchers, can use their new perspective to help those they work with better understand families and why individuals behave in certain ways in the family unit.

ACKNOWLEDGMENTS

Over the years during which we developed the ideas presented in this volume, we received support and help from dozens of individuals. We wish to express our deepest thanks to many people who so freely gave of their support, time, ideas, and assistance. Our wives, Carol and Eve, deserve much credit. They were very supportive throughout the process and helped by providing input on the clarity of drafts of the book as it was being developed. We also want to thank our children, David, Sara, Aubrey, and Julia and our parents, Bernice, Milton, Ruth, Marilynn, and Burril, for their patience, loving support, and generous help. Finally, we want to thank our brothers and sisters, Bob and Claudia, Dan and Anita, Paul and Karen, and David and Beth.

Over the past several years, we have benefited greatly from discussions with our colleagues and students about families and family members. In this connection, we thank Marilyn Coleman, Brenda Donnelly, Ryan Dunn, David Gately, Larry Ganong, Larry Kurdek, Stephanie McIver, Barry Moss, Maureena Renner, Gregory Smith, Bryce Sullivan, Pat Voydanoff, and Joan Williams for helping us to clarify and advance our thinking with regard to the ideas presented in this volume.

Finally, we want to acknowledge the support provided by our publisher, Lawrence Erlbaum, the thoughtful assistance we received from Hollis Heimbouch and Judith Amsel, the quality editorial attention Robin Weisberg paid to the manuscript, and the energetic assistance provided by Sharon Levy.

Andrew I. Schwebel
Mark A. Fine

I

THEORETICAL AND
CONCEPTUAL PERSPECTIVES

This book contains two parts. Part I has four chapters that provide the conceptual context for the cognitive-behavioral family (CBF) model. Chapter 1 explores the many ways to understand the family unit and the various forms it takes, the functions it serves, and the changes it experiences. Chapter 2 describes the cognitive-behavioral perspective and how it has been used to help individuals deal with personal problems, relationship difficulties, and other adjustment challenges. The chapter briefly reviews the history of this approach and the thinking of several influential scholars. Chapters 3 and 4 provide a detailed description of the cognitive-behavioral perspective as we have applied it to understanding families. More specifically, chapter 3 presents an overview of the CBF model and its major tenets, whereas chapter 4 focuses on specific types of family-related cognitions that are central to the model. As a unit, these chapters provide a foundation for the exploration in Part II of applications of the CBF model in research, theory, assessment, family life education, counseling, therapy, and so forth.

1

THE STRUGGLE TO
UNDERSTAND THE FAMILY

Excitement peaked in the sanctuary as Candy and Tom stood nervously in front of their pastor and lovingly exchanged vows. The guests wore smiles on their faces at the moment when the two of them became Mr. and Mrs. Johnson, except for a scattered few who found themselves shedding tears of joy.

As the ceremony drew to a close and Candy and Tom stepped down from the pulpit a married couple, each of them began a new task, adjusting to the demands of their freshly created circumstances and to the environment that they would be creating in the weeks and years ahead. This book focuses on the processes by which spouses, like the Johnsons, work to build and maintain healthy family relationships. Using a cognitive-behavioral perspective, we delineate a model that shows how individuals proceed, step-by-step, to create shared and mostly unspoken rules that enable them to live in ways they find at least acceptable, if not fulfilling.

BASIC CONCEPTS IN UNDERSTANDING THE FAMILY

Most definitions of family have focused on the formal nature of the relations between individuals. Formal relations are ones that are either biologically created (e.g., parents and children) or institutionally sanctioned through law (e.g., marriage). For example, *The American Heritage Dictionary* (1985) defined *family* as "a fundamental social group in society consisting especially of a man and woman and their offspring; a group of persons sharing a common ancestry; lineage; or all the members of a household under one roof" (p. 488). Family scientists use similar definitions. For example, Beutler, Burr,

Bahr, and Herrin (1989) defined the family realm as that which "is created by the birth process and the establishment of ties across generations" (p. 806).

Individuals' Working Definitions

When Candy and Tom exchanged rings and thereby established their family of procreation, each of them had a dictionary-level, working understanding of the concept of a family that emphasized biological and legal bonds. Like most people, neither one had ever spent any period of time thinking about "the family" as a social entity or considering or seriously talking to each other about what they expected would be involved in building and maintaining a healthy family unit. It never occurred to them to invest time in such efforts because each of them "assumed," without considering the matter, that marriage and family building comes naturally and are not tasks for which one prepares.

In this regard, Tom and Candy are typical of individuals in this society. Imagine randomly selecting 100 people, whether married or single, and asking them a series of questions about family life. You would undoubtedly discover that, beyond homing in on the issues of "love and being in love," individuals have thought little about what it takes to build and maintain a healthy family.

For example, imagine the response one would expect to the following question: "I'm trying to understand families. Please tell me enough about your family to give me a sense of what it is like to be a member." Most respondents would smile, wondering why you asked them what they think is a simple question with such an obvious answer. You would discover, however, that nearly all of them would struggle before they supplied you with the information necessary to effectively address your question.

Although the respondents queried would verbalize their replies in various ways and emphasize somewhat different factors, we suspect that there would be regularities in their reactions and comments. First, most people would enjoy sharing information about this important aspect of their lives and would experience little difficulty at the outset. Almost inevitably, they would begin by naming and describing family members, perhaps identifying their occupations, personality characteristics, and likes and dislikes. Next, respondents might comment about the family atmosphere—noting how much love and caring exists or is lacking between and among people.

After making basic points like these, however, respondents would experience a sense of having reached a "dead end" in their report. Nothing else would readily come to mind. They might say, "we're typical, you know," and would soon conclude that they had already shared the relevant material necessary to convey an understanding of their particular family.

In sum, the respondents would have focused mostly on the individuals, and a bit on what connects family members. It would not have occurred to them to mention the work that their family unit performs and how it is structured to accomplish these tasks.

A Broader Conception of Family

Whether held by dictionary authors, family scientists, or laypersons, we consider views of the family that focus only on formal ties as unduly limiting. In this book, consistent with Aldous and Dumon (1990), the concept of *family* is broadened to include intimate, committed relationships that may not involve biological or legal ties (e.g., homosexual and cohabiting couples). Marciano and Sussman (1991) referred to families that meet this broad definition as "wider families" (p. 1). Consequently, rather than focus only on the formal aspects of relationships, we place our emphasis on the nature of the commitments and relationships among individuals (i.e., interpersonal processes). Goldenberg and Goldenberg (1991) provided a definition that is consistent with our broader focus:

> . . . [the family] has evolved a set of rules, is replete with assigned and ascribed roles for its members, has an organized power structure, has developed intricate overt and covert forms of communication, and has elaborated ways of negotiating and problem solving that permit various tasks to be performed effectively. The relationship between members of this microculture is deep and multilayered, and is based largely on a shared history, shared internalized perceptions and assumptions about the world, and a shared sense of purpose. Within such a system, individuals are tied to one another by powerful, durable, reciprocal emotional attachments and loyalties that may fluctuate in intensity over time but nevertheless persist over the lifetime of the family. (p. 3)

The elements of this definition emphasize the processes that characterize families and are relevant to traditional and nontraditional families alike. Even if pressed, the Johnsons and most of the 100 randomly selected respondents would be unable to identify many of the ideas detailed in this definition. This is at least partly because much of individuals' knowledge about how their family operates is stored at a low level of conscious awareness and is not easily accessed. Because Candy and Tom, like most of the randomly drawn respondents in the imaginary survey described earlier, think of the family unit in limited terms, they are handicapped in diagnosing family problems they encounter and in fixing them.

THE UNIVERSALITY AND FLEXIBILITY OF FAMILIES

Societies can survive only if they find ways to organize human beings so they can work together productively and live harmoniously, relatively free of fear from whomever or whatever might do them harm. This is true whether the societies are situated in the densest tropical rain forests of Brazil or in the most advanced industrialized nations of the 20th or 21st centuries.

The family unit has played an instrumental part in helping solve the complex problems of human organization, serving as the most basic social institution in the multitude of societies that human beings have created around the world and over the ages. In fact, Murdock (1949) argued that among human beings, the nuclear family is a universal social grouping. He stated, "Either as the sole prevailing form of the family or as the basic unit from which more complex familiar forms are compounded it exists as a distinct and strongly functional group in every known society. No exception, at least, has come to light in the 250 representative cultures surveyed for the present study" (p. 2).

In the decades since Murdock (1949) made this statement, some social scientists have challenged his position, citing a few possible exceptions. Even so, the family can be viewed as societies' institutional workhorse and the most basic unit of human organization.

Variation in Family Forms

The two-parent nuclear family form was the typical one some 35–40 years ago. Stereotyped versions of that form were portrayed in situation comedies aired initially in the 1950s and 1960s, but that are still being shown on reruns. Examples include "Leave It to Beaver," "Father Knows Best," and "Ozzie and Harriet."

In contrast to the statistics of that era, a relatively small percentage of today's families are of that kind. For example, 44% of American women work outside of their home and more than 50% of all youngsters in the United States dwell in households in which both their parents or their single-parent household head work(s) (Select Committee on Children, Youth, and Families, 1987). Of course, the number of single-parent households and stepfamilies is substantially greater as well.

Family units of today have a variety of forms, all of which involve individuals living under one roof. These include:

1. The nuclear family: two adult partners and frequently, but not always, children.

2. The single-parent family: one adult and one or more children. This household, usually formed after divorce, out-of-wedlock birth, or the death of one parent, is sometimes connected to another household that contains the second biological parent or other adults significant to household members.

3. The stepfamily: two adult partners, children from one or more previous relationship(s) and, sometimes, children from the present marriage.

4. The cohabitation family: two unmarried adults who are committed to a long-term relationship and, sometimes, children from this union or from previous relationships. This can include heterosexual or homosexual partners.

5. Cross-generational family: two or more adults from different generations of a family, who intend to share a household during the foreseeable future and, sometimes, children.

Of course, these changes in prevalent family forms in recent decades did not take place in a vacuum. Rather, they were a product of the complex industrial, technological, and social changes that were unfolding, including those that forged the new prevailing attitudes about women working outside of the home, about divorce, and about single adults. Naturally, as the make-up of family units began to shift, this, in turn, promoted other changes in society.

For example, society's acceptance of or tolerance for this variety of family forms has provided new lifestyle opportunities for people and, at the same time, has impacted on the nature of the beliefs that they hold. Today, individuals dissatisfied with their marriages may soon consider divorce whereas some years ago, when the idea of divorce was "frowned upon," they might have held beliefs and values that would have discouraged them from separating, instead directing them to try harder or to accept their plight. Similarly, decades ago pregnant single women might have felt great shame, been sent to a home for unwed mothers, and been encouraged to have their babies adopted immediately after delivery. Today, many individuals seek to become single parents and value the goal of raising their children in a one-parent household.

The centrality of the family as a social institution has been challenged by some in light of the fact that in the United States, since the 1950s, the divorce rate has more than doubled, although the rate has seemed to reach a plateau (Norton & Moorman, 1987). Further, the number of out-of-wedlock births has also increased dramatically during this same time period (Moore, 1989).

Prompted by statistics like these, social critics, popular writers, and members of the media have argued that, at least in these contemporary times, the family is "dead" or, at minimum, doomed to passing quickly into extinction.

Although great changes have taken place in the nature of families in American and in Western societies, contrary to the predictions of some, the family unit has not passed into oblivion (Fine, 1992). For example, marriage remains as popular as ever. Data indicate that more than 90% of American adults will marry during their lifetime (Norton & Moorman, 1987). Among those who divorce, about 76% of the men and 83% of the women remarry within 5 years (Glick, 1984). One reason why people desire family life is that it provides a setting in which they can meet their needs.

THE FUNCTIONS OF FAMILIES

No other social institution yet invented has been able to equal the family in its ability to satisfy the diverse needs of its members while, at the same time, meeting the needs of society. To accomplish the need-meeting role given to it by society, the typical family unit performs many of these basic tasks:

1. Providing shelter, food, clothing, and health care for its members.
2. Meeting family costs and allocating such resources as time, space, and facilities, according to each member's needs.
3. Determining who does what in the support, management, and care of the home and its members.
4. Assuring each member's socialization through the internalization of increasingly mature roles in the family and beyond.
5. Establishing ways of interacting, communicating, and expressing affection and sexuality, within limits acceptable to society.
6. Bearing (or adopting) and rearing children; incorporating and releasing family members appropriately.
7. Relating to school, church, and community life; establishing policies for including in-laws, relatives, guests, and friends.
8. Maintaining morale and motivation, rewarding achievement, meeting personal and family crises, setting attainable goals, and developing family loyalties and values (Duvall, 1977).

Families that perform these tasks satisfactorily benefit both their members and society as a whole. Society benefits because the individual family members contribute their productivity to the work force and because such families socialize children who, in the future, will become the adults charged with the responsibility of maintaining society in its present or in an improved form. At the same time, members benefit because, as a result of the tasks they as a family accomplish, they create a comfortable setting in which they can meet their needs.

Family Roles

Accomplishing the tasks outlined in Duvall's (1977) list is time consuming and requires determination and psychological investments that extend over a period of decades. For instance, one family member or more must fill the provider role over his or her lifetime to supply the financial resources necessary to provide food, clothing, and shelter for all family members. Nye et al. (1976) identified eight roles that they believed had to be filled by families if their units were to function in effective and healthy ways:

1. Housekeeper role: This entails completing the many and varied tasks required to keep the family's living quarters in order as well as the chores associated with keeping family members fed, their clothes clean and available, and so forth.

2. Provider role: This involves earning the monetary and other material resources necessary to support the family members.

3. Child-care role: This involves "the physical and psychological maintenance of the child . . . [and] [a]ctivities such as keeping the child clean, fed, and warm, as well as protected from physical dangers and frightening experiences . . ." (p. 34).

4. Child-socialization role: This "is limited to the social and psychological development of the child. It refers to those processes and activities within the family which contribute to developing the child into a competent, social and moral person" (p. 33).

5. Kinship role: This role concerns the maintenance of relationships with extended family members through communication, participating in holiday gatherings, and so forth. Support and assistance is exchanged in the kinship relationships and a sense of identity is developed.

6. Therapeutic role: This consists of assisting other family members in dealing with the day-to-day difficulties they encounter. When practicing this role, the help-giver may engage in careful listening, offer sympathy or assistance, and express reassurance or affection.

7. Recreational role: This concerns organizing family members and involving them in leisure-time activities.

8. Sexual role: This role is unique in that it, alone, applies to the heads of the household, and it subsumes their exchange of affection and sexual gratification.

The amount of labor required to fill these roles adequately and the importance of the role varies across families and within families, over time. For example, the amount of work necessary to adequately fill the child-care, child-socialization, recreation, housekeeper, therapeutic, and provider roles would depend greatly on the number of children in a household, their ages, and their level of health. Table 1.1 shows how the importance of each role and the amount of work it demands changes over the course of a family's developmental history (Vess, Moreland, & Schwebel, 1985).

THE ROLE OF COGNITIONS IN FAMILY LIFE

As discussed further in chapter 2, cognitions are thoughts, ideas, beliefs, values, expectations, and perceptions and many cognitions play important roles in the development of a family and the interaction of its members. Some of the

TABLE 1.1
Life Cycle Family Changes

Stage of the Family Life Cycle	Stage-Critical Family Developmental Tasks	Roles							
		P	H	T	R	S	K	CC	CS
Married Couple	Establishing a mutually satisfying marriage Adjusting to pregnancy and the promise of parenthood Fitting into the kin network								
Childbearing	Having, adjusting to, and encouraging the development of infants Establishing a satisfying home for both parents and infant(s)								
Preschool Age	Adapting to the critical needs and interests of preschool children in stimulating, growth-promoting ways Coping with energy depletion and lack of privacy as parents								
School Age	Fitting into community of school-age families in constructive ways Encouraging children's educational achievement								
Teenage	Balancing freedom with responsibility as teenagers mature and emancipate themselves Establishing postparental interests and careers								
Launching Center	Releasing young adults into work, military service, college, marriage, etc., with appropriate rituals and assistance Maintaining a supportive home base								
Middle-Age Parents	Rebuilding marriage relationship Maintaining kin ties with older and younger generations								
Aging Family Members	Coping with bereavement and living alone Closing family home or adapting it to aging Adjusting to retirement								

Note. From Vess, Moreland, and Schwebel (1985. Reprinted by permission of Baywood Publishing); based on the ideas of Nye et al. (1976) and Duvall (1977). Width of band indicates relative importance of the role within a given stage and the amount of labor or work family members must do to fill the role. P = Provider; H = Housekeeper; T = Therapeutic; R = Recreation; S = Sexual; K = Kinship; CC = Child Care; CS = Child Socialization.

vast number of marriage- and family-related cognitions Candy and Tom each hold shaped their choice of partner. Others provide them with expectations about what their relationship "should" and "will" be like, what they "should" be getting from and putting into their marriage, what every important aspect of their relationship "should" be like, and so forth. For example, Tom's cognitions tell him that to have a happy marriage, the husband should attend to traditional responsibilities, should allow his wife to voice her concerns and state what meets her needs and, in turn, she should recognize that he has "final say" in areas ranging from the budget to the bedroom.

Candy's cognitions, in contrast, tell her that to have a happy marriage she should follow tradition but she should have rights and responsibilities equal to Tom's. Further, she believes that she should have primary responsibility for all decisions regarding the home and child rearing and equal input with regard to decisions about vacations, sex, and major purchases.

To state the obvious, Candy and Tom have major differences in what their cognitions tell them about interactions in "happy families." That this is true is not surprising. As discussed further in chapter 3, like any two partners, they grew up in unique and different environments, had distinctive sets of experiences, and came to understand their world in a unique way.

As different as their marriage- and family-related cognitions appear in the areas previously mentioned, Candy and Tom have many similar and compatible cognitions that will ease their adjustment. In this regard they were aided by two factors that operate in partner selection: endogamy (Buss, 1985) and homogamy (Honeycutt, 1986). Respectively, these are the tendencies to marry an individual who comes from the same social group and who has similar personal characteristics. Because Candy and Tom share the same ethnic background, social class, age group, religion, and so forth, they are more likely to have many similar cognitions (including attitudes, values, and beliefs) than partners who do not.

However, regardless of similarities in spouses' backgrounds and the apparent compatibility of their values and goals, they inevitably encounter conflict that is directly related to differences in their marriage-related cognitions. For example, as Tom and Candy go about their day-by-day business of sharing time, money, space, and other resources, and as they divide household chores, conflict will inevitably develop over what unfolds. Most differences will be minor but, inevitably, more substantial ones will emerge.

For example, during the first weekend in their apartment Candy made an apple pie. Sunday evening Tom asked Candy if she wanted part of the last piece that was left. She said "No." As he put it on a plate he yelled out to Candy in the living room, "Are you sure?" "Yes," she replied. As he ate the last bite she walked into the kitchen and said unhappily, "You didn't even save a piece for me." Tom could not understand her reaction. Weeks later the Johnsons figured out the problem developed because in Candy's family of origin the protocol was to ask three times before assuming the answer to this type of question was truly "No."

More serious differences develop when one partner finds that what he or she is receiving from or giving to the relationship does not match what his or her cognitions dictate should or ought to happen in marriage. As elaborated in chapter 1, when individuals sense such disparities, their family problem-solving cognitions come into play, as do cognitions that dictate their level of flexibility and toleration for situations unlike what they expected.

For example, as was inevitable because Candy and Tom's cognitions differed so, soon after they returned from their honeymoon, they experienced conflict over who would make decisions about their budget. Fortunately for the Johnsons, both spouses were relatively adept as problem solvers, although Tom's impatience as a listener sometimes hampered him.

Another obstacle stemmed from differences in Candy's and Tom's family-related problem-solving cognitions. Tom's direct him to problem solve only after a concrete problem has emerged and has caused visible upset in a family member. More specifically, his problem-solving cognitions tell him to address the problem only after it is verbalized in a way that conveys that the speaker has experienced discomfort, pain, or another type of hurt. Candy's family-related problem-solving cognitions, in contrast, tell her to monitor family members' interactions and to anticipate and address problems that are brewing. When she does this and describes a problem-in-the-making to Tom, she smiles (as directed by her cognitions so she can concomitantly communicate caring). Tom discounts Candy's comments in this situation because she is smiling (Tom's cognitions tell him that smiling people have no serious concerns) and because his problem-solving cognitions do not direct him to look ahead and avoid problems. Therefore, he typically responds with, "I don't see any serious problem. You're imagining things. I don't know what you are talking about."

Figure 1.1 shows that the nature (content and flexibility) of the marriage- and family-related cognitions that each partner (Candy and Tom) holds is important to their ability to resolve conflicts, adjust, and find marital and family happiness. Put another way, spouses' family-related cognitions, including their family-related problem-solving cognitions, shape the course of their adjustment by mediating their ability as a couple to provide, obtain, process, and act upon information about themselves in their relationship. Applying Weiner's (1954) ideas about how feedback loops allow systems to regulate themselves, it is clear that how effectively the Johnsons (or any couple) can adjust is limited or enhanced by how well they access and use information as it develops, moment by moment, in their relationship.

Candy and Tom's Problem: When should they fly home?

Candy: Tom, I think we should fly home late on December 24th.

Tom: (assertively) But Mom's birthday is on the 23rd.

Candy: (Feeling badly for failing in a task important to her, remembering her mother-in-law's birthday, but, at the same time, not wanting to miss her Christmas Eve office party.) I knew that, but I just did not want to push you at work by suggesting that we leave for home a day early.

Candy and Tom's Ability to Find a Solution Depends On: The flexibility and effective meshing of their individual, family-related cognitions, including their family-related problem-solving cognitions. Some cognitions they hold are listed below:

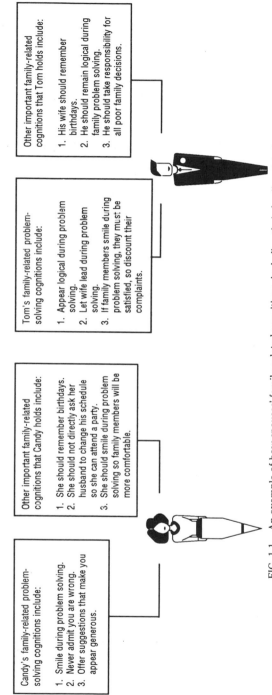

Candy's family-related problem-solving cognitions include:

1. Smile during problem solving.
2. Never admit you are wrong.
3. Offer suggestions that make you appear generous.

Other important family-related cognitions that Candy holds include:

1. She should remember birthdays.
2. She should not directly ask her husband to change his schedule so she can attend a party.
3. She should smile during problem solving so family members will be more comfortable.

Tom's family-related problem-solving cognitions include:

1. Appear logical during problem solving.
2. Let wife lead during problem solving.
3. If family members smile during problem solving, they must be satisfied, so discount their complaints.

Other important family-related cognitions that Tom holds include:

1. His wife should remember birthdays.
2. He should remain logical during family problem solving.
3. He should take responsibility for all poor family decisions.

FIG. 1.1. An example of how spouses' family-related cognitions, including their family-related problem-solving cognitions, shape the course of their adjustment.

A LIFE-SPAN DEVELOPMENTAL PERSPECTIVE

To be fully understood, the family unit must be considered in the context of the life-span developmental perspective. The Johnson family of today, for instance, will look vastly different on many dimensions 5, 10, and 20 years hence. Viewing the Johnsons at a given point in time is informative, but has limitations that parallel those faced by the scientist who examines a photograph of a caterpillar to understand a butterfly. A movie picture that captures the insect before, during, and after the metamorphosis would provide the scientists with a fuller and more useful set of data.

When viewing the family from a developmental perspective, one can identify a pattern of change or a course of movement through which each particular family unit passes as its life as a social unit unfolds. For heterosexual couples in Western societies, the inception of a given unit occurs when two individuals, who will eventually date, first meet. At that point their history together begins. At a later point in time, the two individuals will decide to change the nature of the relationship by having a date. Put another way, they leave the stage of friendship or acquaintance, in which they had been, and make a qualitative change in their relationship by entering the dating stage.

As they continue to date and court each other's affection, the development of their relationship proceeds in quantitative ways. Eventually, however, they reach the point at which one or both of them initiate another qualitative change. Specifically, one partner, or both, decide(s) to no longer romantically date the other and their progress toward becoming a family terminates or, alternatively, both decide to move one qualitative step forward in the relationship and they begin seeing each other exclusively.

The cycle begins anew as the two individuals now relate to one another with a new sense of future, fostering further quantitative development of their relationship. In time, they reach the point at which one or both of them are ready for another qualitative change, ending the relationship or moving it one further step forward, into engagement, and making public their permanent commitment to each other. And so the relationship develops, with quantitative and qualitative changes propelling the couple to marriage and through the predictable stages that partners encounter as the years go by. Inevitably, of course, every marriage and love relationship ends, either through death or divorce, although the families created by the unions may continue, especially if the partnership gave birth to or adopted children.

Candy and Tom and the other couples in the imagined survey would be advantaged in many ways by understanding the normal course of family development and what typically happens as the developmental process unfolds. For instance, they would know that when a family's normal course of development is interrupted (Carter & McGoldrick, 1989), problems often occur and that as families pass through transition points (Haley, 1973), family members are often stressed. Such awareness could lead informed family members to be vigilant during times of change in their family unit's development and to be prepared to prevent or cope with any problems that emerge.

Developmental Stages in the Family

Several authors have named and described a set of stages that they believe family units encounter as they pass through the family life cycle. Lewis (1979) described these six: courtship, the early marriage stage, the early parenthood stage, the adolescent children stage, the empty nest stage, and the postretirement stage.

Duvall (1977) identified eight stages and associated them with their approximate duration in time: the married couple stage, which she suggested lasted typically about 2 years; the childbearing family stage, which runs 2.5 years, from the birth of the oldest child until that individual reaches 30 months; the family with preschool children stage, lasting 3.5 years, from the oldest child's 30th month to his or her 6th-year birthday; the family with school-children stage, running the 7 years from the oldest child's 6th through 13th birthdays; the family with teenagers stage, lasting the 7 years from the oldest child's 13th through 20th birthdays; the family as launching center stage, running the 8 years from when the first child leaves home until the last leaves; the family with middle-age parents stage, covering the 15 years between the beginning of empty nest until retirement; and, finally, the aging family members stage, running about 10–15 years from retirement to the death of both spouses.

Another model for understanding the stages that families pass through over the course of their life cycle is provided by Carter and McGoldrick (1989). They also described the emotional adjustment that family members need to make as they move through the stages and the second-order shifts that are necessary in individuals and in the unit as they move forward. Table 1.2 conveys key aspects of the Carter and McGoldrick model. An inspection of it suggests how Tom and Candy and other couples would benefit by having a working knowledge of this model.

As Table 1.2 suggests, family units can move forward only when individuals take important steps in their own personal adjustment and development. For example, for unattached young adults to proceed from the first to the second stage in family development, they must do the work necessary to achieve the age-appropriate adult development at this point in life; that is, they must separate from the family of origin, learn how to develop an intimate relationship and trust the self to do so, and find a job and adjust to the world of work. When these personal developmental tasks are success-

TABLE 1.2
Developmental Stages and Tasks in the Family Life Cycle

Stages of the Family Life Cycle	Developmental Tasks
1. Beginning Family	a. Differentiating from family of origin
	b. Negotiating boundaries between friends and relatives
	c. Resolving conflict between individual and couple's needs
2. Infant/Preschool Family	a. Reorganizing family to deal with new tasks
	b. Encouraging the child's growth while maintaining safety and parental authority
	c. Deciding how to implement personal and family goals
3. School-Age Family	a. Renegotiating work load
	b. Sharing feelings when child can't handle school
	c. Deciding who helps child with school work
4. Adolescent Family	a. Renegotiating autonomy and control between adolescents and parents
	b. Changing parental rules and roles
	c. Preparing to leave home
5. Launching Family	a. Separating from family
	b. Leaving home appropriately
	c. Entering college, military, or career with assistance
6. Postparental Family	a. Renegotiating marital relationships
	b. Renegotiating time and work
	c. Adjusting to retirement

Note. From Brown and Christensen (1986. Reprinted by permission of Brooks/Cole).

fully accomplished, then individuals are prepared to proceed to the second stage of family development, committing to another to form a family of procreation.

The material in Table 1.2, although quite informative, is strikingly simple, partly because it outlines only the course taken by continually intact nuclear families as they progress over the years. When household heads divorce or one dies, and when remarriages occur, sometimes forming stepfamilies, the process is much more complicated. Nonetheless, the steps involved for these family units in the course of their development have also been described (Carter & McGoldrick, 1989; Schwebel, Fine, & Moreland, 1988; Whiteside, 1983).

THE BENEFIT OF A COGNITIVE-BEHAVIORAL FAMILY APPROACH

Although Candy and Tom faced a significant challenge as they began adjusting to the shared home they established, the process of adjustment itself was not a new enterprise for them. Like every other individual who has married, they each had a lifelong storehouse of experiences with this task, and were well versed in the two actions involved in personally adjusting to life circumstances: "First, the individual attempts to *relate* effectively to the environment in which he or she lives—by developing skills, traits, patterns of thoughts, and behaviors that will bring success, happiness, and other valued goals. Second, the individual attempts to *master* the environment—that is to modify it for his or her own advantage" (Schwebel, Barocas, Reichman, & Schwebel, 1990, p. 6).

Will the Johnsons adjust effectively and be happily married 5, 10, or 20 years hence? Although social scientists cannot yet identify and measure enough relevant factors to accurately make predictions about the Johnsons' future happiness, this type of assessment will be more possible in the future. Along with the ability to predict more accurately will come an understanding of how to intervene on behalf of couples (whether their prospects are good or poor), providing them with the information and skills they need to avoid difficulties and to greatly enhance their prospects of lifelong marital satisfaction.

The cognitive-behavioral family (CBF) model developed in this book suggests that healthier families, and thus healthier members of society, would emerge if those responsible for each family, the adults who form and maintain a unit, had a better understanding of families and how they work and were skilled at teaching this to their children. Furthermore, the CBF model suggests that two factors are the key to making accurate predictions about the likelihood of two spouses making successful adjustments and building a successful marriage: the family-related cognitions the spouses bring into the relationship and the quality of their problem-solving skills. CBF also suggests that these same factors provide indicators to help-givers, enabling them to select the potentially most beneficial relationship-strengthening interventions to apply with couples seeking premarital training or assistance in addressing marital problems.

Of these two factors, the importance of problem-solving skills has been much more widely recognized over the years (D'Zurilla, 1988). Problem-solving skills conventionally thought to be essential to happiness in marriage include the ability and willingness to: listen, perspective-take, engage in give and take, compromise, reason in a rational way, explore alternative solutions, seek and work toward equity, use third parties to find solutions, engage in new experiences, and so forth.

The other set of key predictors of future marital happiness, the spouses' family-related cognitions, have received comparatively little attention until recently. The CBF model suggests that family-related cognitions are important predictors because they function to provide meaning, order, and a sense of control to individuals as they interact on a day-to-day basis with their spouse, children, and other family members. When the content of these cognitions is understood, effective predictions can be made about how spouses in a couple will function and about the likelihood of their sharing a happy future.

The CBF model maintains that the marriage- and family-related cognitions individuals hold shape what they perceive, what they feel, what they think, and how they behave. This volume examines how individuals draw upon these powerful cognitions to guide them in creating a satisfactory marriage and family life. Toward the goal of extending theory in the area of family life, the book considers issues such as: how individuals develop marriage- and family-related cognitions; how these cognitions affect their thoughts, feelings, and behaviors in their marriage and family environment; the impact these cognitions have on individuals' level of life satisfaction; and the kinds of cognitive-behavioral interventions that therapists can use to help individuals and families improve the quality of their lives.

As shown in chapter 2, the cognitive-behavioral approach has provided an effective way to understand individuals and, further, a vehicle to use in individual therapy (Dobson & Block, 1988). Although the use of the cognitive approach can be fruitful, it challenges those that apply it because the search for underlying cognitions in an individual can be difficult, because differentiating between one's perceptions and reality is often difficult, because individuals are unaccustomed to such self-study, and because of a multitude of other reasons. However difficult applying a cognitive-behavioral model to one individual is, the task is still a good deal easier than applying it to a family. To gain understanding of a family, one must consider the intrapersonal dynamics of each member, the interpersonal relations among family members, and systemic issues pertaining to the family unit as a whole.

2

THE COGNITIVE-BEHAVIORAL
PERSPECTIVE

An early psychologist, Herman Ebbinghaus (1910), once described psychology as "having a long past, but only a short history" (p. 9). His comment is as applicable to the cognitive-behavioral perspective as it is to psychology in general.

A key notion in the cognitive-behavioral perspective—that perceptions play a critical role in determining how individuals will respond to events—has its roots in works by the Stoic philosophers. For example, Epictetus, a Stoic philosopher, has been quoted as saying, "People are disturbed not by things but by their view of things" (Ellis, 1989, p. 202).

The British empiricists further developed the idea that perceptions play an important role in human experience. According to Locke (1706/1974), ideas arise from external stimulation or by reflection on the remnants of previous stimulation. He drew a distinction between the primary and secondary qualities of objects. Primary qualities are attributes of physical reality, whereas secondary qualities refer to psychological experiences of the physical world. Thus, secondary qualities are related to the notion of cognitions, as cognitions represent our interpretation of events in our environment.

Berkeley (Armstrong, 1965), also writing in the 18th century, took a more extreme position than Locke. He agreed with Locke that all knowledge is based only on ideas. However, he disagreed with Locke that ideas stemmed from the physical world. Rather, he argued that objects in the physical world have no existence apart from our perceptions of them. As such, reality consists of our perceptions and nothing else:

> Some truths there are so near and obvious to the mind that a man need only open his eyes to see them. Such I take this important one to be, viz. that all the

choir of heaven and furniture of the earth, in a word all those bodies which compose the mighty frame of the world, have not any subsistence without a mind; that their *being* is to be perceived or known; that consequently so long as they are not actually perceived by me, or do not exist in my mind, or that of any other created spirit, they either have no existence at all, or else subsist in the mind of some Eternal Spirit: it being perfectly unintelligible, and involving all the absurdity of abstraction, to attribute to any single part of them an existence independent of a spirit. To be convinced of which, the reader need only reflect, and try to separate in his own thoughts the *being* of a sensible thing from its *being perceived*. (Armstrong, 1965, p. 63)

The important legacy of the British empiricists is their demonstration that reality is affected by individuals' perceptions. In opposition to the notion that reality is an objective and external entity, Locke and Berkeley argued that our experience of reality is largely based on our perceptions. Thus, this claim and others laid the groundwork for later cognitive theorists who argued that perceptions determine reactions to the environment and that individuals may differ in their interpretations of events in the external world.

In this chapter, the cognitive-behavioral perspective that forms the foundation of the CBF model to be described in the next two chapters is presented. After a review of the model's modern historical roots, its basic tenets are outlined. Next, some of the major cognitive-behavioral theorists' contributions are reviewed. Finally, two common themes of cognitive-behavioral models—cognitive mediation and metacognition—are discussed.

HISTORICAL ROOTS

Alfred Adler was among the first modern psychoanalytic or psychological theorists to clearly identify the association between ideas and behaviors. He noted that " . . . *a person's behavior springs from his ideas*" (Adler, 1964b, p. 19) and "The individual . . . does not relate himself to the outside world in a predetermined manner, as is often assumed. He relates himself always according to his own interpretation of himself and of his present problem. . . . It is his . . . attitude toward life which determines his relationship to the outside world" (Adler, 1964a, p. 67).

The "modern era" of cognitive-behaviorism dates back to the 1950s with the beginning of cognitive models of individual functioning. At this time, several forces converged to make a cognitive-behavioral model possible and, in fact, according to Dobson and Block (1988), necessary:

1. There was growing discontent with the strictly behavioral view of psychological functioning.

Research by Bandura (1969) and others demonstrated that such a view was not exhaustive enough to explain many types of human behavior. In particular, the phenomenon of vicarious or observational learning demonstrated that a "mediational" model (i.e., cognitions mediate the relations between stimuli and responses) was necessary. Because individuals who learn from observing others do not directly experience environmental contingencies, they must have engaged in cognitive activity to process their observations.

2. There was also dissatisfaction with several features of psychoanalytic models (Ellis, 1986).

Not only was the therapeutic effectiveness of psychoanalysis challenged, but its reliance on unconscious processing, long-term work, and a nondirective stance was also questioned. Therapists were drawn to the emerging cognitive schools of therapy because they focused on conscious processes (i.e., cognitions), were time limited, and were directive and structured.

3. Within the field of cognitive psychology, information-processing models of cognition were being developed.

Information-processing psychologists, many of whom trace their philosophical roots to Kant's notions of how thought gives structure and meaning to sensory information, argue that humans function in a manner similar to computers. Both receive input, process these data, have a memory, and produce output. The processing of input data includes such activities as encoding, storage, and retrieval. Information-processing psychologists typically focus their efforts on understanding such higher mental processes as language, thinking, perception, problem solving, concept formation, memory, learning, intelligence, and attention (Lachman, Lachman, & Butterfield, 1979).

These models included a mediational component that was soon applied to further understanding of clinical constructs. Lazarus and colleagues demonstrated that anxiety and stress are mediated by cognitions (Lazarus & Folkman, 1984). For example, several studies have suggested that individuals who believe that they have the coping resources to manage a stressful event experience less anxiety than those who believe that they are not able to manage the situation (Lazarus & Alfert, 1964; Lazarus, Opton, Nomikos, & Rankin, 1965).

4. During the 1950s, 1960s, and 1970s, there was the emergence of several theorists, researchers, and clinicians who identified themselves within a cognitive-behavioral framework.

Ellis, Beck, and Meichenbaum were strong and articulate advocates of this approach to understanding human psychological problems. Their emergence created a *Zeitgeist* that led to increased attention and development of the model. To illustrate, several scholarly journals (e.g., *Cognitive Therapy and Research*) were developed during the latter portion of this period to provide a forum for research and theory into this model. In addition, numerous outcome studies in the late 1970s showed that several variants of cognitive-behavioral individual psychotherapy were promising in their efficacy and were, to the surprise of many, potentially as potent as antidepressant medication (Hollon & Beck, 1979; Rush, Beck, Kovacs, & Hollon, 1977).

5. Cognitive models are attractive because they focus on the rational and intellectual mental processes that are very comfortable and familiar to many highly educated, bright therapists.

Although emotions are not ignored, cognitive-behavioral models clearly place more emphasis on the intellectual than on the affective side of human experience. This emphasis is quite consistent with the cognitive and rational focus that characterizes the higher education that mental health professionals have received. Thus, assisting clients in identifying their "irrational beliefs" and "cognitive errors" is a process well within the "comfort zone" of most mental health professionals.

There has continued to be a vast amount of interest and research in cognitive phenomenon. At this point, several features of this work need to be recognized. First, the primary focus of scholarly activity has been on understanding the development and treatment of psychopathology. Relatively less attention has been directed to understanding healthy functioning. Second, the major unit of interest has been the individual. Only very recently have efforts been devoted to understanding couples, marriages, and families. Some work of this nature is described in the next two chapters.

MAJOR TENETS

At their core, cognitive-behavioral models share several basic assumptions:

1. Individuals are proactive, autonomous agents capable of influencing their environments.

Human beings uniquely process information derived from their environment because they respond primarily to cognitive representations of their environment, rather than to the environment per se. Thus, the radical behaviorist notion that individuals merely respond passively and reactively to stimuli is rejected.

This assumption has been institutionalized within some areas of personality and social psychology in terms of the notion of *phenomenology*. The phenomenological approach has as its basic tenet that the key factor in determining how individuals will respond to situations is their unique experience of the event rather than the event itself. Within personality psychology, the humanistic approach has emphasized the importance of understanding the unique perspective that each individual has of any given situation (Maslow, 1954; Rogers, 1970).

Within social psychology, some of the best known studies in psychology have demonstrated that perceptions of the situation, to a greater degree than the situation itself, influence behavior. For example, the Asch (1956) conformity study, the Milgram (1963) study of obedience, and Zimbardo's (1975) prison experiment all demonstrated that human behavior can be altered by changing individuals' interpretation of the meaning of their environments. In fact, social psychology has a long tradition of exploring the behavioral effects of manipulating individuals' perceptions of the meaning of a given situation. This practice can be understood as empirical verification of the usefulness of the phenomenological perspective.

2. Cognitions affect behavior and well-being. Not only is it postulated that cognitions are related to behavior, but, in addition, a causal relation is proposed.

Thus, individuals' cognitive appraisals of environmental situations play a causal role in determining their responses to specific situations and, on a larger scale, their overall well-being. This is the basic tenet of the mediational hypothesis.

3. Cognitions can be monitored, assessed, and modified.

Although some cognitions occur outside of conscious awareness, cognitive-behavioral models postulate that individuals can be helped to recognize their cognitions and change them if they so desire (Schwebel & Fine, 1992). This assumption forms the basis of the many assessment strategies that have been developed to measure cognitions, which are discussed in more detail in chapter 6.

4. Changes in cognitions will lead to changes in behavior and well-being.

Although cognitive change is not the only way to effect behavior change, cognitive-behavioral models suggest that this approach is a potent and widely applicable method. This assumption has provided the context for the development of cognitive-behavioral therapeutic approaches, as discussed further in chapters 7 and 8.

Changes in cognitions may be set in motion by internal forces, as individuals think about themselves and their interactions with others. The change process can also be instigated by external stimuli. Mental health professionals have employed many techniques to help individuals develop more accurate and health-promoting cognitions, including, for example, training in cognitive coping skills, anxiety management, and problem solving. Finally, individuals are helped in the process of developing more accurate and health-promoting cognitions by being taught about cognitive behavioral theories and how to apply them in their own lives (Ellis, 1986).

SELECTED THEORISTS

Of the vast number of theorists, clinicians, and researchers who have advanced our knowledge of cognitive-behavioral models, the works of Ellis, Beck, Meichenbaum, Kanfer, D'Zurilla, and Spivack and Shure are highlighted here. Their contributions have helped therapists, counselors, and educators, aided adults and children, and laid the groundwork for many of the concepts used in the cognitive-behavioral family model presented in the next two chapters. Thus, a review of their works provides a context in which to understand later material.

Ellis.   According to rational-emotive therapy (RET; Dryden & Ellis, 1988), the root of psychological disturbance lies in the human tendency to make "devout, absolutistic evaluations of the perceived events in their lives" (p. 220). These evaluations are reflected in the form of dogmatic "shoulds," "musts," and "have tos." These beliefs often obstruct individuals in the pursuit of their life goals. In addition, this philosophy of *musturbation* (e.g., "I *must* do this. I *must* do that. I *must* be perfect.") leads disturbed individuals to have a number of distorted beliefs. For example, *perfectionism* reflects the belief that, although a job may have been performed well, the fact that it was not performed "perfectly" indicates that the person is actually incompetent.

According to Ellis, individuals can generally accept personal shortcomings and weaknesses if they are able to resist the tendency to "awfulize" them. Thus, there is nothing inherently unhealthy about believing that one is only average in intelligence and attractiveness; the distress stems from the additional belief that "If I am only average in these areas, it would be terrible and I would be a complete disgrace."

As a result, an RET therapist attempts to help clients realize that illogical beliefs and logical distortions underlie their emotional problems. Although most clients blame their troubles (C) on activating events (A), RET therapists probe for the irrational beliefs (B) that mediate the relationship between A and C. Once identified, these irrational beliefs (B) are logically challenged by the individual who learns to *d*ebate and *d*ispute (D) them and, hopefully, will modify them in a more rational direction (Ellis, 1986).

Beck. According to Beck and associates' (Beck & Emery, 1985; Beck, Rush, Shaw, & Emery, 1979) cognitive model of emotional disorders, maladaptive and inaccurate cognitions lead to the development and maintenance of a variety of upsetting emotions. The notion of a *schema* is central to Beck's cognitive model, as it constitutes " . . . the underlying cognitive structures that organize the client's experience and that can form the basis for the individual instances of bias or distortion. . . . and can be called core beliefs" (DeRubeis & Beck, 1988, p. 275). For example, depressed individuals have a negative self-schemata, which leads them to consistently overemphasize the negative elements in themselves, their environments, and their futures.

Stemming from the maladaptive or inaccurate schemata are a variety of *cognitive errors*. These refer to thinking errors that are particularly likely to occur during periods of emotional distress. For example, *overgeneralization* refers to the pattern of drawing a general rule or conclusion based on one or more isolated incidents. Suppose one receives negative feedback on one particular project at work, but generally is praised for performing well. A nondepressed individual would likely attempt to improve future performance and would not be overly distressed. By contrast, a depressed person might overgeneralize and conclude, "This one failure experience really shows my incompetence. My boss has finally seen through my facade."

Similar to RET, cognitive therapists attempt to assist clients in identifying and changing their maladaptive cognitions. Unlike RET, however, there is a greater emphasis on empirically (rather than logically) testing the veracity of various beliefs and assumptions. Clients are encouraged to engage in a process of *collaborative empiricism* to establish an empirical foundation for their beliefs about themselves, their futures, and their environments.

Meichenbaum. Meichenbaum has developed two related therapeutic approaches that have been used both with adults and with children. The first—self-instructional training (SIT-1; Meichenbaum, 1977)—is a form of self-management that focuses on the importance of a person's instructions to him or herself. This approach is based on the assumption that these self-instructions affect behavior and behavior change. Thus, this approach suggests that psychological problems may be caused by maladaptive self-statements, and the modification of these statements may yield therapeutic benefits.

SIT-1 can effect change in either of two ways. First, in the acquisition of new skills, self-statements can serve as useful cues for the recall of desirable behavioral sequences. Second, in the correction of maladaptive behavioral patterns, self-instructional statements can serve to interrupt automatic behavioral or cognitive chains and to encourage the use of more adaptive coping strategies.

In the early phases of SIT-1, the therapist and client collaboratively work to generate a conceptualization of the problem. An important goal is to help the client understand the notion that his or her cognitions may play a role in his or her problematic behaviors.

After this shared conceptualization has been developed, the client is helped to develop skills that would allow him or her to change the problem behavior or cope in problem situations. For example, the client is taught more adaptive self-statements and how to substitute them for those currently contributing to the problem. The specific strategies used to elicit these changes vary considerably depending on the nature of the problem and the age of the client.

Although SIT-1 has been used extensively with adults, perhaps its greatest impact has been with children. According to Kendall and Bemis (1983), self-instructional training is perhaps the most widely studied cognitive-behavioral strategy employed with impulsive, hyperactive, and behavior-problem children. Much of this work has been designed to help these children modulate their impulsivity through deliberate and task-oriented "self-talk."

Meichenbaum (1985) also developed stress inoculation training (SIT-2), which is a strategy designed to help clients develop and use a repertoire of skills that will enable them to cope with a range of stressful situations. As implied by its name, an analogy with medicine is evoked, as this approach is held to build "psychological antibodies" and enhance resistance through exposure to stimuli strong enough to arouse psychological defenses but not powerful enough to overwhelm them.

Meichenbaum (1985) also identified phases in SIT-2. The first stage—education—is designed to develop rapport with the client, to educate him or her about the transactional nature of stress, to show how cognitions and emotions play a role in generating and maintaining stress, and to delineate a situational analysis of the nature of the presenting problem.

The second phase—skills acquisition and rehearsal—teaches clients effective coping responses. Depending on the nature of the presenting problem, a variety of approaches can be utilized to teach these skills, including relaxation training, cognitive restructuring, problem-solving training, and self-instructional training. Thus, SIT-2 is a broad approach to stress management and subsumes many of the specific strategies developed by others.

The final phase—application and follow through—is designed to encourage clients to implement coping responses in their daily lives and to maximize the chances that treatment improvement will extend to other life areas (i.e., treatment generalization). The therapist uses paced mastery, in which small, manageable amounts of stress are presented to the client to foster the development of *psychological immunization.*

Meichenbaum's contributions are many and far-reaching. First and foremost, SIT-2, in particular, has provided an overarching framework for integrating a variety of specific strategies developed by other authors (Kendall & Bemis, 1983). For example, depending on individual needs, cognitive restructuring, testing inaccurate beliefs, correcting cognitive distortions, challenging irrational beliefs, problem-solving training, self-monitoring, relaxation, and other strategies can be employed. The underlying unifying theme across all these modalities is that they help individuals cope more effectively with stress and this, in turn, is assumed to help resolve emotional problems.

An additional contribution is that Meichenbaum expanded the range of cognitive-behavioral interventions to include children. Before his work, children, because of their limited cognitive abilities, were not considered good candidates for cognitive-behavioral approaches. Since Meichenbaum's early work, a number of clinicians have developed such interventions for children, many of which are based on the self-instructional model (Braswell & Kendall, 1988).

Kanfer. According to Kanfer's (1980) self-management model, self-control is viewed as a series of processes that a person engages in when a change in behavior is desired. For example, a person who comes to perceive himself as overweight may initiate a series of activities to attempt to lose weight. In these and other instances, the person engages in a three-stage feedback loop involving self-monitoring, self-evaluation, and self-reinforcement processes.

At the self-monitoring step, the individual observes his or her behavior, either in a systematic or nonsystematic fashion. At the second stage, self-evaluation, the person compares his or her performance (from the self-monitoring stage) with some standard or criterion. Based on this comparison, the individual makes a judgment that his or her performance either did or did not meet the standard. At the final stage in the self-control feedback loop, individuals reinforce themselves. If their performance was satisfactory, they are likely to reward themselves.

Kanfer (1980) emphasized two additional concepts. First, because of the extensive amount of effort required to change behavior, it is important that an individual is *committed* to engaging in self-correcting behavior. Second, self-management is facilitated to the extent that an individual believes that the desired behavior is under *personal control*.

Therapists using the self-management approach attempt to help clients engage in this process in a systematic, rational, and realistic manner. Thus, strategies of effectively monitoring one's behavior are taught, the importance of developing realistic standards is emphasized, and the value of making an effort to reinforce oneself for successful performance is stressed. If performance does not meet the standard, clients are encouraged to maintain an optimistic stance and, after modifying one or more aspects of the procedure, to try again.

D'Zurilla. In D'Zurilla's (1988) problem-solving therapy, *problem solving* is defined as "a cogntive-affective-behavioral process through which an individual attempts to identify, discover, or invent effective or adaptive means of coping with problems encountered in everyday living" (p. 86). D'Zurilla argued that individuals often take a nonsystematic and haphazard approach to coping with daily problems. As a result, the problems are not adequately resolved and, eventually, lead to substantial distress.

Several basic assumptions underlie the problem-solving approach. First, it is assumed that the quality of one's ability to solve problems is positively related to social competence and negatively related to psychopathology. Second, for individuals who do not currently have significant emotional problems, it is assumed that training in problem solving will lead to increases in social competence and reduce the risk of psychopathology. Third, for those who already have emotional problems, it is assumed that enhanced problem-solving skills will reduce the magnitude of their impairment.

As described by D'Zurilla (1988), the problem-solving process involves five stages: problem orientation, problem definition and formulation, generation of alternative solutions, decision making, and solution implementation and verification. The tasks of each stage follow:

1. During the *problem orientation* phase, the individual becomes sensitive to problems, focuses attention on generating positive expectations about solving problems, maximizes motivation to resolve the problem, and minimizes emotional distress.

2. During the *problem definition and formulation* stage, the individual gathers as much relevant, factual information as is available, sets realistic goals for resolving the problem, and appraises the significance of the problem for personal and social well-being.

3. During the *generation of alternative solutions* phase, the individual generates as many alternative solutions as possible to maximize the chances that a desirable solution will be identified. This stage involves the technique of *brainstorming*, which encourages the construction of as many alternatives as possible, the withholding of judgment, and the emergence of a variety of different solutions.

4. During the *decision-making* stage, the individual "objectively" evaluates the available solutions and chooses the one judged to have the greatest probability of addressing the problematic situation. This is the solution that maximizes the likelihood of achieving the problem-solving goal, while maximizing benefits and minimizing costs. Of course, the process is not objective, as different individuals may rationally weigh the same evidence in contrasting ways. Rather, clients are encouraged to conduct their evaluations with a minimum of subjectivity and bias.

5. During the *solution implementation and verification* phase, the solution is actually implemented and the outcome evaluated. If the solution is judged to have satisfactorily resolved the problem, the process has been successful. If the solution partially addressed the problem or if it does not help at all, the problem-solving process is initiated again. In this case, the problem may be reformulated, new alternatives may be generated, a different evaluation strategy may be employed, and a modified implementation approach may be utilized.

The primary benefit of the problem-solving process is that it provides individuals with the tools necessary to consciously, systematically, and rationally resolve their daily problems. Potential disadvantages are that it may take a considerable amount of time to employ and the process is not as objective as it is often described. There are many subjective judgments made at each and every step of the procedure.

Spivack and Shure.   Spivack, Shure, and associates have extended D'Zurilla's (1988) work to children. They have approached child or family difficulties as problems requiring effective resolution, rather than as the inevitable outcome of mental disorders, behavioral problems, or family dysfunction. Spivack, Shure, and associates hypothesized that effective interpersonal cognitive problem solving (ICPS) demands a number of skills, including a sensitivity to problematic situations, the ability to generate alternative solutions, the capacity to identify appropriate means to achieve a given solution, and an awareness of consequences and cause–effect relationships in human behavior (Spivack, Platt, & Shure, 1976; Spivack & Shure, 1974).

Spivack, Shure, and associates argued that problem-solving deficits underlie many child adjustment difficulties. However, empirical findings related to this assumption have yielded mixed results. Some studies have found that maladjusted children do have social cognitive deficits and biases, whereas others have found small or nonexistent relations between ICPS skills and adjustment (Braswell & Kendall, 1988).

This group has also suggested that problem-solving training will enhance the interpersonal competence and adjustment of children. As such, formal problem-solving methods have been developed for children, using methods such as that described earlier for D'Zurilla. With these, children are taught skills related to identifying problems, generating solutions, developing means to achieve the most desirable solution, and evaluating the effectiveness of the results of employing the solution. Spivack, Shure, and colleagues have suggested that such training may be beneficial for children who already have interpersonal difficulties or as a preventive measure for children who may be at risk for developing later problems.

COGNITIVE MEDIATION AND METACOGNITION

The cognitive-behavioral approaches described earlier, and the others in the literature, rest on the common assumption that individuals' experiences, thoughts, emotions, and behaviors are heavily shaped by the manner in which they cognitively structure their world. Given this common assumption, the similar goals of the cognitive-behavioral intervention programs and therapy techniques make sense: to help participants become aware of and correct the unhealthy cognitions that they, as human beings, tend to make. Toward this end, interventions help participants to identify and replace inaccurate and maladaptive cognitions; to learn self-instruction, self-control, and self-management skills and techniques; to prepare themselves to cognitively manage stress; and to acquire effective problem-solving skills.

Cognitive-behavioral interventions, including psychotherapy, assume that help-recipients have learning deficits which, if eliminated, would enable them to live happier and more fulfilled lives. Therefore, cognitive-behavioral-oriented help-givers function as teachers who try to empower individuals to overcome these deficits. As teachers, they serve as mediators of their clients' experiences, standing between them and their environment in order to help them discover new and more productive ways to perceive and interpret their world (M. Schwebel, Maher, & Fagley, 1990).

A common element of successful cognitive-behavioral approaches is that help-givers "give away" their knowledge to help-recipients—they transfer to them information, skills, and favorable attitudes toward problem solving. For this to occur during cognitive-behavioral interventions, help-givers first serve as *cognitive mediators* for helpees. The term cognitive mediation refers to the process through which one individual helps another to perceive and interpret in new ways significant social or physical features in his or her current or past experiences (M. Schwebel et al., 1990). Then, over time, help-recipients become their own cognitive mediators, learning what was taught to them by the help-giver and integrating it into their *metacognition*. The term metacognition describes the process through which individuals think about the thoughts they have and about the products of their thoughts. This process is explained further later.

Cognitive Mediation

Parents are typically individuals' first cognitive mediators. They help offspring make sense of the stimuli that continuously bombard them. Most mediation done by parents is "automatic." As parents react to situations, people, and events in the household, their reactions and behavior mediate for their children and teach them how to react and adjust. Other times, of course, parents intentionally mediate, using messages like, "Pick up your toys. It's improper to have a messy house when guests are coming."

Automatically or intentionally, parents provide children with mediation messages hundreds, if not thousands, of times a day. As well illustrated in a study by Lewis and Michalson (1983), the nature of the lessons parents teach varies greatly. These researchers observed one hundred and eleven 1-year-old children who were distressed because their mothers had left them alone in a playroom. Upon returning to their upset child, some mothers explained to the children that they were "sad or tired," whereas others labeled the children's reaction with words like *angry, mad, scared*, or *frightened*. Still other mothers asked their babies, "Did you miss me?" The mothers, each in her own way, mediated the experience for their children and taught them the "appropriate" cognitions to use in the situation.

Adults benefit from mediation as well as children. The value of mediation to an adult is more obvious in certain circumstances. Imagine flying to a city halfway around the world where you have business but little knowledge of the language or customs of that society. You would probably hire a guide to mediate for you. The value of mediation is less obvious but as helpful to an unhappily married person who also feels frustrated by career-advancement problems at work. A cognitive-behavioral therapist could help that individual mediate his or her experiences and find more satisfying ways to function.

Targeting Interventions. Help-givers in cognitive-behavioral programs assist help-recipients in filtering, organizing, and making sense of the stimuli in their environment. To assist help-recipients in gaining new insights into the temporal, spatial, or causal relationship among factors associated with an issue at hand, help-givers need to determine the recipients' level of understanding of the problem. This assessment informs help-givers about what lessons the recipients are ready for.

Figure 2.1 depicts the learning process that help-recipients experience as they are assisted in building more accurate and effective cognitions about an issue at hand. At the top of Fig. 2.1, A represents the point in the past at which a client had no understanding whatsoever about the concepts key to a particular issue. Since then, during the course of living, the client's understanding of the relevant concepts has advanced to Point B. Now, as the intervention process begins, the ultimate goal is to help the client advance at least to Point D, where he or she will possess cognitions that will provide a better understanding of the issue and that will facilitate his or her functioning in a healthier way with regard to it.

For example, the Stones brought their 3½-year-old son Kenny in for treatment. They reported that he does not obey his day care center teachers and that he is biting his classmates. Soon after the consultation began, the help-giver noted that the parents let Kenny wander around the office and lift books,

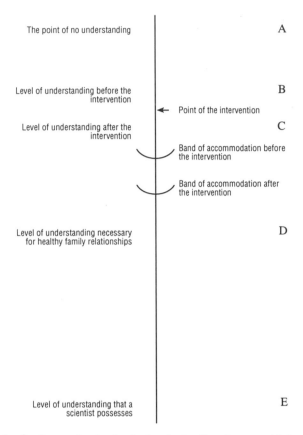

FIG. 2.1. Continuum showing levels of understanding of a concept before and after an intervention that successfully fosters better understanding of that concept.

paperweights, and other objects from the desk and shelves. Instead of asking him to sit with them, the parents commented on how cute, creative, and inquisitive the boy is. To tailor an intervention, the help-giver drew on this and other information and asked questions that helped assess where, on the continuum shown in Fig. 2.1, the parents were in their understanding of Kenny's problem behavior.

Once the help-giver determined the parents' level of understanding, potentially effective interventions could be designed. Assume that the help-giver determined that the mother and father were both at Point B in their understanding of the fact that children need externally imposed discipline in order to develop self-control. Based on this assessment, the help-giver designed an appropriate intervention for the Stones, drawing on the *band of accommodation* concept described by Piaget (personal communication, May 1967).

The band of accommodation concept suggests that any cognitive mediation or interpretation given to individuals that falls at a point between their level of understanding and the band of accommodation will be usable by the individuals and, therefore, will advance their understanding and also their band of accommodation. In this case, as Fig. 2.1 shows, the help-giver designed an effective intervention that moved Mr. and Mrs. Stone's respective understandings forward to Point C, as well as advancing their bands of accommodation. Figure 2.1 also suggests that additional interventions will be necessary to advance the Stones' understandings to Point D.

The band of accommodation concept also suggests that when help-givers provide a cognitive mediation or intervention beyond the recipients' band of accommodation, it has no benefit to them. As Fig. 2.2 shows, such a failed intervention leaves the recipient's level of understanding and band of accommodation unchanged. To illustrate this, imagine that Mr. Stone entered treatment believing that Kenny had an "active personality" and this factor alone

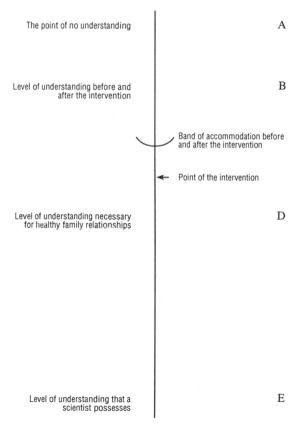

The point of no understanding   A

Level of understanding before and   B
after the intervention

Band of accommodation before
and after the intervention

◄— Point of the intervention

Level of understanding necessary   D
for healthy family relationships

Level of understanding that a   E
scientist possesses

FIG. 2.2. Situation after unsuccessful intervention.

was causing his son's problems. An example of an intervention that would be beyond Mr. Stone's band of accommodation, and therefore ineffective, would be if, early in the first meeting, the help-giver said, "Your conception of this problem is all wrong. Kenny's problems have nothing to do with an 'active personality' but rather stem from his history of little discipline. . . ." Because this intervention would fall beyond Mr. Stone's band of accommodation (falling near Point D), he could not "digest it" and, therefore, it could not help him advance his understanding beyond Point B.

Vygotsky's (1978) concept of the *zone of proximal development* (ZPD) is similar to Piaget's concept of the band of accommodation. Vygotsky wrote about two development levels that need to be considered when evaluating an individual's learning potential. First, he referred to individuals' *actual* level of development, or in this case, the cognitions individuals have to help them understand how families operate and how they can function effectively in theirs. Second, he also referred to individuals' *potential* level of development. The difference between the two levels is the zone of proximal development. Individuals cannot use skills or knowledge in this zone independently but, with help from mediators and with practice, can develop to the point where they eventually can function independently (i.e., skills from their potential level of development move into their actual level).

Both concepts—the band of accommodation and the zone of proximal development—underline a key point with regard to effective cognitive-behavioral interventions. Specifically, they indicate the importance of assessing the kinds of cognitions individuals hold and where they are in their development. With such information at hand, help-givers can provide lessons at the appropriate level for the recipients. Assessment of family members' cognitions is discussed further in chapter 6.

Metacognition

The final step in completing the transfer of knowledge and skills from the help-giver to help-recipients takes place as the help-recipients substantially increase their practice of and abilities in *metacognition*. This occurs when individuals show significant improvements in their abilities to effectively monitor and think about their own thought processes and the products of their thoughts.

The value of using metacognition skills is made apparent by a study of school children, some of whom were taught to use this in mastering their school lessons. When these youngsters encountered problems in learning a reading assignment, they could tap into the following metacognition skills: (a) monitoring progress, which leads them to establish a goal for the lesson and to assess their understanding as they go through the assignment, (b) awareness, which informs them when they are not understanding the lesson and directs them to overcome it, and (c) regulating, which leads them to change their functioning by utilizing strategies to overcome the problem, such as re-reading and asking for help (Haller, Child, & Walberg, 1988). In Haller et al.'s (1988) study, and in 20 others they examined in the area of reading comprehension, when students were taught to use metacognitive skills, their gains were substantial. Adults can find equally powerful benefit from meta-cognition.

The process of acquiring metacognition skills begins in childhood. During this period, individuals first learn to monitor their own thinking and to evaluate their own responses to the environment. Of course, learning to identify cognitions operating within the self and discovering how they affect thoughts, feelings, and behaviors is a challenging task. Just as individuals cannot easily understand subtraction until their mind has physically and intellectually developed to the point where they can master addition, they cannot experience shame and guilt about their behavior and thoughts until they have acquired self-awareness. Similarly, they cannot engage in metacognition until their minds have developed sufficiently and until they have mastered more basic understandings.

Over the years of childhood and adolescence, as their biological and cognitive capabilities develop, individuals learn to be reflective and introspective and to use cognitive skills that allow them to engage in more sophisticated metacognition. Effective cognitive-behavioral help-givers understand this and conduct their assessments and interventions accordingly.

CONCLUSIONS

The works of Ellis, Beck, Meichenbaum, Kanfer, D'Zurilla, and Spivack and Shure illustrate a variety of attempts to derive cognitive explanations of and treatment for maladaptive functioning. Several concepts from these approaches have applicability to the model presented in the next chapter: irrational beliefs, cognitive errors, comparison of perceived experiences with internal standards, self-monitoring, self-reinforcement, coping self-statements, stress management, the importance of an optimistic approach to problems, and conscious problem-solving strategies. In addition, the processes of cognitive mediation and metacognition are common themes across these approaches.

The major limitations of these models are that they are better suited to understanding individuals than larger systems and they primarily explain how emotional problems develop. They have placed relatively little emphasis on how cognition is related to healthy or adaptive functioning.

CHAPTER

3

THE COGNITIVE-BEHAVIORAL
FAMILY MODEL

Building on the work described in chapter 2, the cognitive-behavioral family (CBF) model argues that to understand why individuals function as they do in a given family situation, observers need insight into the family-related cognitions they hold. The following example illustrates how, if observers knew family members' cognitions, they would be empowered to better understand individuals' behavior and to predict the kinds of problems a family unit would encounter over and over again:

> The night was dark and still, and it was late when the Procios boarded their car to drive home from the company office party. Almost immediately Carl complained to his wife, Janet, "Next time, please don't talk in that high squeaky voice at parties. When the out-of-town associates heard your irritating, ear-piercing tone, they immediately discounted everything you said."
>
> Janet did not respond to Carl but sat in an obvious, passive–aggressive silence for the rest of the trip.
>
> The next evening during dinner, Janet, Carl, and their son Jeff were discussing the day's events. Janet asked Jeff about his math test and Jeff curtly replied, "It was hard and I didn't understand the last three problems."
>
> Carl, who enjoys spending time with his children, immediately offered to help Jeff study math. Jeff responded with a brief, unenthusiastic "yeah," but then sat silently for several minutes.
>
> "Tonight," Carl pondered, "as soon as Jeff's favorite television program ends, I'll again suggest doing math with him."

To predict Jeff's reaction when later in the evening his father again offers to help, the CBF model suggests that observers must have knowledge of Carl,

Jeff, and Janet's family-related cognitions. These cognitions dictate to them what family life is supposed to be like and will guide each of them in interpreting and reacting to each other's behaviors. At the same time, these cognitions shape the thoughts and feelings each of them will have as events unfold and how they will behave.

Although observers wanting to understand the Procios would seek to identify the family-related cognitions they hold, the Procios themselves are only vaguely aware of having cognitions and possess little knowledge about the role cognitions play in shaping the quality of their family life. In fact, like most people, the Procios do not ordinarily engage in much metacognition regarding their family life.

For example, neither Carl nor Janet engaged in self-reflection about the "drive-home" and the "math test" issues or tried to analyze what happened between and among them over these issues. If an observer had asked about these incidents, the couple would have indicated that the two were separate problems and were nothing more than the type of difficulties that arise in most people's day-to-day lives.

Because the content varies in the "drive-home," the "math test," and other problems the Procios face from day to day, they are unaware of the fact that in terms of family dynamics, they repeatedly encounter the same type of problem. As a result, after the Procios come to manage today's problem, tomorrow they will have to start all over again. That is, they will have to address what to them will feel like a new problem but what will, in fact, be a variant of the same ones that recur because of their individual family-related cognitions.

BECOMING AWARE OF FAMILY-RELATED COGNITIONS: POWERFUL, INVISIBLE TOOLS

Only a small portion of an iceberg is visible above the water. It does not occur to vacationing, Alaska-bound cruise ship passengers who pass a massive iceberg to even think about what might be underwater and unseen. That is so because, in general, naive observers are deceived by their own perceptions. They "know" what they perceive and what they perceive is true and real to them.

Because Janet, Carl, and, for that matter, most people lack basic conceptual tools to understand the nature of interpersonal relationships, they are naive observers of them and are comparable to cruise ship passengers who steam by an iceberg. Because they, and anyone who lacks these tools, are essentially "interpersonal tourists" who know what they perceive, that alone is what is real to them.

Lack of Awareness

Family-related cognitions are mostly acquired from observational, non-systematic, piecemeal learnings. Few individuals recognize that they hold this set of cognitions that underpin their understandings of family life and of their role in it and few recognize that their set of cognitions is unique. As a result, although most individuals are aware that their behaviors, reactions, and so forth are sometimes different from family members,' few recognize that the differences are caused by differences in their cognitions about how families and individuals should function.

Although individuals are not at all or only vaguely aware of having their own unique set of family-related cognitions, most, nonetheless, operate as if they see the world the "right" way—the same way other "decent" or "logical" people do. Because of this, few individuals recognize that they view family life through a lens and that the lens itself affects their family-related thoughts, feelings, and behaviors.

Consider Carl and Janet, for instance. Neither one of them considered in a disciplined way the differences between the family-related cognitions that operated in each of them during their drive home from the party (described earlier). However, both concluded that they were "in the right" and the spouse "in the wrong."

Janet and Carl and most people can be helped to better understand family interactions and themselves by becoming more aware of their family-related cognitions and learning how these shape their thoughts, feelings, and behaviors. People so empowered have tools that will help them understand and bring about changes they desire in their own families.

No Formal Training

Janet and Carl's lack of awareness about their cognitions and lack of sophistication in handling problems related to the differences between their cognitions is certainly understandable. In contrast to some content areas, like mathematics, science, history, and English, in which they received formal instruction, the Procios built understandings of family life and families without benefit of structured and planned lessons. As discussed later in this chapter, they learned by watching and listening to their caretakers and observing them as they interacted with their immediate environment. In other words, instead of being taught how to think systematically about family life, the Procios developed family-related cognitions in unplanned and unsystematic ways and were left with inadequate understandings of families.

The process of learning family-related cognitions, besides having a "hit-or-miss" quality, presents children with other obstacles. For example, parents often issue conflicting directives. One conveys that joking during dinner or throwing a ball in the living room is enjoyable family fun, whereas the other conveys that it is unacceptable behavior. Further, parents often give different messages about the same behavior at different times. For example, when a parent is in a good mood, he may be physically affectionate with the child at bedtime, yet withdraw and be distant the next night because his mood changed. Similarly, parents may unintentionally and simultaneously, or almost so, send conflicting messages. For instance, a mother may intervene when a boy is hitting a younger sibling by saying, "Don't hit your sister," while at the same time delivering a swat to the offender's buttocks. Or instead, a 5-year-old hears her parents verbalize, "Be a little lady with your friends," but discovers she is ignored by them when she does so, whereas she earns great attention from them when she pushes to the front of a line or punches a boy who tries to play with her toy.

Some cognitions that individuals construct during childhood to help them function in their family of origin remain part of their repertoire into adolescence and adulthood, when they are no longer appropriate. For example, Jeff Procio constructed cognitions of himself that led him to function as "the helpless child," and although this earned him attention then, these cognitions could remain with him and cause difficulties in his marriage and career.

Unfortunately, society has no institution that formally teaches children effective family living. Recognizing that the task is assigned primarily to parents, family members, and other caretakers, the CBF model maintains that healthier families, and thus healthier and more functional members of society, would emerge if the responsible adults in each household had, first, a better understanding of families and how they work and, second, the skill to teach this knowledge. For example, imagine the impact of providing parents with an easy-to-follow instructional program that enabled them to teach their children to be more effective family members.

The Power of a Theory: Making Visible the Invisible

Although we offer no such detailed, step-by-step instructional program, knowledge of the CBF model would help parents better understand family functioning and teach it to their children. The utility of a model in this connection is addressed by Lewin (1951) in his classic statement, "nothing [is] so practical as a good theory" (p. 169).

Once individuals are introduced to the CBF model of family functioning, they become more aware of their cognitions and the impact they have on their thoughts, behaviors, and feelings. Concomitantly, they become aware that other family members have their own unique sets of cognitions and of the impact these have on their functioning.

When individuals obtain a working familiarity of the CBF model, they are empowered to become more effective change agents on their family's behalf. The model provides them with a vocabulary to understand and a framework in which to analyze what is happening in their family unit. The model can also guide them in thinking systematically about the discrepancy between what is happening in their family life and what they want to happen, and about changes they can make to reduce it.

If Carl and Janet Procio had been taught the CBF model, they would have brought their formerly unseen and unconsidered family-related cognitions into the forefront. Both Carl and Janet would have recognized that their own perspective on family life was unique and as valid as their spouse's. As the postparty drive-home episode unfolded, Janet might have asked herself, "Why do I feel hurt by Carl's comments? Am I reacting to the situation at hand, or to factors (like memories of Mother's criticism) from my past? What is Carl wishing to convey when he asks . . . ? How do I interpret what he is conveying and how does that fit with what I expect from a loving husband?" Carl might have asked himself, "Why am I irritated by Janet's manner? Why do I want her to change? Am I being reasonable in asking her to change? Does she want to change and if so, how can I help her?"

Had Carl and Janet raised questions like these, they would have probably identified the cognitions that lead them to repeatedly experience the drive-home type of conflict and the stalemates that follow. Then they could have evaluated each of the problem-causing cognitions by asking, "Does this cognition reflect reality to me today?", "What are the costs and benefits associated with holding this cognition?", and so forth. After assessing each cognition's validity and impact, Janet and Carl could then thoughtfully decide whether to keep, alter, or replace it.

Similarly, had Carl and Janet learned the model and taught it to Jeff, the math test/math homework issue probably would not have developed. But had it, Jeff and his parents would possess tools to help analyze why he avoided working with his father and to find a mutually satisfactory solution. The analysis would have indicated that the incident developed partly because Jeff had acquired cognitions that led him to utilize his mother's style of dealing with his father (Carl); specifically, he had learned to say "yes," pacifying his father, and then to avoid following through to protect himself from his father's corrections (equivalent to lost love, in his cognitions) when he made mistakes.

Put another way, Jeff shielded himself from criticism (or lost love) by (passively) refusing to accept his father's help. Had the Procios understood the CBF model, they would have identified this counterproductive pattern that deprived Jeff of needed assistance and that denied him the opportunity to succeed in math and to develop the self-view that he was a competent math student. They could have replaced their cognitions and interaction patterns with ones that provided father and son with quality opportunities to share work time and to enjoy each other's company.

The end of this chapter and chapter 4 detail the CBF model and explain how families like the Procios can apply it to enrich their understanding of family life. Before that, however, we outline the assumptions that underlie the CBF model and an important theme in it: empowering individuals to identify and control their family-related cognitions rather than allowing family-related cognitions to control them.

ASSUMPTIONS IN THE CBF MODEL

Four assumptions central to the CBF model are discussed in this section.

Assumption I.   Individuals seek to master their environment, working in a committed fashion to receive what they need and want from it. To accomplish this, individuals apply their intelligence and other resources, in the best way they know how, toward the goals of understanding their environment and how they can function at maximum effectiveness in it.

With regard to making the most of family life and interpersonal relationships, individuals function like scientists, following their inborn propensity to want to learn. As they interact with family members, they continually gather data about how the individuals and family work. Those data are used in two ways. First, family members use the information to guide their behavior at the moment. Second, they use the data to help them build and refine the family-related cognitions that, as a group, constitute what we call their *personal theory* (PT) *of family life and family relationships.*

Once established, an individual's PT becomes a force within him or her. It shapes how he or she perceives, processes, and reacts to family members and events that unfold in family life. It directs the individual to function in ways that the theory suggests will help him or her satisfy needs and achieve desired goals.

PTs have the important advantage of providing their possessors with a conceptual framework that they can use to guide them in family settings. The framework organizes the mass of information to which individuals are exposed, coming both from the inside (e.g., thoughts and feelings) and from the outside (e.g., events, others' comments and behaviors). However, these theories have disadvantages as well.

One limitation of most PTs is that they lead family members to react to each other in terms of stereotypical roles, rather than in terms of who they are as individual people. For example, Carl often relates to Janet in ways his PT tells him a man should relate to "a wife." At these times Carl does not give much weight to Janet's unique personality characteristics. Then, when undesired events unfold in their household, Carl attributes them to Janet's attitude and is not at all aware of the role his PT might have played in fostering these specific outcomes. The findings of deTurck and Miller (1986) apply to this unknowing use Carl makes of his PT. They reported that spouses who had fine-grained representations of their partner's attitudes, beliefs, and habits tended to have greater marital satisfaction than their peers who did not.

Perhaps the greatest limitation of most PTs is that individuals are generally not aware of having and using one and, therefore, cannot subject it to careful scrutiny. Although individuals will never have the luxury that scientists enjoy to manipulate one variable at a time, if individuals were taught to engage in effective and focused metacognition, they would discover that they have a PT and learn much more about the impact their PT has. This activity would be particularly worthwhile in helping people like the Procios recognize that their PTs lead them to repeatedly encounter the same kinds of problems and, each time, to experience the same types of difficulties in finding solutions. For example, because neither Carl nor Janet effectively analyzed their drive-home interaction and worked to change aspects of their PTs, they are doomed to use their PTs in much the same way the next time a similar situation arises and to re-experience the same types of problems.

Assumption 2. Individuals' cognitions affect virtually every aspect of their family life. One begins to get a sense of the impact that cognitions have on individuals in family life by considering the five categories of cognitive variables identified as important in close relationships (Baucom, Epstein, Sayers, & Sher, 1989). Specifically, cognitions include selective attention (what is noticed), attributions (how individuals explain why any given event occurs), expectancies (what individuals predict will occur in the short-, medium-, or long-term future), assumptions (how individuals think the world "works"), and standards (what individuals believe "should" be). When the content of these and of other cognitions family members hold are understood, effective predictions could be made about how they will function as a unit and about the likelihood of their sharing a happy future.

Dattillo and Padesky (1990) suggested that family-related cognitions exist in individuals at three levels of depth: in their automatic thoughts, in their underlying assumptions, and in their core beliefs. Automatic thoughts are those that spontaneously thrust themselves from moment to moment into the individual's awareness or preconscious, presenting ideas or images relevant to what is happening at the moment. Automatic thoughts, which stem from (and follow the themes and logic of) the deeper level cognitions, affect the thoughts, feelings, and behaviors of the individual.

Underlying assumptions lie between automatic thoughts and individuals' core beliefs (Dattillo & Padesky, 1990). They carry the stable rules that individuals apply across situations and serve as a bridge between levels. The core beliefs are a set of highly valued and relatively difficult to modify cognitions that the individual constructed as he or she experienced the world. The core beliefs form the heart of the individual's family-related schemata. They guide the individual's thoughts, feelings, and behavior in the family, and have a major impact on his or her experiences in family life.

Assumption 3. Romantic relationships and family units develop in healthy directions unless their progress is blocked by problems or other obstacles. The roots of such blockage typically lie in the cognitions and PTs of the romantic partners or family members.

In making this assumption, the CBF model follows conceptual models in the fields of child psychopathology (Wenar, 1990) and sexual dysfunctions (Masters & Johnson, 1966), both of which assume that development naturally follows a healthy course, unless obstacles are introduced that cause problems. Respectively, they assume that child development and healthy sexual expression inevitably unfold on course, unless obstacles block the processes involved.

Similarly, the CBF model assumes that when romances end or when families can no longer live as physically intact units, there are identifiable obstacles that blocked the processes that otherwise would have led the individuals forward in healthy ways. The CBF model assumes that the roots of the obstacles lie in family members' PTs. More specifically, the cognitions within their PTs were such that the individuals were unable to find ways of relating to each other (see discussion of family constitution in chapter 4) that provided them with sufficient benefits to compensate for their costs of being involved (see discussion of cost–benefit cognitions in chapter 4).

Assumption 4. Individuals would better achieve individual and family goals if they were more aware of the cognitions in their personal theories of family life and family relationships (PTs) and of how these cognitions impact their functioning. Further, with such awareness, family members would problem solve more effectively and gain more benefits in family life with fewer costs.

Methods are outlined later in the book that can be used to teach individuals, in therapy or in other programs, the CBF model and how to use it. The techniques presented can be used to help individuals develop their skills in: (a) becoming more aware of the family-related cognitions they hold, (b) identifying how specific cognitions affect them in certain situations, (c) noting when specific cognitions are causing distress in them or in family members, and (d) replacing unhelpful cognitions with health-promoting ones. Next, we briefly discuss the value to individuals of learning to effectively use the CBF model.

THE CBF MODEL: A VEHICLE
FOR IMPROVED FAMILY PROBLEM SOLVING

Carl, Janet, and Jeff Procio encountered the ride-home and the math-homework problems on consecutive days. In each case, Carl made a suggestion to a family member, hoping to teach that individual something he "knew" and thereby spare that individual the heartaches that result from not knowing. In both cases, Carl's efforts were resisted. Neither Janet nor Jeff thought about why they resisted or about the value of what Carl offered. Instead they reacted "automatically," guided by cognitions that told them: "It's 'awful' to be criticized by a family member," "Do whatever possible to avoid it," and "Ignore or resist Carl's suggestions, even if they might help you achieve a goal to which you aspire."

If a practitioner using the CBF model worked with the Procios, a challenging but achievable goal would be to teach them to function as if they were their own cognitive-behavioral therapists. More specifically, the practitioner would show the Procios how to identify troublesome situations as they were brewing, to isolate cognitions in their PTs that had contributed to causing the situations, and to replace these cognitions with more health-promoting ones.

A successful intervention would help the Procios avoid many problems in the future, better handle the inevitable stresses of family life, and gain fuller satisfaction from their day-to-day activities. The practitioner would achieve these ends by teaching the Procios about the CBF model and this would lead them to be more self-reflective—to develop their metacognition skills, to become more aware of the value of taking the interpersonal perspective, and, finally, to come to understand the origins of their PTs.

Metacognition

As explained in chapter 2, metacognition refers to the process of actively reflecting on one's cognitions. The Procios would become better problem solvers by strengthening their metacognition skills. They would come to recognize that they, like all individuals, are susceptible to making generalization errors in building cognitions and in developing their PTs. For example, through metacognition, Janet and Carl could discover the nature of the "errors" that were involved in their ride-home and math-problem episodes. Specifically, without thinking about the issue, Janet and Carl applied cognitions in their family of procreation that were drawn directly from their lives in their families of origin.

Janet might discover that she "heard" and reacted to Carl's comments as if they were from her mother to her—the little girl. Through metacognition she could discover that she learned cognitions in childhood that said, "Don't let a family member criticize you; it amounts to losing love. Don't fight with powerful family members. They might take away love. Act helpless and you will get attention." Whereas Janet's parents did provide attention when Janet followed these cognitions, Carl has not. His cognitions direct him to act in a logical way and to deal with matters that are out in the open.

With continued use of metacognition, the Procios could identify other types of family problems that stemmed directly from their cognitions and PTs. For example, Carl, after engaging in metacognition, could discover that he had been assuming that Janet and Jeff would react to him the way he and his siblings reacted to Carl's father, Mr. Procio. That is why when he made his comments to Janet and when he offered to help Jeff, he expected positive responses, even though many previous efforts had been passively rebuffed. Through more self-reflection, Carl might become aware that his comments and suggestions often have an entirely different meaning to Janet and Jeff than what he intended. Recognition of this could lead Carl to monitor his comments for any condescending qualities and to be more aware of the impact he is having on his wife and son.

With continued and systematic use of metacognition, Janet could work on being less resistant and more receptive to his suggestions. She could come to recognize that she was handicapping herself by having these cognitions in her PTs. With this recognition, a measure of determination, and support from her family, she could then come to accept suggestions and criticisms from Carl and others, and become more productive and self-fulfilled.

Continued use of metacognition could help Jeff, too. In ways consistent with his level of intellectual development, he could first come to recognize that he had learned from his mother a set of cognitions that guide him in reacting to his father. Next, he could come to see the consequences of these cognitions, some of which lead him to resist his father's assistance. Through metacognition, he could come to recognize that he would be better off if he and his father learned to relate to each other in more effective ways or, more broadly, if he had the fullest possible relationship with both parents.

The Value of Taking an Interpersonal Perspective

Deal, Halverson, and Wampler (1989) made an extremely important, albeit obvious, point: To understand a relationship, observers (and family members) need data that shed light on that relationship itself, not simply the individually oriented data that provide information about each participant. Clinical experiences suggest, however, that individuals' PTs tend to explain interactions and household events in terms of what is within the individuals involved (e.g., personalities, motivations), rather than in terms of what goes on between people or what connects them.

For example, parents who see their daughter physically poke her older brother for no reason apparent to them would likely apply an intrapsychic explanation, concluding that she is in a bad mood or is behaving this way because of her "ornery" personality. Nonetheless, the parents could not fully understand the physically aggressive behavior unless they took an interpersonal perspective and recognized that the two siblings often compete for parental attention and were in fact yesterday engaged in an angry battle that was not settled.

This example illustrates the CBF model's position that the behavior of each family member is inextricably connected with the current and/or past behavior of others, and usually can be fully understood only in this context. It also shows why the Procios' problem-solving skills would be strengthened if they came to recognize that when they experience and react to events unfolding in their household, they almost inevitably apply an intrapsychic perspective. This is how they learned to think as they observed others in various kinds of interactions and heard them talk about these interactions. Similarly, the Procios as young children with impressionable PTs, like most people, came to understand their interactions with others in simple, "me" versus "them" terms. At present, only through metacognition, self-reflection, and learning to apply their PTs in new, disciplined ways can they begin to overcome this tendency.

As they learn to look at issues from an interpersonal perspective, they will discover that they more fully understand what happens within their unit. This discovery, in turn, will lead family members to expand their PTs so that they go beyond the intrapersonal perspective and direct their possessors to seek insight into what is happening between people in the household as they communicate, work together, and share dreams.

Another way to help the Procios take an interpersonal perspective is for them to think about their family as an organization that initially involved a merger (Mirvis & Marks, 1992) and that involves coordinated efforts to help it achieve its goals (Peters, 1982; Sandy, 1990). Although families can be considered organizations, they are unique in that members typically enter through marriage, birth, or adoption, and maintain a high degree of affection and loyalty to each other.

The Procios' problem-solving abilities would also be strengthened if they learned to view their family as an organization. By doing so, they would be more likely to take into account the issue of *organization rules and by-laws* when they engaged in metacognition. The CBF model suggests that families are guided by a family constitution (discussed in chapter 4)—an unwritten set of rules created by family members that regulates interpersonal relationships in the household. Although family members are only vaguely or not at all aware that this set of rules exists, it creates expectations, directs family members' thoughts and reactions, and shapes the nature of their interactions.

For example, when Jeff announced his poor showing on the test, the Procio family constitution dictated that the parents had to act quickly and, more specifically, that the father, who is college educated, had to be in charge of helping Jeff correct matters.

Finally, viewing the family as an organization would also alert the Procios of changes that they will face in the near future. The family, like its members, changes over time. As Jeff approaches adolescence and becomes more mature, his needs will change and so will the nature of their family. If the Procios engage in effective metacognition, they will be better able to prepare for and adjust to these changes.

The Origins of PTs and Their Associated Cognitions

The Procios would strengthen their problem-solving skills by coming to understand how individuals build their PTs. Such understandings serve many functions including helping individuals become masters of their cognitions, instead of vice versa, and helping them recognize that cognitions are learned and, therefore, can be eliminated or replaced by new ones.

To understand their family-related cognitions, the Procios would first start by examining their childhoods. For example, they would imagine Carl and Janet, moments after their births, lying peacefully in their mothers' arms. Then they would ask, what happened in their lives from that point, when they had no family-related cognitions, until they reached young adulthood and met and married each other?

As they reflected on this they would recognize that, as the weeks, months, and years passed, Carl and Janet experienced an uncountable number of interactions in their environments and, as a result, constructed and continually refined a model of the world and how to operate effectively within it. Through these efforts, Carl and Janet learned how to accurately predict the impact their behaviors would have and, therefore, learned how to adjust to the requirements of the environment. Of course, many of these learnings related to family life and formed the cognitions that constitute their PTs.

The experiences that Carl and Janet had were unique, partly because of who they were, partly because of how their parents thought of themselves and of them, and partly because of the family interactions that emerged after they joined their respective family units. For instance, some newborns face a greater challenge from the outset because of the environments in which they were conceived and into which they were born. Janet's parents waited for and planned the conception and joyfully looked forward to the birth. They felt a sense of accomplishment when it took place and enjoyed the opportunity to care for their newborn (Rayner, 1986). Had Janet's mother adjusted poorly to pregnancy and experienced marital discord, soon after birth Janet might have lagged behind her peers developmentally. Instead, Janet was, in a sense, part of a family and a social network before her birth, and this had an impact on her mother and the environment she experienced within the womb (Gottlieb & Pancer, 1987).

At birth and in the months and years that follow, individuals' gender, temperament (Chess & Thomas, 1987), birth order (Leman, 1991), growth rate, and interactions with parents (Belsky, 1984) are among the other factors that affect what individuals experience in their families. These factors also influence what they learn about family life and, therefore, the contents of their PTs.

Parents, Grandparents, and Great-Grandparents. Parents, of course, are the principal force in shaping individuals' developing cognitions and PTs. To understand the origins of individuals' family-related cognitions, we can look at their parents' family-related cognitions, and those of their parents' parents, and so forth. By engaging in self-reflection and tracing their psychohistory (see chapter 8), individuals can make useful discoveries. For instance, Janet saw that her "a family member's criticism means lost love" cognition that played a significant role in shaping the drive-home and math-problem episodes were first acquired by Janet's foreparents several generations earlier, and handed down from parents to child ever since.

Janet and Carl and their son (like all individuals) began acquiring family-related cognitions early in childhood, absorbing a great deal of what they saw and heard from caretakers and others in their social environments. From this raw material, they unknowingly built the foundation of their PTs. Although their family-related cognitions continued (or, with Jeff, will continue) to develop throughout childhood, adolescence, and adulthood, these early learnings anchored their PTs and will always retain a disproportionately strong influence. This is why it can be said that Carl's present behavior with Jeff and Janet is partly shaped by what happened to his foreparents decades ago.

Carl's parents, Mr. and Mrs. Procio, immigrated to the United States from Italy in their teens. When Carl was born, his young parents were struggling financially, trying to keep solvent their newly established plumbing business. Carl's first-learned family-related cognitions were heavily influenced by his parents' thinking and behavior as they worked to avoid bankruptcy.

During early childhood, Carl observed his parents "bending over backwards" to be well liked by customers. He learned much by observation and what he noticed was validated by the comments of his take-charge father who often explained, "Be popular. Customers will trade with you if they like you and if everybody in the company sounds competent and self-assured. Present yourself in a friendly, know-what-you're-doing manner and you'll do well in business and be popular." These early-learned lessons remain at the core of the cognitions that guide Carl's interactions with others.

When Carl married Janet, he was awe-struck by her physical appearance, an attribute he associated with popularity. He did not look ahead to a time when he might also want his wife to be an able conversationalist. Now, as he struggles up the executive ladder, he wants her to interact effectively with his colleagues and superiors. To accomplish that, he knows (from his upbringing) that she must be more than attractive. She must be friendly, self-assured, and confident, qualities not well demonstrated if one's voice trails off into the high-pitched, shrill range.

Janet's upbringing differed greatly, and this is reflected in the family-related cognitions that guide her interactions with Carl and the children. Janet's mother dominated her family of origin and controlled everything that went on in the household. Unbeknownst to Janet's mother's conscious mind, whatever the issue, she "had to be right." If Janet said "day," her mother said "night," and vice versa. Janet felt "put down" whenever she was corrected, which was often, and that depleted her self-esteem.

Janet's mother behaved as she did for reasons traceable to her own upbringing. Ironically, however, she was a good-hearted woman who only wanted the best for her children. She never recognized this behavioral pattern in herself and, therefore, could not consider that a consequence of her "I'm right and I'll correct everybody else" behavior would be the sapping dry of her daughter's self-confidence.

Over time Janet learned to cope with her mother's corrections in several self-protective ways. These included: disguising her comments and opinions by vocalizing them in the form of questions; making partial statements of her thoughts and stopping in midsentence so that her mother could finish them; and speaking in a high-pitched voice and using body language that conveyed vulnerability and weakness, discouraging others from attacking.

Besides presenting herself as being weak, Janet also used a passive–aggressive style she unknowingly acquired by observing how her father dealt with her mother. Like her father, Janet learned to let mother "be right" and think that she was "directing" family activities. Often that meant that Janet, like her dad, said "yes" to mother but then went ahead and did exactly what she (Janet) felt like doing. The cognitions in her PT that led her to function in this way throughout childhood and adolescence still guide her behavior. That is, Janet, as an adult, often interacts with Carl and others using the same types of behaviors she used with her mother in her family of origin.

By becoming aware of the origins of the cognitions in her PTs, Janet saw that she had come to apply childhood-learned cognitions (that had in many ways worked for her as a child) in her family of procreation (where they do not work well for her). As a result of this discovery and the changes she made, Janet became a happier and more effective person. Carl, too, made progress in understanding the origins of his PT cognitions.

The Procios' problem-solving abilities were further advanced when they were given a "tool" to help them bridge the gap between their unique PTs. The tool was an understanding of the CBF model. This provided them with a model of how families function and with concepts and a common vocabulary that enabled them to communicate and problem solve more effectively. The next section describes a concept at the heart of the CBF model, the family schema.

FAMILY SCHEMA

The CBF model locates the PT and all other family-related cognitions individuals hold in a construct called the *family schema*. As suggested in Assumption 2, the model assumes that an individual's schemas or knowledge structures have a major impact on his or her thinking, feelings, and behavior and, therefore, on his or her mental health and functioning within the family setting.

Beck et al. (1979) explained that schemas are the stable cognitive patterns that direct individuals to selectively attend to particular aspects of situations and, moreover, to interpret what they perceive in specific kinds of ways. Put another way, schemas are mental structures individuals construct that then screen, mold, and shape the raw perceptions they experience and the sense they make out of them. In the context of family life, Epstein, Schlesinger, and Dryden (1988) proposed that an individual's schemas are "the longstanding and relatively stable basic assumptions that he or she holds about the way the world works and his or her place in it" (p. 13). Further, schemas direct individuals to behave in situations in particular ways.

Family schema is the term used in the CBF model to describe all the cognitions that individuals hold about their own family life and about family life in general. Included among this set of cognitions are an individual's assumptions about family life, attributions about why events occur in the family, and beliefs about what should exist within the family unit (Baucom & Epstein, 1990). The family schema also contains ideas about how spousal relationships should work, what different types of problems should be expected in marriage and how they should be handled, what is involved in building and maintaining a healthy family, what responsibilities each family member should have, what consequences should be associated with the failure to meet responsibilities or to fulfill roles, and what costs and benefits each individual should expect to have as a consequence of being in a marriage (Schwebel & Fine, 1992).

The CBF model assumes that family schemas not only shape how individuals perceive, interpret, and react to events that unfold in family life, but also provide the foundation for their consistency in responses to situations. To illustrate, persons who are feeling depressed have schemas that focus upon the negative and rejecting elements in interactions with their spouse and in

those with their children. The same schemas also lead them to tend to ignore positive elements in situations (Beck et al., 1979; Norman, Miller, & Dow,
1988) and to behave in ways that result in reactions from others that reinforce their initial negative interpretation. Parallel kinds of patterns develop
when individuals function with other styles that influence how they perceive
and react to events in their family. For example, styles characterized as "full
of zest and enthusiasm," "quiet," "timid," "pensive," and so forth, would each
affect individuals' thoughts, feelings, and behaviors and how other family
members would behave toward and react to them.

People's awareness of having and using a structure like a family schema
is limited. Consider Carl again and the fact that all his memories of family
life are stored in one part of the family schema. He uses these memories regularly but is only sometimes aware of doing so. The part of Carl's family schema that contains memories relevant to his family life, like his memory system
in general, is mostly a passive system that stores facts, or declarative
knowledge, and skills, or procedural knowledge.

Both Carl's memory system and this part of the family schema have many
components, but only one part, the working memory, is always active. As
Carl functions in the environment and interacts with family members, he
draws on his working memory in the family schema to guide his behavior
(Bourne, 1992). Sometimes Carl draws on memories to guide his behavior
and is aware of doing so. For example, when he recently dined at his in-
laws, before he asked for seconds he recalled what happened last year when
he asked. In this case his "explicit memory" of his mother-in-law's comments
about his waist led him to forgo seconds. Other times, Carl draws upon
memories without accompanying awareness, such as after dinner when he
was sitting comfortably on the patio conversing informally with his father-
in-law about his plans for the garden.

In sum, individuals are sometimes aware of using memories from their
family schema but more often use them without being consciously aware of
doing so. This "automatic" functioning simplifies day-to-day family living, and
helps individuals avoid the barrage of decision making that would otherwise
follow. However, because automatic functioning is rarely brought out on the
table and considered, it may remain in place when the associated behavior
is no longer healthy.

Family Schemas and Kelly's Personal Constructs

The concept of the *family schema* can be further understood in reference
to Kelly's (1955) theory of personal constructs. Kelly suggested that humans
are active in the process of trying to make order out of the world and, by
nature, direct their efforts toward the goal of predicting the future. To make
such forecasts, individuals operate like research scientists. They develop

hypotheses about future happenings and, after testing their hypotheses, will accept, modify, or reject them.

Through this process, each individual assembles a unique set of *personal constructs*, which are ideas or thoughts about how the world works—a minitheory derived from observations and other learnings. Kelly suggested that individuals, on an ongoing basis, observe and refine their personal constructs, so that they can make increasingly more accurate predictions and reduce the uncertainties in life. Extending Kelly's ideas to the family, one expects individuals to be actively and constantly working at building a more effective family schema that accurately predicts how events in family life will unfold.

Jean Piaget and the Development of the Family Schema

Children begin the process of constructing their family schema during the first days of life when they interact with their environment, engaging in reflex and reflexlike behavior. In the first 2 years, or the *sensorimotor period of cognitive development* (Piaget, 1965), as is the case throughout life, individuals use the tools at their disposal to build an understanding of their environment. For instance, during the first month, the sucking reflex not only brings warm milk, but through this activity the infant comes to discover that the nipple she sucks is not part of her.

Although much work using Piagetian theory has been directed at showing how children acquire basic knowledge about the properties of concrete objects, little attention has been focused on the more complex issues of how individuals build understandings of their social world and family life. Nonetheless, an awareness of Piaget's theory gives scientists and practitioners an appreciation of children's abilities and limitations in understanding family life and in building family schemas that give them a veridical picture of family life.

Viewed from the point of view of psychological adjustment, learning about the environment and about the behavior of people in it are important activities for young children. Through observation, imitation, experimentation, and other means, they come to acquire many elementary understandings, including those related to the issue of causality. For example, Piaget's daughter, then somewhat older than 2 years, had her hand slip when she was bathing. Delighted by the splashing water that resulted, she joyfully repeated the behavior several times. However, indicative of her developmental stage, each time she wanted to produce a splash, she started by grabbing her hair, just as she had done the first time.

Over the months and years, as children's cognitive capacities develop (Piaget, 1965), so do their family schemas. At about 2 years of age, when children develop a growing ability to use language, the first stage of development gives way to the second, the *concrete operations* stage (2–11 years). This stage is divided into the preoperational subperiod (2–7 years) and the concrete operations subperiod (7–11 years).

The literature lacks studies describing the sense that a 2-year-old like Piaget's daughter has of family life and her role in it. However, the fact that this period is popularly known as the "terrible twos" suggests that children are working to develop understandings of themselves and how they can and cannot relate to others. Among characteristics of children's thinking that affect their developing family schema during the first part of the preoperational subperiod (2–4 years) are: (a) Their desires distort their thinking, (b) their memories of previous experiences can now help them think concretely about their current situation, and (c) they reason from particular to particular, without reference to the general. This latter characteristic can lead to the child thinking along these lines: "Daddy runs the water in the sink when he shaves. I like to watch him shave, so I'll run the water."

During this period, children are no longer limited in their thinking by the necessity for direct interaction with the environment and those in it. Instead, albeit in a concrete way, they can mentally process symbols that represent aspects of their environment. More specifically, children can engage in thinking that involves mentally imaging a sequence of events, exactly as they would occur if they actually happened. Drawing from their family schema, they can think by "running through" what they expect would happen if, as their mother requested, they put away the toys in the den.

During the latter part of the preoperational subperiod (4–7 years), children use this mental experiment method to solve more complex tasks requiring logical thought. Although their functioning remains limited and rigid, they have the potential to function more effectively in the family environment and to develop more sophisticated ideas in their family functioning. However, they remain limited by the number of dimensions they can mentally consider at one time and by the power of their perceptions. These limits are illustrated by the well-known Piagetian conservation task of rolling a ball of clay into a cylinder shape. After observing the clay rolling, the child is asked, "Now, is there more clay, less clay, or the same amount?" The child at this stage will answer either "more" or "less," responding to the perception of change in the one dimension he or she had focused upon—the clay's length or its "fatness."

Although children's thought continues to remain dependent on their perceptions of concrete events and actions, significant developments occur during the concrete operations subperiod (7–11 years) that strengthen their thinking capacity and enable them to extend their family schema. For example, children become more capable of appreciating that their perspective differs from others. As a result, they become more capable of practicing sociocentered thought and limiting their egocentric thought (in which the world is viewed only through their own perspective). Further, children learn to classify objects and to handle, albeit in concrete ways, two changing dimensions, such as in the rolled clay example. This growth enables children to make further advances in their social interactions and to further refine their family schemas. For example, they can decide to behave in certain ways to concretely learn how their parents and others will react.

At about 12 years of age, children enter the *formal operations stage* and acquire the potential to reason in logical, scientific ways. At this point, young adolescents have the capability to go beyond the concrete and abstractly reason the way to a problem's solution. Their problem-solving approach may involve generating hypotheses, taking many elements of a situation into account, and wrestling with apparent contradictions in a situation. Another key change in this stage is development in individuals' ability to engage in metacognition—their skills in reflecting upon their own thoughts or upon the product of their thoughts (see chapter 2).

Armed with skills in metacognition and the capacity to think like scientists, individuals continue to develop their family schema throughout adolescence and adulthood. From experiences with family members and their increasingly more mature perspective, individuals continually refine their family schema. For example, as they build friendships and date during adolescence, they learn how new friends and associates react to their behaviors in comparison to their family members. Their observations enter their family schema and they engage in metacognition. This could lead them to experiment with new ways of interacting with others. Often, for example, individuals discover that interaction techniques and strategies that "work" with parents in the family environment do not bring desired reactions with peers in the school environment. Thus, the relevant cognitions must be accordingly modified. However, much of the process of adjusting cognitions and behaviors occurs at a low level of awareness in individuals and, therefore, is not as efficient as it might be if individuals thought systematically about these matters.

The Uniqueness of an Individual's Family Schema

Although individuals are very much affected by the society and subculture in which they live, and these have a major impact on individuals' family schemas, family schemas are nonetheless constructed by individuals as they work to make sense of the unique environment in which they live. It is not surprising, therefore, that individuals' family schemas differ. The newborn is welcomed into an environment that is unique and is reacted to in a unique way. Each individual's unique set of experiences and interpretations of them shape his or her family schema and, of course, as the family schema develops, it, in turn, helps determine and shape the experiences an individual has and the interpretation given to them.

Because the family schema contains the entire set of cognitions an individual holds about family life, it can be said to be the lens and vehicle through which an individual views and experiences family life and, at the same time, the guidance system that directs the individual's family-related behavior. Because the construct of the family schema is broad and all-encompassing, researchers, practitioners, and people learning about the CBF theory find it helpful to think in terms of *family schema subconstructs* (FS-SC). Four FS-SC are introduced and discussed in chapter 4: the relationship script, the family constitution, the cost–benefit analyses of family involvement, and the problem-solving strategies.

4

COGNITIONS WITHIN THE
FAMILY SCHEMA

We hope that the CBF model will serve two related, but diverse purposes: to support the work of family scientists and practitioners and to help family members solve problems and create a healthy family unit. Toward these goals, the present chapter focuses on describing the CBF model in detail.

As discussed in chapter 3, the CBF model locates all family-related cognitions individuals hold in a construct called the *family schema*. The cognitions within the family schema can be likened to computer software. They help their possessors function in the family setting, shaping their perceptions, thoughts, reactions, feelings, and behavior, and guiding them through the "challenge" of living family life.

Many cognitions in the family schema provide their possessors with short-cuts through their day-to-day family activities. For example, some cognitions enable individuals to make nearly instantaneous, automatic decisions when faced with theoretically unlimited choices in commonly encountered situations. To illustrate, consider the parent arriving home from a busy day at the office. When stepping from the car, he or she is bombarded by demands for attention from the spouse, children, and family pet. That individual's family schema cognitions will enable him or her to react "automatically," prioritizing the actions to take.

A different set of family schema cognitions operate when the individual cannot react automatically. For example, consider a situation when a teenager requests to stay out somewhat later than usual. The parents may not react automatically because they are experiencing conflict between two sets of cognitions in their family schema—those from their relationship script that want to please the adolescent and those from the family constitution that suggest there is danger in failing to "draw the line." The mother and father will resolve this conflict in their cognitions by utilizing other cognitions that will dictate how they should proceed.

Although the family schema has a finite number of identifiable family-related cognitions that are stored in an organized fashion, thinking about an individual's family-related cognitions as an entire set is inefficient for heuristic and practical purposes. Hence, we partitioned the family schema into *family schema subconstructs* (FS-SC), each of which holds a group of powerful cognitions that guide individuals in their daily functioning in the family environment.

Figure 4.1 depicts the family schema and identifies several FS-SCs: the family constitution, the relationship script with the PT within it, the cost–benefit ratio, and the problem-solving strategies. These FS-SCs contain cognitions that work in a coordinated fashion within the family schema, each performing a unique function. Specifically, the cognitions within the family constitution subconstruct spell out the "rules" regulating family functioning whereas those within the relationship script subconstruct direct individuals in interacting with family members and others. The cognitions within the cost–benefit analyses subconstruct provide individuals with yardsticks for measuring relationships—enabling them to determine whether they are gaining sufficient benefits from their family membership, given their costs. Finally, the cognitions in the problem-solving subconstruct guide individuals in solving the inevitable difficulties they encounter in family relationships.

The discussion of these four FS-SCs begins with consideration of the family constitution. This FS-SC is considered first because, on a time line, it exists

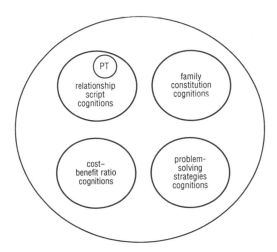

FIG. 4.1.   Family schema and the family schema subconstructs. The family schema contains all of an individual's family-related cognitions.

in the household before an individual joins the family, whether by birth, adoption, or other methods.

THE FAMILY CONSTITUTION

The family constitution contains the unwritten and ever-changing collection of rules that govern family life. Each family member carries a unique version of the family constitution in his or her family schema and this represents his or her understanding of the rules. To state the obvious, families function much more effectively if members hold similar understandings of (have similar cognitions in) their family constitution, or, put another way, if they have similar models in their family constitution about how family members and the family unit should function.

The family constitution delineates broad issues, like how family members should communicate, make decisions, solve problems, share resources and responsibilities, and interact with nonhousehold members. It also specifies detailed procedures and policies, ranging from how the shared toothpaste tube should be squeezed to who is responsible for clearing the dishes from the Sunday breakfast table. As the family and family relationships develop over time, the family constitution changes as well.

A small sample of the range of rules found in family constitutions is listed in Table 4.1. As the rules enumerated suggest, the family constitution serves as a glue, binding members of a household together by organizing and regulating family life and structuring spousal, parental, and sibling interactions. In these ways, the family constitution gives order to family members, making life today more predictable, while, at the same time, providing feelings of security about the future.

Viewers who have seen episodes of the classic television program "All in the Family" could likely identify important aspects of the Bunker family constitution. It specifies that although Archie is "lord and master" of the family and is to be recognized as such, household members also know that Edith is the pillar of strength in the unit, committed to him and comfortable in letting him be in command.

Archie and Edith's constitution helps them maintain the kind of family life they value: They aspire to have a loving marriage, a close-knit family, a happy, successful daughter, and earthy but livable black-and-white rules about work roles, being affectionate in public, which easy chair is Archie's, and so forth. Their constitution also helps maintain closeness by mandating how the spouses should solve a difference: Edith is to back down, allowing Archie to "save face" by solving the problem. However, if the issue greatly concerns Edith, she and Archie may negotiate a settlement. In some circumstances, the constitution directs Archie to distance himself from Edith. For

TABLE 4.1
Sample Rules in a Family Constitution

Rules about family relationships
   * How affection and other feelings will be expressed
   * Benefits and duties of being a spouse, parent, child
Rules about the division of labor
   * Work assignments for individuals
   * Criteria dictating how tasks are assigned
Rules about the use of resources
   * How each person's time is to be budgeted
   * How space in the family home will be used
   * Priorities regarding the spending and saving of money
Rules about how the family constitution can be changed
   * Procedures to be followed (including who has what power)
   * How family will initiate and react to change
   * Special procedures in emergency situations
Rules about how conflict will be resolved
   * Procedures for handling spousal conflict
   * Procedures for handling conflict between children
   * Procedures to limit aggressiveness and to mend hurt
Rules about privacy
   * What privacy individuals are entitled to
Rules about interactions with individuals outside the unit
   * Procedures with members of extended family
   * Procedures with friends
Rules indicating penalties invoked for each type of violation

---

Note. From Schwebel (1992). Reprinted with permission from Aspen Publishers.

example, if he grows anxious about what is happening in the marriage (i.e., too much closeness) or in their extended family, he may flee to his neighborhood tavern.

If one asked Edith about unspoken rules in the Bunker family constitution she might say, "Archie's personality leads him to run the family like a captain runs his ship. But under the surface, Archie's a teddy bear who cares for and protects me, our daughter Gloria, and Mike (her husband) from harm and misfortune.

"My personality leads me to mother—to love and nurture everybody— and to support Archie in doing what he believes is best for us. Although Gloria and Mike would probably dispute it, I believe Archie and I are 50–50 partners. Long ago we agreed, without ever discussing it, that he'll run things unless he gets agitated and so outraged that we need a cool head to prevail. Then I step in and, although he complains vigorously, he doesn't really object."

As was the case with the Bunkers', an effective family constitution structures a household's development and, at the same time, is modified by family members so that it can meet their needs as they and their unit grow and develop. For example, the family constitution building begins when two individuals who will eventually form a household first interact. They unknowingly begin the process of creating a dating version of their family constitution. As their relationship progresses, they add and change rules so that the constitution can serve their needs.

The family constitution building process that first unfolds is illustrated by Betty and Jason's relationship. Jason phoned Betty and after a brief chat asked her out. She agreed and he invited her to help plan their date. This discussion, by precedent, established a rule about how future shared time would be planned, should the relationship continue.

During their date, and without discussion, they established many other rules. For example, Jason's PT told him that door-opening behavior was "appropriate" and he did so for Betty, whereas Betty's told her how to dress and behave on a first date that involved dinner and a movie. She wore a "feminine" outfit and set limits on the extent of physical contact. On their second date, and without being consciously aware of thinking about what kind of relationship she wanted, Betty decided to "beat Jason to the door," thereby amending the previously established rule about traditional patterns of behavior at doorways.

At all times, but perhaps most noticeably at the beginning of a relationship, partners, guided by their PTs and other family schema cognitions, steer interactions in directions they deem favorable. Partners engage in a bargaining process because each person has emerged from a family of origin with family schema cognitions that direct him or her to try to create a certain type of family constitution in their romantic relationships and family of procreation. Because both partners have this aim and will inevitably have many different wishes, if their relationship is to endure, they must forever be resolving door-opening issues and a multitude of others.

As the example of Betty and Jason shows, from the moment the earliest rules are introduced (e.g., who takes responsibility for initiating and maintaining conversation, who decides how they are going to structure their time, who makes arrangements for future get-togethers), family constitutions begin to require modifications. This occurs because developing relationships, changed circumstances, and new personal needs affect how partners can and want to interact. Therefore, ongoing constitutional change is necessary and vital in support of partners' and family members' efforts to achieve their goals and have harmony. Family constitutions, therefore, contain rules that regulate the process through which they can be "amended."

The *rules for change* are established in the family constitution much like other ones, with minor amendments often being instituted by precedent and without discussion, such as the first time a couple has two dates in one weekend, or when the partners first kiss. In contrast, as the following example illustrates, major changes usually occur one step at a time when family members amend old rules or form new ones, using discussion, behavioral precedent, societal traditions, cultural or peer group norms, and other means:

> Last summer Lily and Harvey, and their 3-year-old, Pat, moved to a snow-prone mountainous region. When they arrived, their family constitution rules assigned food-shopping responsibilities to Lily and those for driving on difficult or dangerous roads to Harvey.
>
> One Saturday in October, the couple awoke to discover snowy conditions. Because they needed cereal and milk for Pat, Harvey announced that he would drive to the market; Lily told him what aisles to search for the goods. The couple had amended its constitution to meet its current needs and the unique circumstances that had emerged. From that point on, Harvey went shopping from time to time when no emergency conditions existed.
>
> Two weeks later the couple was challenged again. The ground was snow-covered, the cupboard was empty, and Harvey was in bed with an oppressive case of the flu. Lily, after seeking Harvey's advice about steering out of skids, drove to the market, amending the family constitution.

As soon as new and amended rules enter the family constitution, they acquire their own "power," directing individuals' behaviors and, concomitantly, influencing their perceptions, thoughts, information processing mechanisms, and feelings. For instance, Harvey's thoughts and feelings about himself changed forever when he shopped for his family, as did Lily's a fortnight later, when she drove through several inches of snow.

Transition Points

As mentioned earlier, the constitution-rewriting process intensifies at points of change in the relationship, such as when the partners "go steady," become engaged, marry, establish a household, have a baby/adopt a child, launch an adolescent, or retire. The undefined future leads partners to engage in a usually benevolent struggle, directing the family constitution in ways suggested by their PTs and closer to their own personal preferences. Typically, partners push in directions that mirror what they experienced in the constitution that governed their family of origin (Whitaker & Keith, 1981). However, as each person tries to pull the family in directions he or she desires, family members may resist or actively push in other directions, as in the following example:

> The newlywed Wilsons are adjusting to life with shared bank accounts. Phil came from a family that spent freely and used credit cards to accumulate significant debt, whereas Tanya's budget-oriented family of origin prided itself on careful money management, conservative spending, and paying with cash. In the months ahead each spouse will subtly and not so subtly attempt to have his/her PT-based financial style become "family law."

Of course, if the relationship is to endure, compromises must be struck and the spouses must become tolerant of the other's view. However, even after the initial agreements and compromises are made, the battle may continue indefinitely, producing ever-evolving rules in the constitution. As this unfolds, family members who engage in limited self-reflection and metacognition will fail to recognize that their partner's persistence in championing particular family constitution rules comes from their PT and long-held family schema values concerning what makes for successful family life. Spouses who do not recognize this may misattribute their partner's persistence to undesirable personality characteristics (Baucom, 1987). Phil, for instance, called Tanya "stubborn, miserly, and cheap" after she criticized his use of credit cards to buy what she considered a foolish and unnecessary "luxury" item—a big-screen television.

Family Typologies

During early phases of a romantic relationship, important aspects of their family constitution take shape, leading the couple to interact in ways that may be predictable to observers. Those who know them might say, "The Smiths are a unique family . . . they have a particular kind of character . . . we know even before we ask them to see a play with us that no matter who answers the phone, they won't accept the invitation immediately. They check with each other, call back and apologize for the delay, and ask us to join them for dessert." As Constantine (1986) noted, although all families are confronted with the same problems—both the daily trifles and the larger issues—they differ in their methods of dealing with them.

These differences are what *family typologies* (Constantine, 1986; Kantor & Lehr, 1975) or, in Reiss' (1981) terminology, *family paradigms*, are based on, and they can be used to understand and categorize family members' interaction patterns and styles of functioning. Family paradigms are worldviews or models or images that family members share and that organize their family life. Family typologies and paradigms, which provide holistic characterizations of family functioning, are driven by underlying cognitions. They can be understood in terms of the rules that family members have established in their family constitutions to guide their interactions and to provide them with a sense of predictability and comfort about their interactions.

As discussed further in chapters 7, 8, and 9, it would be helpful for couples to develop a blueprint of the kind of family unit they consider desirable and healthy, and then to thoughtfully develop rules in their family constitution that would help them achieve this. Although individuals do not receive education or training that would lead them to even think about engaging in this kind of planning, familiarity with the CBF model may open new options for them. Not only would it lead them to think about actively building the kind of home environment they desire, but it would provide tools to help them accomplish this.

Couples and family members who proactively consider the kind of family constitution they want to build would benefit by learning about the concept of *family wellness*, a term Mace (1983) used to convey the idea that family health is much more than simply the absence of pathology. A healthy family is a flourishing entity that meets the constantly changing challenges it faces while, at the same time, providing its members with a health-promoting environment. This important topic is discussed further in the next chapter.

THE RELATIONSHIP SCRIPT

Whereas the family constitution is an interpersonal entity that develops as the family does, the *relationship script* FS-SC (see Fig. 4.1) is an intrapsychic one that grows as the individual does. The relationship script contains the set of cognitions that tell an individual how to function and relate to others in the family and outside of it (Schwebel, Schwebel, Schwebel, Schwebel, & Schwebel, 1989). It is prescriptive, indicating what is possible and desirable in relationships, and it regulates thoughts, feelings, perceptions, and behaviors. The relationship script dictates values, coping style, emotional sensitivity, capacity to love, and communication approaches in relationships, as well as governing abilities to cooperate, problem solve, and resolve interpersonal conflict (Schwebel et al., 1989).

As presented in chapter 3, one component of the relationship script is the personal theory of family life and family relationships (PT). The PT reflects the individual's perceptions of what families are like and what they should be like. An individual's PT leads him or her to think, feel, behave, and react to others in ways that move family life and family relationships toward the image the individual's cognitions specify are ideal.

The "Script" in Relationship Scripts

The relationship script directs its possessor much like a character in a movie is directed by the film's script. Although family members believe they are free to act as they may wish to when interacting with others, the CBF model suggests that the individuals are actually following the dictates of their relationship script. Thus, for example, when two teenagers decide they are in love, they follow their cognitions and act toward each other in ways society has taught them that people in love should.

Because individuals consistently follow their unique relationship script mandates, other people notice regularities in their interpersonal behavior and personality (e.g., "Betty is an outgoing and social wife"; "Jason is cheerful"; "Pat rarely takes the lead, but is a loyal spouse and parent").

Groups of people, because of how they are treated by others or what is expected from them, tend to develop some similar cognitions in their relationship scripts. Evidence of this is found in the fact that only children, first-borns, middle-borns, and last-borns tend to have certain characteristics (Leman, 1991) or, put another way, cognitions in their relationship scripts. Because they have some similar cognitions, predictions can be made about how the family constitution of two firstborns who marry might differ from that of two last-borns (Leman, 1991).

Other psychological theories and research findings can also be applied in CBF to explain why groups of people who have had similar experiences (and presumably developed some similar cognitions) behave in similar and predictable ways in given circumstances. For example, Bowlby (1988) developed *attachment theory*, and in his writings he has described certain characteristics and behaviors that are associated with individuals who had certain experiences in their attachment histories. The CBF model argues that people with a given attachment history acquired certain kinds of cognitions in their relationship scripts, and these account for behaviors they exhibit and the relationship script they follow when they interact with others.

Differences between relationship scripts of women and men are illustrated and, at least in part, perpetuated by differences in the use of language. Men's speech tends to be straightforward and often abrupt. Men say, "Jot that down," "Hand me the recorder," and so forth, whereas women's speech tends to be less direct. To achieve this, women use intensifiers ("The movie was *so* fascinating and I had *such* a good time"), construct sentences with helper verbs (e.g., can, should, would, might, will, have, been, etc.), and use longer sentences and sometimes tag questions ("Henry is going to attend that meeting, isn't he?") (Lakoff, 1975). Gender-related teachings are provided to children early, as they master their native tongues.

After viewing a few episodes of the popular situation comedy "All in the Family," one can identify key aspects in Archie's and Edith's relationship scripts by recalling regularities in their behavior. By functioning like a detective or a scientist, one could develop hunches or hypotheses about the kinds of family-related cognitions the characters of Archie and Edith have in their relationship scripts.

Given Archie's behavior, one might deduce that his relationship script gives him the "need to feel superior to others, and he acts this need out by means of a facade of knowing everything, despite his ignorance and unworldliness . . . [He also achieves this] by putting down ethnic and religious groups and individuals, including his wife and son-in-law. In his sledge-hammer style, Archie is open about everything except sex and tender emotions, which he feels but dares not voice. Underneath it all, however, Archie is an insecure man, who is very much in need of the unconditional love he gets from his wife and the not-quite unconditional love and affection his daughter gives" (Schwebel et al., 1989, p. 39).

Archie's PT is also evident. He believes that families should consist of a husband, a wife, and their children. Furthermore, the husband should work outside of the home and should "call the shots," whereas a wife should be a homemaker and care for the children. The children should be taught discipline, to mind their elders, and to learn the value of hard work. His PT indicates that families who deviate from this arrangement are deficient. Because an increasing number of families do not function in this manner, he is distraught with the decay of "family values."

Key concepts of Archie's relationship script are clear to observers who note regularities in his behavior. Archie, however, like most people, is not aware of having a relationship script. Although he does not engage in much self-reflection or metacognition, if asked he would say that "I just act like any regular guy does. I work for a living and I understand how politics works and what a guy has to do to get what he wants. I love my family, I am a patriotic veteran of WWII and I love my country. Although I believe in God, I don't have time to go to church. I'm not a bigot but let's face it, pal, we have too many give-away programs for minorities, protestors, lazy students, women, and everybody else but the hard-working, patriotic American."

In contrast to Archie's, Edith's relationship script directs her to be friendly, loving, warm, and eager to please family members and others. She might be aptly described as an eternal, maternal giver. She openly and proudly expresses love for her family and she enjoys providing caring support for neighbors, regardless of age, race, or ethnic origin. In fact, her relationship script enables her to enjoy serving others and helping them solve problems. This holds whether she is delivering Archie's after-work beer, assisting her children or the neighbor's, or generously donating her time to the seniors in the Sunshine Center.

Edith's PT is similar to Archie's. However, in contrast to her husband, she places a greater emphasis on the socioemotional needs of family members. Although she wants children to learn discipline, she also is concerned that they feel comfortable in the family, receive the support they need, and are happy with their lives. Although she is willing to let Archie control many aspects of family decision making, she is unwilling to let Archie interfere with family members meeting their socioemotional needs.

Family functioning is facilitated when spouses have compatible relationship scripts. In the Bunkers' case, Edith's need to nurture and give love is quite compatible with Archie's need for approval. However, some spouses have conflicting relationship scripts and this can cause difficulties. Helping spouses who are in this dilemma is discussed further in chapters 7 and 8.

Cognitions in Relationship Scripts

Within an individual's relationship script, there are some cognitions with broad applicability (e.g., "Above all, be pleasant while interacting with others"), some with narrowly defined utility (e.g., "At wedding parties be deferent to the newlyweds' parents"), with the vast majority falling in between. Although the CBF model assumes that relationship scripts contain literally hundreds or thousands of interrelated cognitions, an individual's relationship script can be characterized by identifying one or two outstanding features in his or her interactions with others.

Once observers identify outstanding characteristics in an individual's behavior or personality, they can deduce from these the kinds of cognitions that he or she holds. Then, using an MMPI-2-like (Minnesota Multiphasic Personality Inventory-2) approach (MMPI-2 scores on the two highest scales are often used to provide clinical insights), observers can predict from these cognitions the kinds of thoughts, feelings, and behaviors the individual may experience/produce in various types of interactions. Examples of outstanding characteristics that would provide insight into an individual's cognitions and interactions with others appear in Table 4.2.

Janet Procio, who was discussed in chapter 3, has a relationship script that can be characterized by passive behavior that helps keep her from either being, or thinking she is being, evaluated or criticized. Her relationship script also leads her to start sentences and let others finish them.

Another characteristic of Janet's relationship script is to want to be help-

TABLE 4.2
Common Relationship Script Characteristics

* the need to be bright and right
* the need to be seen as attractive and desirable
* the need to be seen as entertaining
* the need to see that rules are enforced
* the need to care for others and be seen as self-sacrificing
* the need to be seen as athletic and in style
* the need to be in control of interactions
* the need to be on guard, so no one will take advantage
* the need to be "daddy's little girl" or "mommy's good boy"
* the need to engage in or avoid confrontation and conflict
* the need to be adaptive, flexible, and "cool"
* the need to share feelings and closeness with others
* the need to avoid feelings of weakness and vulnerability
* the need to withhold information and feelings
* the need to show off expertise
* the need to engage in power plays
* the need to build consensus and good feelings
* the need to disguise ignorance when one does not know an answer

ful and giving. She partly satisfies this by working as a volunteer at her church, but it is harder for her to satisfy this part of her at home, because of her other relationship characteristic—the fear of criticism. This might lead her to respond to her husband in the following manner:

> Carl (who is driving a rented car in a foreign country new to him): What's the speed limit?
> Janet: There's a sign (pointing to what was obviously the route number sign).
> Carl: That's the route number.
> Janet: Right. Oh, I remember. It's 100 kph on this stretch of road.
> Carl: (while stepping on the accelerator) Thanks.
> Janet: (some moments later) Or maybe it's 50 . . .

In this interaction she tried to be helpful while she also tried to avoid making a mistake. However, in this effort, she frustrated Carl and he criticized her for providing misinformation that led him to speed. For all her effort, Janet ended up feeling just as she had when her mother had criticized her during childhood.

Janet's behaviors are directed "automatically" by relationship script cognitions. They require little or no thought on her part. In this way, relationship cognitions limit their possessors' choices in day-to-day opportunities and, in a sense, deprive them of opportunities to experiment and grow. In exchange, however, relationship scripts provide order in individuals' lives and eliminate the stress they would otherwise experience if they had to stop and think more thoroughly about each of the countless decisions they make. The automatic nature of relationship script cognitions has another extremely important function in households: It helps make each individual's behavior more predictable and, therefore, less threatening to other family members.

The Origins of Relationship Scripts

The CBF model assumes that individuals acquire the basic cognitions in their relationship scripts in the family of origin and mostly without being aware that this is happening. The process begins as babies learn basic behaviors, such as how to get their needs met by caretakers. To use an analogy, imagine that infants are born with minds formatted like blank computer diskettes. Over a period of years, their family members, and particularly their caretakers, teach them how to relate to others, placing data sets and files of cognitions on their diskette.

For instance, the techniques individuals use to get fed, changed, and attended to, shape how they come to understand the social environment and the personal style they develop for interacting within it. Some children discover that if they sob softly, caretakers will respond to their needs. Some learn to wail, whereas still others come to recognize that they will be ignored or punished if they cry, and that they must wait until their caretakers come to them.

Of course, one incident does not usually shape cognitions in an individual's mind. However, repeated exposure to patterns of interactions have the potential to do so. Given this, the "invisible fly on the ceiling" who watched caretakers interact with their children would note regularities in their interactions and could develop reasonable hypotheses about the kinds of cognitions the children would eventually acquire. This observant fly, therefore, could also predict with accuracy that certain characteristics will emerge in these children's relationship scripts and be displayed in their behavior.

For example, if observers note that a girl always has to cry or otherwise protest when hungry, thirsty, tired, or bored, they will predict that her cognitions will indicate that the world provides gratification only after she complains. If, on the other hand, observers note that parents continually cater to their son's wishes and needs before he expresses them, they would predict that he will develop cognitions that lead him to expect others to cater to him. If observers further note that these parents do not discipline this boy, they would also expect him to acquire other cognitions. For example, he might come to feel entitled to respond to impulses and to later resist those who attempt to set limits with him. The following example illustrates the long-term effects of relationship-script-shaping experiences.

During Johnny's childhood and adolescence his parents owned a small chain of dry cleaners and these businesses placed a great demand on their time. Johnny and his four siblings were on their own after school and until 9:30 P.M., when the stores were closed and the accounts tallied. The children had to stay home and each one had daily chores. Johnny and an older sister, however, carried most of the burden because two other siblings were younger and the oldest child in the family, a brother, had a slight physical handicap. When any chores were left undone, Johnny and this sister were scolded, sometimes with harsh words. Reflecting on his childhood now, as an adult, Johnny explains, "We never had a family. We were just people who happened to occupy the same house. Moreover, us kids were bossed, bullied, and manipulated by our older brother, and Mom and Dad never recognized this."

The events just summarized shaped Johnny's relationship script and have direct consequences on how he, now 26 years old, views work, housing, and relationships. He refuses to take a job in which a boss directly supervises him or in which he has to directly serve others. Further, he lives in a rooming house, claiming to save rent but pointing out, "You don't have roommates or family members bugging you and you don't really know other residents except to say hello."

Johnny's abrasive interpersonal style stands out. When asked about his social life he explained, "In college people tried to get me to party. I didn't go. They came back drunk and told me how much fun I missed. One night I sarcastically said, 'Wish I could go to a party and get bombed out of my mind.' Then they got mad. See, you can't count on people." Johnny explains his outlook in the following way, "As a child I always had to stand up for myself. I could depend on nobody and nobody cared about me. So why should I care what anybody else thinks? I don't need a big social life. I have a girl-friend who lives about 750 miles away. We call every other week or so."

One episode of the "Golden Girls" situation comedy also illustrates the impact that parents and grandparents have on an individual's relationship script. In it, Blanche hosts her visiting grandson. This adolescent soon gets into minor trouble with neighborhood teens and is criticized by Blanche and her three housemates. The young man excuses his behavior by griping, "My folks don't care about me."

When alone with her housemates, Blanche accepts blame for the lad's behavior and poor outlook because, after all, she failed to raise his mother correctly. "No," the others reacted, "it's not your fault." After a moment Blanche responded, "That's right, it's my mother's fault because of the way she raised me." Implicit in this episode was the idea that aspects of relationship scripts and family constitutions are handed down from one generation to the next. Like recipes, each user adds or subtracts ingredients (cognitions), depending on his or her unique characteristics and experiences. Blanche's grandson related to the world in a particular way, to a large extent because his mother, Blanche's daughter, provided him with an environment that taught him to hold certain cognitions about how he should relate to others. His mother, of course, learned much about how to raise children and how families should operate from Blanche who, years earlier, had learned this from her own parents, and so on.

Change and Continuity in Individual's Relationship Scripts

Although early experiences form the foundation of the relationship script, its contents change regularly. Adolescents and adults, like playwrights, are capable of engaging in the self-reflection and metacognition necessary to intentionally change aspects of their relationship script so it brings them more satisfaction and fewer problems. Nonetheless, most changes they make are reactive—they develop in response to day-to-day demands to which individuals must adjust.

Although most of these demands come from forces outside the individual, sometimes they stem from internal pressures, such as those that emerge when individuals grow. For example:

Peggy, who was raised in a traditional Appalachian family, married young and cared for her four children. In her thirties, she moved to the city with her husband. There she met neighbors interested in women's issues and personal development. In discussions with them, Peggy came to recognize that her relationship script had led to behavior that typically resulted in her receiving the "short end" of the stick. Motivated by this awareness, she worked to change her relationship script and become more assertive.

One force that retards changes in relationship scripts is how they affect family systems. At first, when Peggy tried to change her cognitions and behaviors, her husband and children felt threatened and resisted her efforts. They feared that if she changed they, too, would be forced to change. The family found a comfortable balance between continuity and change and this enabled Peggy to move forward and her family to support her. Kevin, in contrast, changed because his environment demanded it, as the following illustrates:

Kevin, now 7 years of age, lives with parents and 16- and 20-year-old siblings. He entered kindergarten and Sunday School last year with a relationship script that led him to act in "babylike ways." Although at home he maintained the "poor me, help me, feed me, bathe me" style that had long characterized his relationship script, in the other settings he soon learned that his babylike approach was not effective. His teacher and peers did not relate to him as he wanted when he functioned in babylike ways. He soon tried other ways to win attention and friendship in these settings.

Teenagers provide a good example of people who try to intentionally change their relationship script in order to bring desired social outcomes. After engaging in self-reflection, metacognition, and an assessment of "their personality," they may take certain steps in an effort to become more popular. Ironically, how much change and self-improvement they are able to make and their level of success will be partially determined by cognitions they hold about themselves. For instance, those who have cognitions that let them be flexible and adaptive will find change easier than others, as in the following example:

Tiffany, age 13 years, has been a member of a clique that now is becoming more seriously interested in boys. She, herself, has been engaging in self-evaluation and has decided to make more friends and show leadership in school. Her potential for change, however, is limited by her level of intelligence, by traditional views she and her parents hold about girls' roles, and by the fact that her current friends will discourage her from changing.

Chapters 7, 8, and 9 discuss how individuals can be supported in changing their relationship scripts during CBF-model-based counseling, therapy, and education.

COST–BENEFIT ANALYSES OF FAMILY INVOLVEMENT

As individuals go about the business of living their daily lives in family units, they use *cost–benefit analyses (c/b) cognitions*. These cognitions serve several functions. First, they mandate that individuals regularly conduct assessments of whether they are receiving adequate, equitable benefits from family relationships, given the costs involved in maintaining them. Second, the c/b cognitions provide assessment templates that identify and give weights to costs and benefits. These templates dictate precisely what are relationship-related costs and benefits, the weight each particular cost and benefit is to receive, and what the minimum tolerable c/b ratio is for each type of relationship.

Finally, these cognitions motivate their possessor to take action after c/b ratios are determined. More specifically, when c/b analyses indicate that an individual is receiving adequate benefits from a relationship, given its costs, he or she proceeds on the same course with the relationship. However, when c/b analyses indicate inadequate benefits given the costs, the c/b cognitions motivate the individual to take corrective action to remedy the issues, differences, or problems causing the unacceptable cost–benefit ratio. See the following example:

> After 6 years as a homemaker, Wendy took a job outside of the house. Nonetheless, she continued with the same schedule of household chores she practiced before she worked outside the house. Initially, her c/b analyses told her the tradeoff was fair: She wanted to return to the business world, whereas Nick, her husband, wanted her to wait until the children were older. After a few months, however, weariness, exhaustion, and then ill-health set in. This shifted Wendy's c/b analyses to indicate that she was not getting fair benefits, given what she was putting into the family. Wendy identified work equity as the problem and to improve her c/b ratio she asked Nick to renegotiate household responsibilities.

The CBF model maintains that individuals regularly use c/b analyses as yardsticks to assess their family relationships, but do so with little or no awareness. When individuals are told they conduct c/b analyses, they often react, "Not me. That's awful and selfish!" Their reaction is tempered, however, by learning that the behavior is universal—that their spouse and children also conduct analyses to monitor whether their c/b ratios are adequate.

When considered from the perspective of family survival, the benefits of c/b analyses become clearer: Family members use c/b analyses as ongoing "satisfaction indicators," which warn them when problems exist and remedies are necessary. Given this, c/b analyses can be best viewed as ultimately benefiting family members' profit, rather than as being selfish.

C/b analyses can be understood in the context of exchange theory (Homans, 1961). Exchange theory, in its many forms (see Duck, 1988; Thibaut & Kelley, 1959), proposes that individuals try to minimize costs and maximize benefits in forming and maintaining relationships. Benefits from family relationships come when family units enable individuals to meet their basic biological needs, feel a sense of security, and live in an atmosphere in which they feel loved, happy, satisfied, emotionally secure, worthwhile, productive, and motivated to work. Costs related to family relationships include chores and responsibilities and dealing with the inevitable interpersonal conflicts that develop.

Thibaut and Kelley (1959) identified two other factors involved in conducting this type of c/b analysis: an individual's comparison level and his or her comparison level for alternatives. An individual's comparison level is based on the c/b ratios experienced in previous relationships which, it is assumed, shape present expectations (Baucom & Epstein, 1990). In contrast, an individual's comparison level of alternatives is based on how the present relationship's c/b ratio compares to that which the individual believes could be obtained in alternative relationships. Individuals who believe they have alternatives with more favorable c/b ratios may exit the present relationship, whereas those with poorer alternatives will remain, even if their present c/b ratio is only marginally acceptable.

The following example, of Jane and Ted Whitson, illustrates the kinds of processes that might unfold as spouses, with little or no mindful awareness, conduct c/b analyses of their relationship. Having personal, private time is a major benefit Ted seeks in the marriage. However, Jane experiences Ted's private time as a minor cost. As further shown in the equations in Table 4.3, Ted requires a more favorable c/b ratio than Jane, partly because he has experienced this in past relationships and partly because he believes alternative relationships are readily available to him, should this one cease. In contrast, Jane settles for benefits that equal her costs, partly because she experienced this in the past and partly because she abhors the idea of being a single parent. Given these factors, Ted and Jane's c/b cognitions might operate as indicated in Table 4.3 as they, in one instance, evaluate their spousal relationship (the parenthetical numbers indicate their c/b cognitions' weighting of each factor).

Although the CBF model recognizes that individuals do not consciously assign weights to perceived costs and benefits in the precise manner indicated in Table 4.3, it does maintain that they regularly engage in a similar—although probably less quantitative—process. The CBF model further asserts that the c/b ratios that spouses experience are partly determined by the attributions they make about family confict that follow, of course, from the cognitions in their family schemas. Thompson and Snyder (1986) reviewed this literature and discussed the association between relationship satisfaction and attributional processes.

TABLE 4.3
Cost–Benefit Analysis of Ted and Jane Whitson's Relationship

Benefits in family life for Ted = love of children (5) + caring received from Jane (3) + comfortable lifestyle (3) + luxurious home (2) + physical needs taken care of (2) + Jane's earnings (1) + the couple's place in the community (1) + miscellaneous benefits (8) = 25.

Costs in family life for Ted = recurrent tensions with Jane (5) + irritation with Jane's "consistent, incompetent" behavior (3) + disagreements over child care and socialization (2) + constant bickering (1) + annoyance over checkbook imbalances (1) + miscellaneous costs (5) = 17.

Ted's c/b ratio = 17/25; Ted is satisfied because his c/b ratio favors benefits. However, when opportunities arise he will seek to reduce his costs and obtain more benefits.

Benefits in family life for Jane = love of Ted (10) + love of children (10) + physical needs met (3) + financial comfort (5) + team feeling in life's undertakings (8) + having an environment that supports her goal achievement (6) + miscellaneous benefits (6) = 48.

Costs in family life for Jane = Not getting deserved respect (10) + frustration of daily spousal arguments (10) + being ignored by Ted at times (8) + distress children experience when couple fights (7) + dissatisfaction with social life (5) + unhappiness that the children and Ted don't have a closer relationship (4) + miscellaneous costs (4) = 48.

Jane's c/b ratio = 48/48; her minimum desired ratio is 1/1, so this outcome will not "push her" to act to reduce costs or increase benefits. Nonetheless, because she would prefer a more favorable ratio, she will likely seize opportunities that arise to improve the quality of her family life.

Changes in C/B Assessment Templates

The CBF model assumes that as individuals, their relationships, and their life situations change, so do the c/b assessment templates that identify and give weights to costs and benefits in their relationships. For example, as individuals mature, they may value their partner's companionship more than in the past. Similarly, as their relationship develops (e.g., entering the empty nest stage), and as new circumstances emerge (e.g., the addition of a child to the family), the weights they assign various factors are also likely to change (Berg & Clark, 1986).

Murstein's (1976) stimulus-value-role (S-V-R) theory, which focuses on early stages in relationships, illustrates how c/b analyses templates change. The theory proposes a developmental sequence in what individuals value at different points in romantic relationships. First, stimulus factors, such as physical qualities, attract them. Next, as the relationship grows, individuals attend most to whether the other's values and attitudes mesh with theirs. Finally, they focus on the match between their views about roles (e.g., "wife" and "husband") and what they determine to be their potential partner's willingness and ability to perform those roles they think are necessary for a healthy family life.

Avoiding Unacceptable C/B Ratios by Managing Conflict

If marriages and families are to endure as physically intact units, those involved must maintain favorable c/b ratios and this means finding ways to help them avoid and/or manage conflict. If they fail in this endeavor, the c/b ratios of adult family members may grow so unfavorable that they manage their costs by moving out of the household.

As soon as individuals' c/b ratios become unsatisfactory, their c/b cognitions direct them to try to correct matters as quickly as possible. If, at this point, individuals engage in disciplined self-reflection and metacognition, they would improve their chances of success and might choose one of these options:

1. Family members can work cooperatively to alter their home environment (and, therefore, the family constitution and perhaps their relationship scripts), making it more benefit producing:

> Mr. and Mrs. Easton spend most weekends attending to household chores. When summer began, the children asked to spend one Saturday at the lake, swimming, fishing, and picnicking. Mrs. Easton, feeling overloaded, vetoed this, citing the housework that she was "stuck with." That week, however, the Eastons held a family meeting and this plan emerged: Everybody would awake early Saturday and pitch in to finish the household chores by noon. Then they would spend the rest of the day at the lake. By adhering to this plan, they succeeded in increasing the benefits to all family members on this Saturday and in setting the precedent for using this approach on other Saturdays.

2. Family members can work cooperatively to alter their home environment (and, therefore, the family constitution and perhaps their relationship scripts), making it less cost generating:

> Mr. and Mrs. Gerald argued several times a week about money-related issues. After months of disagreements over how much clothing she bought and how many CDs, coins, and hobby items he purchased, they engaged in enough self-reflection to recognize the costs their arguments were placing on the marriage. At this point, the spouses decided to open separate checking accounts. After contributing a specified amount to the monthly family budget, each could spend as they wished. This arrangement immediately reduced the couple's quantity of arguments and the costs of their marriage.

3. Individuals can improve their c/b ratios, without cooperation from family members, by engaging in metacognition and changing their c/b assessment templates:

> Phil, 35 years of age, yearned to start a family with Ellen, age 25 years, his wife of a year. He had thought, "We want three children, and science says they should be 3 years apart. That's 9 years so we need to start having children immediately. Even so, after I retire we'll still be paying for their educations." Ellen was not yet ready and asserted that waiting 12 more months would make little difference. Phil engaged in metacognition that enabled him to revise the weights in his c/b assessment templates. He recognized, "In fact, it is okay to wait a

year before starting the family—that way Ellen will be ready and we can get our credit card balances under control."

Whereas Phil and Ellen's cognitions were not aligned, and that caused their differences, Jane and Nate's were aligned, but unrealistic. They expected "instant love" between stepchildren and the stepparents. After struggling alone with their disappointment in this area, they spoke with friends, also in stepfamilies, and engaged in self-reflection and metacognition. As a result of these efforts, they replaced idealistic and unreasonable expectations with more reasonable goals, and thereby reduced the costs of their marriage.

Many family members harbor another kind of unrealistic expectation: If they are skilled or persistent, they can create a conflict-free household. Epstein and Eidelson (1981) found that holding unrealistic assumptions like this one is associated with marital dissatisfaction. Family members benefit from recognizing that no matter what talents and qualities they possess, interpersonal differences are inevitable. Once family members recognize this, although they still experience the costs associated with interpersonal conflict, these are not compounded by distress stemming from feeling like they failed because they had conflict. The next section explores cognitions family members hold that enable them to cope with these inevitable differences.

PROBLEM-MANAGEMENT STRATEGIES COGNITIONS

Although much research has addressed how individuals function when relationships begin and when they end, relatively few investigations have studied how they behave in the interim. Duck (1988) predicted that this gap will soon close and the issue of relationship maintenance "will be the backbone of books on relating to others" (p. 85). Undoubtedly, a central concern in this area will be identifying and understanding the strategies that partners and family members use to avoid, cope with, and resolve their inevitable interpersonal differences.

The difference in the amount of work directed at the various phases of relationships is due to several factors. First, the early phases are easiest to investigate: Researchers bring unacquainted subjects into a laboratory and observe them interact. Second, research focused on the beginning and the end of relationships has more immediate utility for practitioners and their clients. A third factor involves a lack of heuristic models: Those concerned with the question of how individuals maintain relationships have few concepts available in the literature to guide their work. The CBF model begins to address this deficiency.

Assuming that interpersonal conflict represents a substantial cost, it follows that individuals who maintain family units intact over the years must develop ways to cope with such conflict. The CBF model seeks to identify the kinds of cognitions that individuals have in their family schemas that empower them to effectively handle interpersonal differences.

Families need a range of strategies to help them cope under the challenging circumstances in which they live. The kinds of conflict that emerge when people must divide chores, share limited resources, and live in close physical proximity range from heart-wrenching difficulties in which one spouse discovers the partner has been unfaithful to the more mundane, such as when a spouse comes home late for dinner. Family members react to such incidents by drawing on their problem-solving strategies FS-SC. These problem-management cognitions, in conjunction with those in their relationship script and family constitution, direct individuals' thoughts, feelings, and behaviors vis-à-vis the incident.

This chapter considers three problem-management strategies thought to be found in the problem-solving strategies FS-SC of most family members in today's industrialized societies. In operation, each of these help family members keep their c/b ratios at acceptable levels while, concomitantly, ensuring that their interpersonal differences do not become a threat to the viability of the unit. Of the three, family members use the first two—*routine problem-solving strategies* and *intentionally developed problem-solving strategies*—to address problems at hand. They also use these two strategies, or solutions they have generated from them in the past, to prevent family problems from developing. The third strategy involves the use of *family defense mechanisms* (FDMs). FDMs, operating at a low level or outside of individuals' awareness, prevent new conflicts from developing by limiting the degree of expressed conflict in the household. These three problem-solving strategies are discussed next.

Routine Problem-Solving Strategies

Figure 4.2 suggests that when family members encounter an interpersonal problem that involves sufficient costs to take action, their family schema directs them to take a first step: Apply an everyday or routine problem-solving strategy available in the family repertoire. These strategies typically include taking a moment to briefly discuss the problem at hand, disciplining or "telling off" the offender(s), apologizing for the past wrongdoing, offering a gift to heal the psychological wounds, and so forth. These strategies are implemented without much thought.

Dindia and Baxter (1987) studied 50 married couples and identified 49 relationship-maintenance problem-management strategies they used. These strategies, which fall within the routine problem-solving category, ranged from keeping in touch (e.g., daily calls at lunchtime, asking about each other's day), which can serve to prevent problems from developing or recurring,

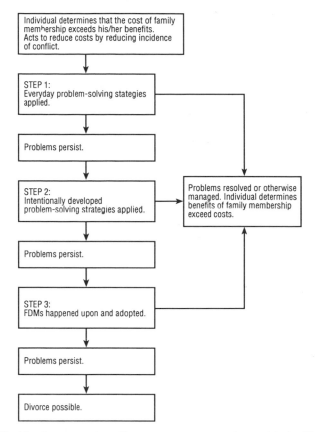

FIG. 4.2.   Sequence of conflict-management strategies used in families.

to conflict resolution efforts (e.g., discussing an issue, "giving in" to the partner).

The enactment of spouses' everyday or routine problem-solving strategies is guided (with little or no awareness on their part) by many cognitions from their family schema, including attributions about their partner's intentions and about their afficacy, as a couple, to solve issues at hand. Doherty (1981a, 1981b), for instance, suggested that the cognitions partners hold about their problem-solving efficacy effects their behavior. Those who believe in their efficacy are more persistent than those who do not. In fact, Doherty stated, those who hold low efficacy cognitions may act with "learned helplessness" behaviors and generate additional negative feelings in their relationship. Fincham and Bradbury (1987) also identified attributions that spouses would draw from during their routine problem solving, making a distinction between the attributions individuals use to determine the cause of and responsibility for their interpersonal differences.

Intentionally Developed Problem-Solving Strategies

As Fig. 4.2 shows, if routine problem-solving strategies fail to sufficiently reduce the costs of a situation, the problem-solving strategies FS-SC may next guide family members to use intentionally developed problem-solving strategies. In contrast to routine strategies that are practiced almost automatically and mechanically, individuals act with deliberation in creating and implementing the intentionally developed strategies. In contrast to when routine problem-solving strategies are used, family members are likely to have more (but still relatively little) awareness of the cognitions that are guiding them.

A popular gift item several years ago was a mug with this "hook," a cliff-hanging message inscribed on its outside: "If you don't want to be disappointed by me . . ." After reading that enticement, one had to drink some coffee to reveal the rest of the message, which was printed inside the cup. The punch-line read, ". . . then lower your expectations"—words of wisdom delivered on a coffee cup, evidently by a designer with a crisp sense of humor and a good intuitive sense of cognitive-behavioral models.

Romantic partners who expect a vintage marriage of the type portrayed by Hollywood in the 1950s (e.g., Ozzie and Harriet Nelson, June and Ward Cleaver, Rock Hudson and Doris Day) are more likely to be disappointed by the conflicts they inevitably encounter than those who expect considerable give and take. Individuals holding unrealistic cognitions will inevitably experience disappointment and this, in turn, will cause unhappiness and additional costs in their family relationships.

It seems counterintuitive to speak about people today holding such "stars-in-the-eyes" expectations about their love and family relationships, given the widely known statistics about divorce rates, unhappy marriages, and dysfunctional families. However, just as we believe accidents only happen to "the other guy," so too do we think that marital problems and divorce only happen to "other couples" (cf. Nisbett & Ross, 1980).

This point is illustrated in data collected by Ryan Dunn and one of the present authors. College students, many in dating relationships, were asked to indicate, on a scale from 0 to 100, how many points they would require to stay in a 1-year-old marriage. The means of more than 100 respondents were as follows: level of love, 90.2; level of physical intimacy, 88.4; communication quality, 86.5; conflict resolution skills as a couple, 86.0; decision-making skills as a couple, 85.7; level of psychological intimacy, 88.4; and amount of joy and laughter, 81.7.

These high scores indicate that the respondents may be holding unrealistically high expectations for marital relationships in their family schema and those who do so are "at risk" for experiencing disappointment in their love and family relationships. The key here, of course, is the term *unrealistic*. Having high but achievable expectations can motivate individuals to succeed and may help them make the self-fulfilling prophecy process work on their behalf. But to be realistic, individuals' expectations must take into account factors like their skills, support systems, the economic and social conditions they face, and so forth.

One intentionally developed problem-solving strategy individuals can use when routine strategies fail them is to intentionally change unrealistic or seemingly unachievable expectations, as illustrated in the following example:

> Jack had expected Becca to be responsive whenever he had the desire for physical intimacy, which was nightly. Jack's family constitution cognitions told him that a woman's willingness to make love was an important sign he could use to tell whether she "really cared" for him. After they had applied several routine problem-solving strategies in an unsuccessful effort to resolve this, Jack engaged in sufficient metacognition to recognize that Becca could care a great deal even when she was not interested in sex.
>
> Jack soon adjusted to a less frequent love-making schedule and, once this happened, he found the marriage providing him with an improved c/b ratio. In fact, once Jack changed his cognitions and learned to recognize other signs of Becca's caring, she, through metacognition, developed new ideas about his interest in love making and, as a result and much to her own surprise, she experienced a significant increase in her level of desire.

Intentionally developed strategies may involve cooperative efforts among family members. In the healthiest scenario, spouses or parents and children, as their ages permit, engage in metacognition and talk about the problem until it is well understood from the perspective of everyone involved. After accomplishing this, participating family members develop a joint ownership of the problem and for the task of addressing it. Then, they work cooperatively to find and implement a mutually acceptable solution. The McRoys illustrate a healthy use of intentionally developed strategies:

> For the third consecutive month, the McRoys discovered that they lacked the funds to cover what they owed. Last month they had used routine problem-solving strategies, including laughing together about married life in debtor's prison and a friendly scolding of each other. This time they took a harder look and created an intentionally developed problem-specific strategy. They agreed to end their deficit-spending lifestyle and, together, the McRoys destroyed their bank cards, wrote a new budget, and decided to check with each other each day to make sure they were living within their means.

More often, however, intentionally developed problem-solving strategies are used after one individual's c/b ratio grows so unacceptable that he or she has to search alone (at least at first) for a solution to correct matters, as in the following example:

Jean worried about her children engaging in excessive bickering and, as a result, tried several routine problem-solving techniques. Next, Jean shared her concerns with husband Fred, but he seemed uninterested, answering only, "The kids'll be OK. Besides, I'm busy watching the ball game right now."

Over time the bickering not only persisted, but worsened. After wrestling with the problem further and accepting that Fred would not get involved in finding solutions, Jean drew on her family schema and intentionally developed a problem-specific strategy. Guessing that the bickering was a cry for parental attention, Jean developed a plan in which both she and her husband would spend time individually with each child.

Jean presented the plan as a finished package to Fred. He rejected it, however, and laughed at her request for his participation. "I don't have time for this nonsense," he explained. Although unaware of the reasons behind his reaction, Fred objected partly because he had no ownership of the problem-solving process and partly because, given his family schema, he understood the children's behavior in ways different from Jean.

Although rebuffed by Fred, Jean put her part of the plan into practice and obtained encouraging results. The children's battling dropped, but not to the level she felt was healthy. Next, she asked the children about the arguments, refusing to accept "the baloney they first dished out." Eventually the children talked about the rule in their family constitution that "all children were to be treated equally."

The youngest and middle child complained that the oldest had fewer chores. The oldest rebutted, "My chores take less time, but involve hard physical labor, and I have more homework." After more talk, Jean and the children, together as a group, developed new assignments that all felt were equitable. This further reduced the bickering.

Another use of intentionally developed strategies is when one person believes he or she cannot directly get what is wanted from a partner. Ayres (1983) identified three types of strategies that individuals might use when they want more psychological intimacy than the partner is providing: *avoidance strategies, balance strategies*, and *directness strategies*. Rusbult (1987) identified strategies that an individual might intentionally develop to deal with significant dissatisfaction in a marriage. Her set of four types has similarities to Ayres: *exit*, which involves leaving or threatening to leave the relationship; *loyalty*, staying with the partner and hoping matters will improve; *neglect*, allowing the relationship to deteriorate or paying minimum attention to the partner; and *voice*, talking about the difficulties and engaging in problem-solving activities.

Whether intentionally developed or drawn from the everyday repertoire, individuals, guided by their family schemas, try to improve their c/b ratios by using a range of strategies to solve marital and family problems. When these strategies do not bring success, they usually leave individuals' c/b ratios out of balance and family members faced with the dilemma regarding what to do next.

Family Defense Mechanisms (FDMs)

When routine and intentionally developed problem-solving strategies fail, family members might consider ignoring their seemingly unsolvable problems, but they most often recognize that this course would run contrary to their family schemas and would leave them with unfavorable cost–benefit ratios. Discouraged by the circumstances at hand, they might recognize that human relationships sometimes become so complex and intertwined that people find themselves unable to understand what is causing their family problems and unable to find appropriate solutions. Thoughts of separation, divorce, and moving out of the house may cross family members' minds.

At this point, as Fig. 4.2 shows, family members may happen upon another strategy, the use of FDMs (Schwebel, 1993). FDMs address the problem by dictating a pattern of activities to family members that enable them to live together and avoid the costs of the seemingly unsolvable problem. The pattern of activities is such that it reduces the number of incidents of expressed conflict among family members.

As the following example shows, family members practice FDMs with little or no awareness of the relationship between the prescribed patterns of behavior and the resultant "solved problem" and reduced level of conflict. They believe they follow the prescribed behavior pattern for reasons unrelated to their family problems, such as the enjoyment or accomplishments the behaviors bring:

> Emalee and Jasper, parents of Nancy, age 2 years, now work opposite hours from each other at a real estate office and do well financially. When Emalee first returned to work after Nancy was born, they both worked the same hours and used a sitter. However, one week the sitter was sick and the couple had to rotate between child-care and office responsibilities.
>
> That week, the number of arguments and level of tension between Emalee and Jasper decreased sharply, and they very much enjoyed the limited time they had together to share. Without realizing the connection between their schedule and their happy week, they decided to let the sitter go to save money and benefit Nancy with more parental attention. They referred the sitter to friends and began to practice an FDM.

As the example shows, FDMs are cognitive-behavioral coping strategies. By separating Emalee and Jasper, the FDM functioned to help them avoid and manage their interpersonal problems and this, in turn, enabled them to live together with better c/b ratios. By definition, patterns of behavior that do not reduce the number of incidents of expressed conflict are not FDMs.

At first blush, it seems unlikely that family members would function in "self-therapeutic" ways without realizing they are doing so. However, consider the observations made by Weiss (1990), who studied individuals in psychotherapy: ". . . human beings can unconsciously carry out many intellectual tasks, including developing and executing plans for reaching certain goals" (p. 109); and, "What is more, patients enlist these abilities in the service of working to become well—in the service of gaining control over their irrational beliefs, feelings, and behaviors" (p. 103).

Because FDMs are not characterized by the content of the behavior exhibited but rather by the function they serve in reducing the incidence of expressed conflict, a behavioral pattern that produces an FDM in one family is merely a regular part of life in another. For example, because the main function of Emalee and Jasper's work schedules is to reduce conflict by providing distance in the marriage, the pattern is an FDM. However, the same pattern that the Smiths follow is not an FDM because they follow it primarily because of financial need.

The marital relationship is the central one in a family and the one most likely to need management with FDMs. However, families also use FDMs to cope with the interpersonal conflict between parents and children, siblings, and adult children and their parents. Regardless of the focus of an FDM, family members support each other in the practice of FDM-prescribed behavior, implicitly or explicitly. This is true even when they complain about the burden of FDM-prescribed behavior. For example, Emalee, now more content with her marriage, complains, "Poor us. Jasper and I only have a few hours together each week." However, she neither tries to change her schedule nor encourages Jasper to rearrange his, so they could spend more time together at work or at home.

Types of FDMs

Discussed next are the various types of FDMs. As Schwebel (1993) explained, they are:

> escape FDMs, which prescribe the withdrawal of one individual or more from other family members; goal-driven FDMs, which prescribe that two or more family members devote great amounts of time and energy to an all-consuming activity; mood-swing FDMs, which prescribe the cyclical alteration of loving, distant, and other feelings in family members; and multi-household FDMs, which prescribe behaviors that link individuals living in one household with kin in another. (p. 33)

Figure 4.3 provides information helpful first in determining whether a pattern of behavior is an FDM and, if it is, then in determining its type.

Escape FDMs. These dictate that one person or more physically or psychologically withdraw from the other family members, who collaborate in the process. The interpersonal distance achieved during the escape decreases the number of episodes of expressed conflict between family members. When the escape period terminates, family members are often ready to enjoy what

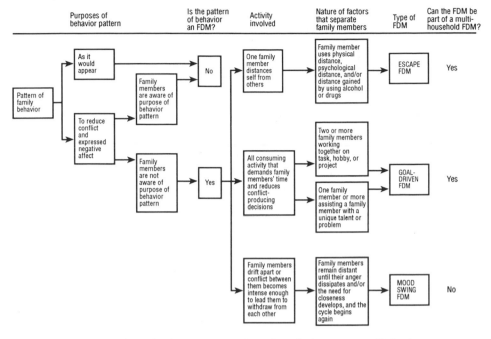

FIG. 4.3. Information helpful in determining first whether a pattern of behavior is an FDM and, if it is, then in determining its type. Reprinted from *The Family Journal*, Vol. 1, 1993, pp. 31–41 © ACA. Reprinted with permission.

has become scarcer: time with each other and opportunities to share and appreciate feelings of psychological intimacy. See the following examples:

> Bill, a 16-year-old, sleeps past noon in summer days and then stays up alone working with his computer late into the night. His parents state, "We wish he'd socialize with us more and keep reasonable hours. Maybe he'll become a computer whiz-kid . . . Anyway, at least we enjoy playing computer games together every Sunday afternoon."
>
> Another family unexpectedly experienced a summer of peace and quiet, living in a vacation beach house, about an hour's commute from New York. The wife explains why the family decided to move from New York to that town that very fall: "On the down side, we know that Paul will have a long commute. But he doesn't mind the train ride. On the up side, the children will attend high-quality schools."

Escape FDMs can involve physical or psychological withdrawal or substance use. With the latter, the substance is the vehicle through which family members create physical and/or psychological distance and, thereby, reduce the number of incidents of expressed conflict. Further, the substance's psychopharmacological action may also act in ways that reduce expressed conflict. Schwebel (1993) provided an example:

The R. family began using this FDM a few years ago. At that point, Mr. and Mrs. R. were "at each other's throats," battling daily soon after they returned home from their high pressure sales positions. One evening, friends invited to dinner brought along martini ingredients. The dinner went well and after the friends left the couple shared another martini and had an intimate night. Soon afterward, they developed an FDM-prescribed pattern of enjoying an after-work martini while their children played nearby. Sometimes they also had nightcaps. They explained their drinking as "a very civilized antidote to the inevitable stress one faces in the 20th century American workplace." (p. 34)

Of course, many family members who use drugs and alcohol are doing so for reasons that do not involve FDMs. By definition, when a family member's use of substances is part of an FDM pattern, it must reduce the number of incidents of expressed conflict and help the family manage. FDMs, like defense mechanisms (Vaillant, 1986), serve similar functions within the family but vary with regard to the costs of their use. Over the long run, in contrast to other escape FDMs, substance-use FDMs are likely to cause other stresses in family members, including exposure to the risk of substance abuse.

Goal-Driven FDMs. These mandate that at least two family members spend substantial amounts of time together in an activity. Frequently, that activity involves a special problem or talent of a family member, economic objectives, or social advancement. There are many ways in which the all-consuming activity prescribed by the FDM helps family members avoid expressed conflict and gain benefits. First, it directs family resources (time, energy, and money) into the FDM priority, reducing the likelihood of conflict over their use. Second, it limits unstructured leisure time during which expressed conflict may occur. Third, it provides family members with a shared goal and with opportunities for shared satisfaction as, together, they progress toward their objective. The following is an example:

Wilma and Frank were going through a difficult time in their marriage when Frank's boss, a successful real estate entrepreneur, decided to take early retirement. Because the boss deeply trusted his long-time handyman, Frank, he offered him the first option and adequate financing on a package deal for his properties. The couple gladly accepted the opportunity, although they recognized that it would require many 12-hour work days.

Wilma and Frank were much overworked soon after they assumed the properties but, to their surprise, their marriage improved. They had happened upon and adopted a goal-driven FDM. As time passed and the couple became established, Wilma begged Frank to take time off so they could be together, relaxing and traveling. Several times they tried this but they soon found that in a matter of days they would "get on each other's nerves." When Frank and Wilma returned to work, although they complained about the hours, they fought less and were able to enjoy the limited evening and weekend time they had as a couple.

Some goal-driven FDMs involve extended family. This may include adult children caring for their elderly parents, or adult children (temporarily) moving back into their parents' home during a life transition, as illustrated in the next example:

> Dolly and Paul, as a result of their FDM, have rarely lived alone as a couple. Somebody in their family has always needed their help. After marrying, they moved into Dolly's parents' farm so Paul could help with the work. Twelve years and four children later the couple bought a house in town so the children could be nearer to friends and activities. However, soon after they moved to this house, Paul's father joined them, needing nursing help from Dolly. Years later and a few weeks before Paul's dad moved into the Methodist Home, the couple's oldest daughter, Darlene, divorced her husband and moved back in with her son, thus enabling Dolly to provide him with day care.

Mood-Swing FDMs. These mandate that conflict and negative affect be expressed during one time period, thereby reducing the number of incidents of expression during each mood-swing cycle. During the FDM-designated period in the cycle, conflict expression and the voicing of anger and negative feelings toward other family members are prescribed behaviors. This cycle period is followed by others during which family members follow other prescribed behaviors, distancing themselves from each other and then becoming close again. Although it seems counterintuitive that mood-swing FDMs would limit conflict in families, these FDMs work by structuring family life so that members express most of their negative feelings and differences in encapsulated and limited time periods, making family life more predictable and manageable. One variant of this FDM involves a period during which a person teases or criticizes one or more family members, causing sufficient angry feelings that the targeted individual(s) withdraw(s) from and/or retaliate(s) against the provoker. During this period, family members express negative feelings and become ready for a period during which there is distance and, therefore, a relatively low level of expressed conflict. After a time period of distance, the negative feelings of family members pass or diminish and they again seek closeness. The closeness phase completes the cycle, providing individuals with opportunities to feel good while "making up." The provocation used must be "within bounds." If it is not, the behavior pattern does not benefit the family in conflict management and therefore, by definition, is not an FDM.

Another example of a mood-swing FDM involves resignation by one family member.

> Marj and Larry had been having marital difficulties and hoped a cruise would help them. When they returned home from their vacation, Larry discovered that a co-worker (whom he felt was less qualified than he) was promoted ahead of him. Larry started thinking of himself as "victimized" and handled his feelings by going home that day, dropping on the sofa, and becoming what he called

a "couch potato." When he shared his despair with Marj, she expressed her sympathy and began waiting on him. In fact, she let him abdicate most household responsibilities and ordered the children to give Dad more respect.

Larry now waits for Wednesday, which he calls "hump day," and Friday, which he calls "made-it-through-another-week day." He explains, "Hey, at first the kids even let me pick which cartoons we watched on Saturday mornings." After a while, however, he became enraged at the way Marj treated him and, concomitantly, she started nagging him about resuming household chores. When this happened, Larry distanced himself from Marj and the children. In time, however, the cycle repeated itself, indicating that the family had adopted this FDM, which required repeated cycles of resignation, closeness, anger, and distance.

Some mood-swing cycles begin when one or more family members has a need to experience intimacy for circumscribed periods, as illustrated in the following:

Dwayne is a reserved person who generally maintains distance from his wife, Trudy, and from their children. After several weeks of being distant, however, he plans a family-camping weekend. On that Friday night, he brings Trudy a flower and a bottle of her favorite apricot brandy. On Saturday, he treats the children by taking them on an early morning fishing expedition and an after-dark swim. By Sunday afternoon, when they return home, Dwayne has had as much intimacy as he can tolerate and he drifts into his own separate activities, usually after conflict over the camping gear, household chores, or other issues. In time the cycle will repeat itself with new periods of buy-offs, closeness, anger, and distance.

Multihousehold FDMs. These operate by mandating behavior to family members in one household that is linked to behavior prescribed to family members in one or more other households. Specifically, multihousehold FDMs prescribe escape and/or goal-driven FDMs in one household that are linked to escape and/or goal-driven FDMs in (an)other household(s), reducing the incidence of conflict and protecting the relationships within each participating family unit, as the following illustrates:

Hanna and George had two children before they divorced 5 years ago. Since the divorce, both Hanna and George remarried and "have had children with their new spouses. Now Hanna's and George's present families are involved in a multi-household FDM, which operates because their households each use goal-driven FDMs, focusing their attention on court battles involving child support, visitation, and custody issues. The ongoing legal entanglement provides each family unit with a common enemy and a substantial problem requiring time and energy" (Schwebel et al., 1989, pp. 154–155). The FDM not only distracts members of each household from problems they would otherwise face in their day-to-day family lives, but it brings them closer in their quest to defeat their common enemy.

Benefits Provided by the Use of FDMs

FDMs improve family life in many ways obvious to observers. They help family members reduce conflict, improve their cost–benefit ratios, and restore equilibrium in their system. Further, because FDMs make unstructured family time a scarcer and more valued commodity, family members tend to put more effort into using it effectively.

FDMs also have positive impact on family members in less obvious ways, such as through the mediation of individuals' cognitions. For example, immediately before FDMs are practiced, couples are typically distressed and, as Fincham (1985) reported, distressed spouses are "likely to see their partner and the relationship as the source of their difficulties" (p. 183). When the FDM brings immediate and significant relief, the spouses will likely create new attributions about their partner and marriage (Acitelli, 1988; Fichten, 1984). Specifically, the kind of attributions they would make would be more likely to be relationship-enhancing ones (Holtzworth-Munroe & Jacobson, 1985).

Other less obvious benefits family members derive from FDM usage include these:

1. Bem's (1972) self-perception theory argues that individuals infer their own attitudes and traits in the same way that they infer others'—by observing their overt behavior. If Bem's position generalizes to an individual's family, then this argument follows: Once FDMs are in operation, family members will experience less open conflict and periods of enjoyed, shared time, even if they are brief. Once individuals note this change, they will, in turn, conclude that their marriage or that their family unit is indeed a happier and healthier one.

2. Once friction is reduced between family members, family members' behaviors and other important parts of family life may be reframed in more favorable ways which, in turn, may make them feel and act more favorably (Watzlawick, Weakland, & Fisch, 1974). Or, put in Milan group terms, once FDMs are operating, individuals may find positive connotations for family members' behaviors (Selvini Palazzoli, Boscolo, Cecchin, & Prata, 1978).

3. Once family members practice FDM-prescribed behavior, cognitive dissonance (Brehm & Cohen, 1962; Festinger, 1957) will lead them to especially value these activities. As a result, not only will they benefit from the reduced number of household conflicts, but they will benefit because they have attributed considerable value to their FDM-prescribed behaviors. For example, they will define the behavior in escape and goal-driven FDMs as being

of great personal or family benefit, the brief period of closeness in the positive phases of the mood-swing FDMs as special ("We have times when we feel absolutely terrific in our marriage"), and the personally exhausting competitive (e.g., with sibling or exspouse) and equally draining cooperative (e.g., with a parent or sibling) behaviors involved in multihousehold FDMs as being essential to the achievement of a valued goal.

4. Finally, dissatisfied spouses voice more anger, sadness, contempt, disgust, and other negative affects than do happier spouses, and the expression of these feelings make family life increasingly stressful (Gottman & Levenson, 1988). FDMs, by reducing the incidence of negative affect and expressed conflict in dissatisfied couples, work like interventions designed to limit the expression of negative affect. These interventions, research shows, bring improved levels of marital satisfaction to dissatisfied couples (Hahlweg, Revenstorf, & Schindler, 1983).

The Costs of Using FDMs

The use of FDMs involves trade-offs. Instead of confronting underlying differences between them, individuals learn to relate in ways that minimize the impact of those differences. Although they benefit from a reduction in the incidents of expressed conflict, they also miss the opportunity to enjoy more shared time, the chance to optimally enhance their relationship, and the sense of shared accomplishment that might have occurred had they effectively addressed the basic underlying differences.

As noted earlier, the costs of FDMs vary by type. The escape and goal-driven FDMs, which involve hobby- or work-related activities that are useful to the individuals, the family, or to society, have fewer costs than do the mood-swing FDMs. These provide fewer secondary gains and involve the costs of having time periods in the cycle set aside for the expression of uncomfortable, stressful emotions. The benefits and costs of FDMs are discussed further in chapters 7 and 8.

CONCLUSION

The elements of the family schema (FS-SC) in the CBF model were discussed in this chapter. The goal was to provide a tool for understanding family functioning that could be used by laypersons, scientists, and practitioners. In Part II of this book, applications of the CBF model are reviewed in the areas of assessment, psychotherapy, education, and research. Before these applications can be considered, some notions of family health need to be presented. This is done in the next chapter.

PART

II

APPLICATIONS

Part II explores a variety of applications that follow from a CBF perspective. Chapter 5 reviews the literature related to characteristics of healthy families and places this material in a cognitive-behavioral context. The chapter provides some sense of what favorable family outcomes can be. Chapter 6 presents material related to how one assesses the relevant cognitive-behavioral dimensions in family members. Assessment strategies and specific instruments are reviewed in the areas of cognition, behavior, and general adjustment.

Much more attention has been directed toward using CBF approaches in psychotherapeutic activities than to using them in assessment, education, or research. The discussion of all these efforts is presented in chapters 7–10. Chapter 7 provides an overview of CBF therapy and describes the stages in this form of treatment intervention. Chapter 8 highlights several specific therapeutic strategies that CBF therapists employ.

The CBF model is also well suited to helping members of healthy as well as distressed families learn to function more effectively. Chapter 9 focuses on psychoeducational topics and strategies that flow from a CBF perspective and that can enrich family members' lives. This material extends traditional family life education content. Finally, because continued research is critical in the development of a theoretical perspective, implications for research are identified and considered in chapter 10. This chapter also provides some recommendations for how the CBF perspective can help improve working relationships between researchers and clinicians.

5

FAMILY HEALTH

This chapter begins the second part of the book, which is designed to illustrate how the cognitive-behavioral family model (CBF) can be applied to helping families, through assessment, counseling and therapy, education, and research. Before the applications can be addressed, it is important to consider the characteristics of family health and the factors that may foster healthy family functioning. In this regard, the CBF model assumes that family members seek to have healthy families and that family members will develop their units in healthy directions unless obstacles emerge in the household that misdirect or block their efforts.

Some obstacles that emerge and hamper family members' progress in creating and maintaining healthy family units develop as a result of the family-related cognitions that they hold. First, family members are handicapped in their efforts to maintain family health because they are only vaguely or not at all aware of holding family-related cognitions and of the power these have in shaping individuals' thoughts, feelings, and behaviors. Second, family members face obstacles in maintaining family health because their thoughts, feelings, and behaviors are affected by family-related cognitions that lead them to engage in irrational thinking, make maladaptive attributions, and/or work toward unachievable goals within the family. Third, family members face obstacles in maintaining family health if, because of their cognitions or lack of communication and problem-solving skills, they cannot work as a team to maintain a family constitution that allows all family members to achieve desired goals.

This chapter addresses the small but growing literature in the area of family health. Studies and conceptual papers have identified a number of attributes that appear to characterize families that function well. These attributes are reviewed and integrated within the cognitive-behavioral framework discussed in Part I of the book. Placing these attributes in the CBF context enriches their meaning and gives them a sense of coherence while also providing concrete goals toward which CBF model-based interventions can be directed. Finally, the chapter concludes with two case studies that illustrate relatively healthy and unhealthy families.

CHARACTERISTICS OF HEALTHY FAMILIES

Numerous family scholars, writing from both clinical and empirical frameworks, have identified characteristics of well-functioning families. Although it has been difficult to operationalize some of these characteristics (Fish, Belsky, & Youngblade, 1991), fortunately there is a high degree of consistency across scholars in their descriptions of healthy families.

Of course, value judgments are involved in delineating what one considers to be a well-functioning family. Some place an emphasis on extrafamilial outcomes (e.g., the extent to which family members achieve desired occupational objectives), whereas others emphasize intrafamilial outcomes (e.g., the extent to which family members relate cohesively to one another). Some focus on individual outcomes (e.g., socioeconomic or professional status of family members), whereas others focus on the family unit's outcomes (e.g., the family's "reputation" in the community).

Our position regarding healthy families is one that is based on the perspectives of the family members themselves—healthy families are ones that are able in their own view to achieve their own subjectively determined mutual goals. These goals are built into their family constitution and personal models (PTs) and, typically, families that meet their own objectives will have positive extrafamilial, intrafamilial, individual, and family unit outcomes. In the descriptions that follow, it should be noted that scholars place differing relative emphases on these possible outcomes.

According to Kantor and Lehr (1975), healthy families set clear rules and boundaries, operate with flexibility, and freely interact with outside institutions. These *open* families have flexible rules and boundaries and operate democratically. They also interact openly with outside institutions. In *closed* families, family members are expected to subordinate their needs for the benefit of the entire family. As a result, these families are rigid in the sense that they allow a minimal amount of interaction with outside systems and have fixed rules and boundaries. The third type of family—*random*—is described as fragmented. Family members do whatever they wish to, regardless of how these behaviors may relate to others. This type of family is the most likely to be unhealthy, as it has few structured rules and guidelines and boundaries are blurred and easily violated.

Similarly, Reiss (1981) identified a typology of families based on paradigms, which are defined as shared assumptions about the social world. These paradigms, which are conceptually similar to PTs (see chapter 4), give family members a sense of order and coherence as they interact with each other and with outside institutions.

Based on a series of empirical investigations that spanned several decades, Reiss (1981) identified three types of family paradigms. *Environment-sensitive* families construe the world as knowable and orderly, and individual members are expected to contribute to developing this understanding. *Interpersonal distance-sensitive* families are comprised of family members who are disengaged from each other. Family members attempt to demonstrate their autonomy and believe that attending to others' suggestions and needs represents weakness. Finally, *consensus-sensitive* families are composed of enmeshed family members. They perceive their world as so chaotic and confusing that they must bond together, agree at all times, and protect themselves from external dangers.

Clearly, there are parallels between Kantor and Lehr's (1975) and Reiss' (1981) typologies. Although there are some conceptual distinctions, open families are similar to environment-sensitive families, closed families resemble consensus-sensitive families, and random families are analogous to interpersonal distance-sensitive families.

According to Olson's (1991) modified Circumplex Model, three dimensions are central to healthy family functioning: *cohesion, flexibility*, and *communication*. Cohesion, the level of emotional bonding that family members have with each other, is ideally balanced between the extremes of disengagement and enmeshment. Flexibility, the ability of a family to change its power structure, rules, and roles in response to environmental stressors, also is optimally experienced between the extremes of rigidity and chaos. Communication includes sending clear and congruent messages, empathy, supportive statements, and effective speaking and listening skills.

Several authors have developed descriptions of healthy families that are consistent with Olson's (1991). Epstein, Bishop, and Baldwin (1982) proposed that healthy families have optimal levels of affective involvement (cohesion); foster behavioral control, problem solving, and clear roles (flexibility); and have members who communicate in an emotionally responsive manner with each other (communication). Similarly, Beavers and Hampton's (1990) description of centripetal forces that pull family members together and centrifugal forces that push them apart is similar to Olson's notion of cohesion. Beavers and Hampton considered leadership style to be an important dimension of healthy families, a notion that is conceptually related to flexibility. The abilities to communicate effectively, resolve problems, and express emotions are also considered to be important correlates of healthy family functioning.

Consistent with our own position, Becvar and Becvar (1988) suggested that the health of a particular family should be judged by the extent to which the unit has achieved its goals. They indicated that the following characteristics facilitate the attainment of goals: a legitimate source of authority that is supported and consistent over time, a stable and consistent system of rules, consistent and regular nurturing behaviors, effective child-rearing practices, stable and well-maintained marriages, a set of agreed-upon goals toward which the family and individuals work, and sufficient flexibility to change in the face of both expected (e.g., birth of another child) and unexpected stressors (e.g., a parent losing his or her job).

Huntley and Konetsky (1992), in an ongoing behavioral observation study, compared communication patterns between families with nonclinical adolescents and families with maladjusted adolescents. Preliminary results indicated that members in families with nonclinical adolescents were more likely to negotiate the topic to be discussed, to use humor, to show respect for differences of opinion, and to clarify the meaning of each others' communications than were individuals in families with maladjusted adolescents. In addition, nonclinical adolescents, when compared to their maladjusted counterparts, had less power and authority, yet were more able to challenge or express dissatisfaction with the current rules.

Clearly, there are commonalities across these descriptions of healthy families. Scholars' reports converge on the following characteristics: (a) a clearly understood system of rules and regulations, including an established authority structure, that can be flexibly modified when necessary; (b) the provision of regular support and nurturance to family members; (c) clearly understood roles and obligations; (d) the presence of homeostatic mechanisms, whereby perceived problems and deficits are recognized, addressed, and modified; and (e) the presence of constructive problem-solving strategies.

It should be emphasized that these commonalities refer to *processes* within families that promote healthy family functioning. These processes provide the necessary context for the achievement of a wide array of family and individual goals. Thus, healthy family functioning is not restricted to the realization of a particular set of goals.

HEALTHY FAMILIES WITHIN THE CBF MODEL

As noted in chapters 3 and 4, the key construct within the CBF model is the *family schema*, which contains a number of subconstructs (FC-SC): the *relationship script, family constitution, cost–benefit analyses*, and *problem-solving strategies*. The relationship script contains cognitions related to how one should function and how one does operate in various family and nonfamily relationships. Notions described previously suggest that healthy relationship scripts include the provision of nurturance and support to other family members and include family members having clear roles. In addition, spouses who have compatible relationship scripts are likely to function more effectively than those who have incompatible ones.

The family constitution consists of the unwritten rules and regulations that govern all aspects of family life. As noted earlier, healthy family constitutions have well-understood rules and regulations, clear authority structures, and provisions for modification (i.e., amendment) in the face of environmental changes. In addition, not only is it important that the authority structure be clear, but many scholars also suggest that it is helpful to place the locus of authority within the marital couple and not in the children (Huntley & Konetsky, 1992). Whereas parents may solicit their children's input, the final decisions are made by the parents. Certainly, children in healthy families are given increasing freedom as they mature, with most teenagers being allowed to make some decisions on their own.

One of the indicators that relationship scripts and/or the family constitution need to be modified is unfavorable cost–benefit (c/b) ratios. As presented in earlier chapters, c/b ratios are regular assessments that individuals make, typically outside of their conscious awareness, of the relative balance of costs and benefits in their present family relationships. If one's assessment indicates an unsatisfactory ratio, given one's standard, individuals in healthy families take constructive steps to address the deficiency. The specific manner in which the c/b ratio is improved can vary widely, but, in all cases, will function according to the amendment clauses within the family constitution. Thus, in healthy families, the c/b analyses operate much like a thermostat does in regulating room temperature. However, compared to the ease with which room temperature is regulated, enhancing the perceived quality of family life is a more difficult challenge.

Problem-solving strategies refer to the ways that families manage both day-to-day and major conflicts in their lives, as well as how family members correct the deficiencies noted in their c/b analyses. As was noted earlier, many families find it useful to engage in an explicit and systematic problem-solving process. In this process, problems are clearly identified, alternative solutions are generated, the advantages and disadvantages of the options are deliberated, a solution is chosen, and the extent to which the solution resolves the problem is evaluated. Although all members in healthy families, when necessary, are able to engage in this process, it is more common for the parents to do so.

In addition, family defense mechanisms (FDMs) are a means to cope with family problems. FDMs serve to reduce the incidence of expressed family conflict and generally occur outside of conscious awareness. Although FDMs do not directly address the core problem, and may involve a bit of self-deception, healthy families may occasionally use them.

An analogy to the Freudian individual defense mechanisms is useful. All individuals, to some extent, use defense mechanisms to help them cope with anxieties in their daily lives. Although the defenses do not directly resolve the actual source of the anxiety, they do not cause any substantial damage when used in moderation. However, when used excessively, they can lead to substantial amounts of personal distress and maladaptive behavior.

Similarly, although FDMs can be used excessively, it is healthy for families to make moderate use of them to assist in the conflict management process. The scope and breadth of the conflicts that FDMs can assist with is somewhat limited, so the more conscious, systematic problem-solving procedure may be necessary for crises and other serious problems.

CASE EXAMPLES

Although family health lies on a continuum, it may be helpful to contrast two families, one of which is considered relatively healthy (the Jones family) and the other which is not (the Miller family). Although, for comparison purposes, both are depicted as being first-marriage families, similar processes are posited to occur in single-parent and stepparent families.

The Joneses.   Mary (age 35 years) and Bill (age 33 years) Jones have been married for 11 years. They have two children, Ben (age 8 years) and Sarah (age 5 years). Both parents work outside the home: Mary is a loan officer in a bank and Bill is a midlevel manager in a large business corporation. Although Mary and Bill are unaware of having done so, they have gradually developed, sometimes through discussion, a family that functions quite well.

In what ways does the Jones family function well? In general terms, Bill and Mary are satisfied with themselves, their marriage, their family lives, and their professional careers. The children appear to be well adjusted and are doing well in school. With reference to the CBF model, the Jones family members have acceptable c/b ratios.

Bill's relationship script dictates that he should be the major financial provider for his family; that he should take care of the yard and major home repairs; that he should allow his wife to assume most of the child-rearing burden, until a "firm" disciplinarian is needed; that he should have outside sports-related friendships with men; and that he should treat his wife romantically.

By contrast, Mary's relationship script dictates that she should be responsible for child rearing; that she should have an outside career; that she should ensure that major family decisions are made responsibly; that she should be attractive to her husband; and that she should assume primary responsibility for cleaning the home and preparing meals. Thus, each spouse has relatively clear roles and the two relationship scripts are generally compatible with one another.

What is the nature of the Jones family constitution? As is the pattern in many dual-career families, Bill takes responsibility for much of the house and yard maintenance, whereas Mary is primarily responsible for child care and housekeeping tasks. Although Mary believes that Bill could do more "around the house and with the kids" than he does, this cost is not greatly distressing to her. Bill believes that he does less than Mary around the house because he has a more stressful and time-consuming job than she has.

The Joneses have a consistent pattern of resolving conflict. When major issues (e.g., when to place the children in kindergarten, moving to another house) arise, Mary asserts herself strongly and Bill typically accepts her preference. On daily issues (e.g., whether to go out to dinner on the weekend, what to eat for dinner), Bill generally is granted his preference. In terms of child rearing, because Mary assumes the major responsibility for this activity, she is considered to "deserve" to make most decisions. When a "firm hand" is needed, however, Mary may call upon Bill to discipline their children.

The Jones' constitution contains relatively clear and straightforward amendment provisions. The constitution underwent major revisions immediately after the two children were born. Mary took time off from her job for 6 months after each birth, and there was a realignment of roles and responsibilities with the additional demands of taking care of an infant. As the children grew older and Mary began to work more outside of the home, Bill was forced, somewhat reluctantly, to assume more responsibility for child care. Although he was somewhat uncomfortable with these extra "duties," he was willing to tolerate them as long as he was permitted to continue his sports activities.

To what extent do the Joneses use FDMs? First of all, Bill and Mary engage in a goal-driven FDM by focusing much of their attention on their children. Although they are not aware of doing so, the parents allow their day-to-day activities to consume much of their energy. On the relatively rare instances when they are alone together, they spend most of their time together talking about the children. Use of this FDM tends to reduce the number of arguments that Bill and Mary have. In addition, Bill's sports activities also serve the function of an FDM, as they reduce the incidence of expressed conflict in the family.

As the case of the Jones family illustrates, healthy families are not "perfect." The parents are not "completely" satisfied with their lives, the children are not "angels," and they use FDMs to some extent to manage conflict. Nevertheless, on the whole, the Joneses are satisfied with their family lives and have established a family system that allows its members to meet their individual goals.

The Millers. Roberta (age 37 years) and George (age 42 years) Miller have been married for 14 years. They have one child, Julie, who is 13 years old. Roberta does not work outside the home, whereas George is an upper level executive in a large and prosperous company. Despite being financially secure, the Millers are not satisfied with their personal, marital, and family lives.

Roberta, who has a college degree in social work, is not satisfied with the direction her life has taken. Although she enjoys having a child, Julie has become increasingly difficult and defiant in the last year. Partly because of this, Roberta feels that she needs some additional challenges outside of the home. She would like to work part time as a Children's Services case worker, but George has told her that he does not think that would be good for Julie, because "kids should have a parent to come home to after school!"

Roberta feels that she and George have drifted apart in the last several years. She perceives him as becoming increasingly involved in business activities, and relatively less concerned with her and Julie. Although she feels that she has attempted to talk about her personal needs for fulfillment outside the home with George, her perception is that he has been unreceptive. She has asked him about whether he could change his 7 a.m. to 8 p.m. work schedule, to give her employment, volunteer, or social opportunities outside the home. He has insisted that he cannot do this, and that "the reason I work so hard is so you don't have to!"

George feels overwhelming pressures to perform well at work. He has very high personal standards, and feels that his performance must improve for him to meet his ever-expanding goals. As his status has been enhanced professionally, he has become aware of nagging feelings of inadequacy and incompetency that he tries to avoid.

George's perception of Roberta is that she does not understand the "dog eat dog" nature of the business world, and that she should be satisfied with her role as a housewife. He does not understand her growing discontent, and, to avoid unpleasant conflict, he finds himself avoiding talking with her. George has found that his professional status leads to opportunities to become involved with other women, and he has sometimes had brief, extramarital affairs. He justifies these affairs by saying to himself, "Roberta spends so much time on Julie that she does not meet my needs." Although he wishes to avoid divorce, this option has entered his consciousness more often in the last 2 years.

Why are Roberta and George's c/b analyses unacceptable to them? To understand this, one must examine their respective relationship scripts, family constitution, and problem-solving strategies. Roberta's relationship script has emphasized the importance of family intimacy, and this led her to focus much of her energy on maintaining a healthy marriage and raising Julie. However, in the last several years, she has realized that she must also feel fulfilled professionally to genuinely enjoy her family life. Thus, her relationship script, which is somewhat different than her mother's, now places a priority on balancing work and family pursuits.

In addition, Roberta's standards for marriage dictate that she expects to spend a considerable amount of time with George. Further, she believes that regular and intimate communication is central to a healthy relationship. With respect to her role as mother, Roberta sees her function as that of "case manager," indicating that she coordinates family functions, carpooling, grocery shopping, and similar activities. She believes that good parents allow their children "freedom to make their own mistakes," so she provides relatively few household rules and trusts that Julie will generally make trustworthy decisions.

George's relationship script is, to some extent, incompatible with Roberta's. He considers his work to be his most important priority, because if he is not successful professionally, he will not be able to provide family members with the standard of living to which they are accustomed. To George, spending substantial amounts of time with Roberta and Julie are appropriate only on vacations or holidays.

George's script also dictates that parents should be "tough" disciplinarians and that children should be "kept in line." Thus, he believes that there should be clear and firm rules in the household, that children should have many chores to do, and that there should be strong punishment if the children do not comply with what is expected of them. He is not pleased with Roberta's emphasis on letting Julie learn from her own mistakes; he concludes that children are most effectively taught how to be responsible and productive citizens by strict discipline.

Further, George's relationship script dictates that men are to be the providers for the family, and that the most efficient way to divide family labor is to have mothers stay home with their children. Thus, he is confused and upset about Roberta's desires to have a professional career. From his point of view, this destroys the equilibrium that he has sought to establish.

What is the nature of the Millers' family constitution? Although it is clear that George is primarily responsible for maintaining the yard and that Roberta is largely responsible for housekeeping and child care, there is some ambiguity about who is responsible for home repairs (e.g., a plumbing leak, nonfunctional furnace). Both George and Roberta feel that the other should take care of arranging for these repairs. As a result, each and every time such a repair is needed, a power struggle ensues, conflict occurs, and one resentful individual "gives in" and arranges for the repair. George and Roberta have never talked about this conflict or attempted to resolve lingering feelings of resentment that one or both may experience.

Another source of ambiguity in the Miller family constitution is the role that Julie plays in house maintenance. George authoritatively sets up chores for Julie to do, but these are not written down, change from week to week, and are not enforced. Further, Roberta does not support her husband in enforcing these chores. Rather, she believes that it is better for Julie to contribute to household tasks on an "as needed basis." Thus, Julie is confused about what she is and is not expected to do, and further receives inconsistent messages about the consequences of not doing what her father wants her to do.

The Miller family constitution lacks effective provisions for amendment. George thinks that "the way things worked in the past should be the way they work now." As such, he is not aware of the necessary changes that all families must make as their members enter new life stages. Thus, he resists making major changes in household routines. This is one of the primary reasons why George has had a difficult time accepting Roberta's desires to have a career outside of the home. Roberta is frustrated by the static nature of their constitution and, without being aware of doing so, struggles to convince George that it needs to be amended. This process, so far, has only resulted in disappointment for her and frustration for George.

Clearly, the Millers are relatively weak in the skill of cooperative problem solving. Neither has the skill to engage in the systematic process of generating alternatives, determining the advantages and disadvantages of possible solutions, choosing the best alternative, and evaluating the results. In fact, conflicts are typically handled by one party giving in to the other and with both spouses feeling dissatisfied with the process and the outcome. Although both give in from time to time, Roberta, modeling her own mother's behavior, is more likely to do so than is George. Because they do not openly discuss these matters with each other, George and Roberta have not been able to solve problems more cooperatively and effectively over the course of their marriage. Rather, each and every dilemma presents them with tension and frustration because they lack the tools necessary to be productive problem solvers.

FDMs are used extensively in the Miller family. With only partial awareness of why he is doing so, George remains at work as long as he can to avoid possible confrontations with Roberta. When George is home, Roberta focuses much of her attention on Julie to avoid arguments and unpleasant interactions with him. To avoid "getting in the middle" of her parents' conflicts, as many teenagers do, Julie spends as much of her time as she can either in her room studying or listening to music or out with her friends.

Although FDMs are not dysfunctional per se, and, in fact, they serve to reduce the incidence of expressed conflict, FDMs serve to maintain the basic problems evident in the Miller family system. Thus, these FDMs allow the Miller family to function at a moderately acceptable level, at least in the short run, but deny them the motivation and opportunity to address the basic underlying problems that have led George and Roberta to have unacceptable c/b ratios.

The Miller family is unhealthy in only a relative sense. Roberta, George, and Julie are functioning adequately in many ways: They have their financial needs met, they are able to fulfill daily responsibilities at work, home, and school, and there is an absence of constant conflict. However, most important, the Miller family is unhealthy because George and Roberta believe it to be—their c/b ratios are barely acceptable to them. Thus, their individual and family-related goals are not being met and some corrective action is necessary. Rather than knowing how to engage in the process of improving their relationship, they feel helpless and without acceptable options. The possibility of divorce has been considered by both spouses and is feared by their daughter.

6

ASSESSMENT

To understand and assist families, particularly those experiencing difficulties, it is important to assess the nature and quality of family functioning. Results from these assessments are important for both family scientists (who extend our knowledge of how families operate) and practitioners (who assist family members function more adaptively). To add to our knowledge of families, scientists require assessments to test hypotheses generated from theories of family life. To design effective intervention strategies, practitioners need assessment techniques to understand a specific family's strengths and weaknesses.

The cognitive-behavioral family (CBF) model addresses three levels of family functioning: cognitions, behaviors, and general family functioning. In this chapter, assessment in each of these areas is reviewed. For information on family assessment instruments not covered in this chapter, readers are referred to Grotevant and Carlson (1989) and Touliatos, Perlmutter, and Straus (1990).

COGNITIONS

Baucom and Epstein (1990) defined cognitive phenomena as "natural aspects of the information processing that is necessary in order for individuals to understand their environments and make decisions about how they will interact with other people" (p. 47). Cognitions provide meaning, order, and a sense of control. Baucom and Epstein described five types of interrelated cognitions that affect interpersonal relationships. We use their taxonomy to organize our discussion of assessment of cognitions in the family context. These cognitions are *perceptions* about what events occur, *attributions* about why events occur, *expectancies* regarding what will occur, *assumptions* about the roles people play and the way relationships work, and *standards* regarding how individuals should perform their roles and the way relationships should work.

Cognitions are relevant to both individuals and multiperson units in the family system. For individuals, these cognitions are individual psychological phenomena. For the multiperson units, we are interested in the consistency of the cognitions held by each member of the unit. The five types of cognitions held by individuals are discussed in the next section, as are examples of standardized and nonstandardized procedures that may be used to assess these cognitions.

Standardized Instruments that Assess Cognitions

Perceptions. Perceptions are those aspects of a situation that an individual notices and fits into categories that have meaning. Here, they include any aspect of family living that a member of the family system notices, gives meaning to, and regards as important. Typically, individuals' perceptions arise automatically without effort. Furthermore, individuals are generally not aware that their perceptions are selective and that there are other aspects of situations that they do not attend to.

Because perceptions determine what will be attended to, they occur before the other types of cognitions. However, one's expectations, standards, assumptions, and attributions also influence what aspects of an event will be noticed (Baucom & Epstein, 1990). Partly because of the idiosyncratic nature of particular family situations, it will be a challenging task to develop standardized instruments that assess perceptions. At the time this volume was written, there are no known instruments.

Attributions. Attributions refer to beliefs about the causes of positive, negative, and neutral events in the family. Attributions help one understand family members, predict events in one's relationships, and contribute to a sense of control in these relationships (Baucom, 1987). As is the case with many types of cognitions, individuals typically do not recognize that they make attributions, are not aware that there may be other possible causes of family events than the one(s) they have identified, and do not realize the impact that attributions have on family life. According to Bradbury and Fincham (1990), attributions can be described along four continua. The ends of these continua include whether the cause of the event is internal or external (the locus dimension), whether the cause of the event is specific or global (the globality dimension), whether the cause of the event is under the person's control or is uncontrollable (the control dimension), and whether the cause of the event is unstable or stable (the stability dimension).

Consider the Johnson family. Frank and Helen have two children, Scott, age 10 years, and Sarah, age 6 years. At the end of the term, a parent–teacher conference is scheduled to discuss Scott's academic progress. The meeting is arranged for midmorning on a Friday. Both Frank and Helen have business meetings at that time. Helen rearranges her schedule so that she can attend the conference, whereas Frank does not feel that he can do so.

In terms of the attribution dimensions described earlier, both Frank and Helen feel that the locus of the event is external to them (the school scheduled the conference and their companies arranged their business commitments) rather than internal and that such conflicts are stable (they occur regularly at the end of academic quarters) rather than unstable. However, Helen and Frank differ in terms of the globality and control. Helen views her conflict between school and work as specific to this situation and believes that she has control over how she responds to this dilemma. By contrast, Frank believes that this type of conflict is global (i.e., it occurs in many situations) and that he does not have control of how he will respond.

A commonly used measure for individuals is the Attributional Style Questionnaire (ASQ; Seligman, Abramson, Semmel, & von Baeyer, 1979). The ASQ measures individuals' tendencies to attribute negative and positive outcomes to internal as opposed to external, stable as opposed to unstable, and global as opposed to specific factors. Each of the three attributional dimensions yields a subscale for both positive and negative hypothetical outcomes, yielding a total of six subscales. Composite scores for both negative and positive events are generated by totaling subjects' scores on the three attributional subscales. Psychometric properties of the ASQ are described in Peterson et al. (1982).

An instrument that assesses attributions for who is to blame and who has control over marital conflict is the Attributions Regarding Conflict Questionnaire (Madden & Janoff-Bulman, 1981). This instrument is a 14-item questionnaire that examines women's blame and control issues within marital conflict situations. Respondents react to two hypothetical conflict scenarios in which jealousy and a financial argument are central themes, and to two actual conflicts they have recently experienced. They are asked to rate how serious and important the conflicts are; to divide blame among themselves, their husbands, other people, and the impersonal world; and to rate other aspects of conflict situations. No psychometric information is available for this scale, but it appears that this scale could also be modified for use with husbands.

Expectancies.   Expectancies represent beliefs about the likelihood that certain events will occur in the future under certain circumstances (Epstein et al., 1988) or, more specifically, what consequences will follow a particular action (Baucom & Epstein, 1990). These expectancies may be based on a history of interactions with actual members of the family unit or they may be based on generalizations made from previous interactions that are carried over to a particular situation that develops in the family unit.

The many and varied expectations of individuals in the family unit are partly shaped by and integrated into the family constitution. The family constitution is the unwritten and ever-changing set of rules that govern interactions among family members. It specifies how family members will communicate, make decisions, share chores and resources, and relate to others outside of the household. Moreover, it dictates procedures and policies that range from how a family develops a budget to how the toothpaste tube should be squeezed. Because it structures spousal, parental, and sibling interactions, the family constitution provides the predictability that family members need to live interdependently and comfortably, in the close psychological and physical proximity of a home. In healthy families, the family constitution is continually modified and rewritten, as family members progress through their developmental stages. The instruments described next assess various components of the family constitution.

The Marital Attitude Survey (MAS; Pretzer, Epstein, & Fleming, 1987) assesses several aspects of marital interaction. In addition to assessing expectancies and attributions, the MAS measures individuals' perceptions of the flexibility of their marital relationships—a concept similar to how modifiable their family constitution is. The MAS consists of a series of 74 statements on eight subscales: perceived ability of couple to change relationship, expectancy of improvement in relationship, attribution of causality to spouse's behavior, attribution of causality to spouse's personality, attribution of causality to own behavior, attribution of causality to own personality, attribution of malicious intent to spouse, and attribution of lack of love to spouse. Preliminary evidence indicates that the instrument is internally consistent and is related to marital distress, communication, depression, and beliefs regarding relationships.

Similarly, Burr (1971) constructed the Marital Role Discrepancy Index to assess congruence between role expectations for spouses and spousal behavior. The extent of this congruence is related to an important aspect of the family constitution—the consistency of spouses' role expectations. Respondents answer each of the 65 items on the instrument twice: once with respect to the extent to which they would be bothered by each behavior, and then with regard to the amount each spousal behavior is practiced.

With respect to expectations for young children, Rickard, Graziano, and Forehand (1984) developed the Maternal Expectations, Attitudes, and Belief Inventory (MEABI). The MEABI assesses components of the family constitution related to beliefs about how children should be raised and how young children typically function. The MEABI is a 7-point, 67-item measure that contains five subscales: parent knowledge of child development norms; need to be liked, which assesses mothers' need for approval for their child-rearing practices; maternal reactions to a child's deviant behavior, which assesses parental use of praise and discipline; should–should not, used to assess maternal beliefs regarding unacceptable behavior by her child; and belief in child monitoring and guidance, used to determine what the mother believes is the optimal level of intervention by a parent in order to promote the child's development. Psychometric properties are generally weak, with only moderate test–retest and internal consistency reliability. It appears that this measure could also be administered to fathers, as well as to other adults responsible for caring for children (e.g., stepparents).

Assumptions. Assumptions refer to cognitions regarding how certain types of people typically behave, how relationships usually work, and the way one sees oneself in certain roles. These kinds of cognitions may represent stereotypes or prototypes that are derived from lifelong experiences with other people. Assumptions may also be internalizations of cultural prescriptions regarding role behavior (e.g., mothers are typically nurturing and self-sacrificing; Thompson & Walker, 1989). In the CBF model, assumptions are a part of an individual's PT and contribute to the development of relationship scripts and family constitutions.

The Family Beliefs Inventory (FBI) taps maladaptive family assumptions held by both parents and adolescents (Roehling & Robin, 1986). Parents and adolescents respond to different forms of the instrument, with items rated by adolescents geared toward behaviors of their parents, and those responded to by parents geared toward behaviors of their adolescent children. Items are divided into 10 categories: (a) who should a youth's friends be, (b) how money is spent, (c) being nice to a teen's friends, (d) spending time away from home, (e) using the telephone, (f) staying out past curfew, (g) cleaning one's room, (h) talking back to parents, (i) earning money away from home, and (j) helping out around the house. Responses are coded on a 7-point scale indicating the extent of agreement with the belief. Parental responses are scored along six dimensions: (a) ruination, or the belief that adolescents will ruin their futures if given too much freedom, (b) obedience, defined as the belief that parents deserve absolute respect and obedience, (c) perfectionism, indicating that teenage behavior should be flawless, (d) malicious intent, (e) self-blame, defined as a belief in the parents' being to blame for their adolescents' undesirable behavior, and (f) approval, the belief that their child-rearing tactics must have the approval of their children. There are four similarly defined dimensions for adolescents: (a) ruination, (b) unfairness, (c) autonomy, and (d) approval.

Psychometric properties of the FBI are reported as adequate, although internal consistency reliabilities are low for some subscales and there has not been much empirical evidence supporting the instrument.

The Automatic Thoughts Questionnaire (ATQ; Hollon & Kendall, 1980) measures the frequency of automatic negative statements about the self, generated from Beck's model of depression. Four aspects of automatic thoughts are assessed: personal maladjustment and desire for change, negative self-concepts and negative expectations, low self-esteem, and helplessness. The instrument has good psychometric properties, primarily tested on populations of clinically depressed individuals. With item rewording, it is possible that this instrument could have utility with families.

A similar instrument, the Dysfunctional Attitude Scale (DAS; Weissman, 1980), taps cognitive distortions thought to underlie depression. The DAS is also based on Beck's cognitive model of depression, as its 40 items represent seven major value systems: approval, love, achievement, perfectionism, entitlement, omnipotence, and autonomy. Psychometric properties are reported to be quite good, although no norms are reported for clinical populations. This instrument may also have utility with families, with appropriate item rewording.

The Irrational Values Scale (IVS; MacDonald & Games, 1972) is a nine-item scale that assesses a respondent's endorsement of irrational values that are based on the work of Albert Ellis. Psychometric properties have not been extensively examined; MacDonald and Games found that the IVS has adequate internal consistency and concurrent validity with several measures that are expected to relate to irrational values. Although this measure may have utility in the assessment of families, it was not developed for this purpose.

Fine and Kurdek (1992) developed the Parenting Perceptions Inventory to assess parent's cognitions related to various dimensions of parenting. There are separate scales for husbands and wives, as well as separate scales for the control/supervision and warmth dimensions of parenting.

As shown in Table 6.1, the nine items on the control/supervision and warmth scales tap how much a typical parent engages in the parenting behavior, how much the respondent performs the behavior, how much the respondent should perform the behavior, how much the spouse should engage in the behavior, how much the spouse does perform the behavior, and how much typical spouses engage in the behavior. In Baucom and Epstein's (1990) typology, the scale taps assumptions, perceptions, and standards related to parental behavior. A particularly interesting feature of this instrument is that it permits an analysis of both intraindividual (e.g., the difference between how much the respondent perceives that he or she supervises the child and how much he or she believes that he or she should do so) and interindividual (e.g., the difference between how much the respondent perceives that he or she should show warmth to the child and how much the spouse believes that the respondent should do so) cognitive discrepancies.

To date, the scale has been used with fathers, mothers, stepfathers, and stepmothers in stepfamilies. With relatively little modification, it could be

TABLE 6.1

The Parenting Perceptions Inventory

Stepfather Version

One of the things that a stepfather does is supervise or monitor his stepchild's activities. For example, he can supervise his stepchild in completing homework or doing chores. Use the following scale to provide the number (1 to 7) that you believe applies to the statements below. WHEN RELEVANT, ANSWER ONLY FOR THE "TARGET" CHILD.

1	2	3	4	5	6	7
not at all			a moderate amount			a great deal

---

1. How much *does a typical stepfather* supervise or monitor his stepchild? _____
2. How much *do you* supervise or monitor your stepchild? _____
3. How much *should you* supervise or monitor your stepchild? _____
4. How much control *do you* feel you have over the job you do supervising and monitoring your stepchild? _____
5. How receptive is *your stepchild* to your efforts to supervise or monitor? _____
6. How much do you think *your wife should* supervise or monitor your stepchild? _____
7. How much do you think *your wife does* supervise or monitor your stepchild? _____
8. How much does *your wife* think you should supervise or monitor your stepchild? _____
9. How much do you think *a typical mother* supervises or monitors her child? _____

Another thing that a stepfather does is show caring and warmth to his stepchild. For example, he can compliment or praise his stepchild, console him or her, or spend time with him or her. Use the following scale to provide the number (1 to 7) that you believe applies to the statements below. WHEN RELEVANT, ANSWER ONLY FOR THE "TARGET" CHILD.

1	2	3	4	5	6	7
not at all			a moderate amount			a great deal

---

1. How much *does a typical stepfather* show warmth and caring to his stepchild? _____
2. How much *do you* show warmth and caring to your stepchild? _____
3. How much *should you* show warmth and caring to your stepchild? _____
4. How much control *do you* feel you have over the job you do showing warmth and caring to your stepchild? _____
5. How receptive is *your stepchild* to your efforts to show warmth and caring? _____
6. How much do you think *your wife should* show warmth and caring to your stepchild? _____
7. How much do you think *your wife does* show warmth and caring to your stepchild? _____
8. How much does *your wife* think you should show warmth and caring to your stepchild? _____
9. How much do you think *a typical mother* shows warmth and caring to her child? _____

---

adapted for use with parents from a wide variety of types of families (e.g., first-marriage, single-parent).

Standards. Standards differ from assumptions in that they refer to how things should be rather than how they are. Standards represent an ideal comparison level against which actual experiences are compared. Whether the resulting comparison meets or exceeds the standard will affect levels of perceived satisfaction (Rusbult, 1983). In CBF terms, standards provide the baseline from which cost–benefit (c/b) assessments are made.

One family-related standard is particularly important. The relationship script is the part of the family schema that tells an individual how she should function and relate to others in family and quasi-family (i.e., dating) relationships (Schwebel et al., 1989). It is prescriptive, indicating what is possible and desirable in relationships, and it regulates how the individual interacts with others. Further, it dictates an individual's values, coping style, emotional awareness, capacity to love, communication effectiveness, and abilities to cooperate, problem solve, and resolve interpersonal conflict (Schwebel et al., 1989). Although a relationship script is limiting in some ways, it also provides order and a sense of control. It guides decisions in the face of countless options, and makes a person's behavior more predictable and, therefore, less threatening to others in the family setting.

Among the instruments available to identify dysfunctional standards are the Relationship Beliefs Inventory (RBI; Eidelson & Epstein, 1982). The RBI is a 6-point, 40-item scale that measures potentially unrealistic beliefs spouses hold about intimate relationships. Five subscales are included: (a) Disagreement is destructive, (b) mind reading is expected, (c) partners cannot change, (d) sexual perfectionism (is possible), and (e) the sexes are different. The instrument is designed to measure beliefs about relationships in general and not about any particular relationship. However, some items refer to the test taker's partner and not relationships in general. This has been cited as a weakness of the RBI and has led to a modified RBI that refers only to a particular relationship (Kurdek, 1992).

A useful screening instrument is the Perceptions of Parental Role Scales (PPRS; Gilbert & Hanson, 1983). The PPRS is a 78-item measure that assesses 13 perceived parental role responsibilities in three areas: teaching the child, meeting the child's basic needs, and interfacing between the child and the family and other institutions. Respondents are asked to indicate how important they believe each item to be as a parental responsibility during the various stages of raising a child under normal conditions. Reliability appears to be adequate, but factor analyses and validity studies have yet to be conducted.

A similar instrument that assesses perceived disagreement regarding marital roles and responsibilities is the Role Consensus (Bahr, Chappell, & Leigh, 1983). This nine-item questionnaire appears to be internally consistent, but validity data are lacking. With some item rewording and additions, the instrument also could be applied to the family environment.

It should be noted that some instruments have been developed that assess cognitions related to living in families that have undergone transition. These instruments are appropriate to assess the cognitions of individuals who have experienced a particular transition (e.g., divorce, remarriage). For example, Kurdek and Berg (1987) developed the Children's Belief about Parental Divorce Scale, which assesses children's problematic attitudes regarding their parents' divorce.

Informal Assessment Procedures

To complement formal assessment instruments for use with families, practitioners may rely on informal assessment procedures—clinical interviews, questioning about family dynamics, household rules, family strengths and weaknesses, and discussions in which individuals report their expectancies, standards, assumptions, and beliefs about the roles family members play in their unit (Epstein et al., 1988). Further, clinicians can continually observe beliefs, expectancies, and attributions spontaneously reported by family members during their interactions, and structure exercises that facilitate family members' becoming more aware of their cognitions.

For example, interviewers can probe for family members' automatic thoughts (e.g., expectancies and attributions) by adapting techniques described by Beck et al. (1979) for use in individual cognitive therapy. When family members report an upsetting experience with a relative, clinicians can inquire about the specific behavioral interaction that took place, the accompanying mood state, and, most important to cognitive-behavioral clinicians, a detailed account of the accompanying cognitions. Similarly, when therapists notice a shift in mood or behavior during therapy sessions, they can stop the proceedings and inquire about relevant associated cognitions. At all times, clinicians must be alert to instances when it might be helpful to inquire about cognitions. Eventually, family members may reveal their automatic thoughts without prompting by therapists.

Different types of inquiries are relevant for different types of cognitions. For attributions, questions such as "Why do you think she acted that way?" and "What do you think caused that to happen?" may be useful. Expectancies may be explored with such inquiries as "What do you think will happen if you do X?" or "What do you think family life will be like in 5 years?" Beliefs and assumptions can be identified by looking for repetitive themes in family members' automatic thoughts and asking progressively probing questions that elicit beliefs about the implications of automatic thoughts. For example, "If that were so, what would that mean?" might be asked of a family member who reported an automatic thought that his family was a failure.

Standards can be assessed by asking "How do you think you should behave toward your spouse and children?" and "What would you have to be like to be a good parent?"

BEHAVIOR

In addition to assessing potentially dysfunctional cognitions, it is also important to assess overt behavioral exchanges within the family. Dysfunctional cognitions can lead to maladaptive behaviors, which, in turn, can lead to poor family functioning. Behaviors by family members can also elicit cognitions. Thus, behaviors are closely related to cognitions and family functioning. Behavioral excesses and deficits that may lead to dysfunctional cognitions and that interfere with family members' abilities to function successfully as a family unit are of particular interest. Relevant behavioral excesses include criticism, threats, defensiveness, and physical aggression; behavioral deficits may include lack of skill in communication, assertiveness, problem solving, and negotiation (Epstein et al., 1988).

Ideally, behavioral assessment consists of the objective recording of discrete acts performed by family members. A comprehensive behavioral analysis consists not only of the behaviors associated with the problem behavior (e.g., an "acting out" child), but also those of other family members that may serve as antecedent stimuli and reinforcement for the problem behavior. For example, the frequency of a child's acting-out behaviors may be high after spousal arguments that the child hears, but low during periods of parental harmony.

The task of gathering objective behavioral data is a difficult one. Some of this information may be collected by a therapist observing the family interacting in therapy sessions, but more systematic methods are desirable. One commonly used technique is to give the family a specified time period to complete a structured task, such as deciding how to spend leisure time or to solve a family problem of its choosing.

Methods of coding this type of information have been developed (see Forehand & McMahon, 1981; Patterson, 1982; Robin & Weiss, 1980). A distinction has been drawn between microanalytic observation codes, which capture the moment-to-moment behaviors of family members toward one another, and rating scales, which rely on summary judgments made by observers with regard to placing an individual, dyad, or an entire family on some dimension (Grotevant & Carlson, 1989). Observational coding schemes have the advantage of greater objectivity, but provide data that are more difficult to collect and interpret. Rating scales, by contrast, are more subjective because they are based on summary ratings, but have greater interpretive relevance. Coding schemes and rating scales have been extensively used in research projects, but not in clinical settings. Of the two, rating scales may be particularly useful clinically because of their ease in interpretation.

Examples of microanalytic observation codes are the Family Interaction Coding System (FICS; Patterson, Ray, Shaw, & Cobb, 1969; Reid, 1978) and the Parent–Adolescent Interaction Coding System (PAICS; Robin & Fox, 1979). With the FICS, after families interact in semistructured home settings for a minimum of 70 minutes, 29 categories are scored, approximately half of which reflect aversive behaviors and half reflect prosocial behaviors. The PAICS, which is based on the Marital Interaction Coding System, records verbal behaviors of parents and adolescents as they attempt to solve their problems. Behavior units are coded into the following categories: positive, negative, or neutral. The data derived from the FICS and PAICS are often used to assess changes following intervention.

Examples of rating scales are the McMaster Clinical Rating Scale (CRS; Epstein, Baldwin, & Bishop, 1982), Global Family Interaction Scales (FIS–II; Riskin, 1982), and the Clinical Rating Scale for the Circumplex Model (Olson & Killorin, 1985). The CRS assesses dimensions considered to have particular impact on the emotional and physical health of family members, including problem solving, communication, roles, affective involvement, affective responsiveness, and behavior control. The FIS–II rates each of 17 dimensions of family interaction that tend to be observable behaviors (e.g., topic continuity, clarity, information exchange, humor). The Clinical Rating Scale for the Circumplex Model allows clinicians to make global ratings of marital and family systems on the basis of a semistructured family interview. Following an interview in which family members are encouraged to engage in a discussion about how they handle general family issues, the clinician rates the family on three major dimensions: cohesion, adaptability, and communication.

Less structured, but also potentially helpful, are systematic interviews with family members, in which questions are asked regarding frequencies of particular behaviors exhibited by each person in the family and the associated behaviors of other members. A potentially more ecologically valid approach is to ask family members to record behavior logs in their homes (Epstein et al., 1988). A sample of the kind of log that can be used with spouses or with family members is presented in Table 6.2. David Gately, Stephanie McIver, Barry Moss, and one of the authors have found that, generally speaking, spouses and dating partners in research studies or in treatment, if asked, willingly and dependably complete this time diary version on a daily basis. Moreover, they found that once individuals collect the data, they look forward to and learn a great deal from their discussions about it.

With help from those trained in the area, family members can be taught to monitor and record their own behaviors in a structured manner. Presenting problems can be broken down into discrete, observable behaviors that

TABLE 6.2
Sample Behavior Log

Please complete your time diary for consecutive 24 hour periods on the sheets provided. Follow the 11 steps below. Complete each step fully before proceeding to the next step. Please review the sample time diary on the next two pages before completing your first day's time diary.

Steps for Completing Your Time Diary:

1. Under column 1, please list separately each activity you engaged in with your spouse or in the presence of your spouse (describe the content of all conversations, including written and telephone communications).
2. Rate how satisfying each activity was.
   1 = very unsatisfying
   2 = unsatisfying
   3 = slightly unsatisfying
   4 = neither satisfying nor unsatisfying
   5 = slightly satisfying
   6 = satisfying
   7 = very satisfying
3. List the activities your spouse was engaged in during the time you were engaged in each activity listed under column 1.
4. Rate how attentive your spouse was toward you during each activity listed under column 1.
   1 = very inattentive
   2 = inattentive
   3 = slightly inattentive
   4 = neither attentive nor inattentive
   5 = slightly attentive
   6 = attentive
   7 = very attentive
5. Please record the approximate starting and ending time for each activity listed under column 1.
6. Rate how angry you felt toward your spouse during each activity listed under column 1.
   1 = very angry
   2 = angry
   3 = somewhat angry
   4 = slightly angry
   5 = not at all angry
7. Rate how happy you were with your spouse during each activity listed under column 1.
   1 = very happy
   2 = happy
   3 = somewhat happy
   4 = slightly happy
   5 = not at all happy
8. Rate how tense you felt toward your spouse during each activity listed under column 1.
   1 = very tense
   2 = tense
   3 = somewhat tense
   4 = slightly tense
   5 = not at all tense
9. Rate how loving you felt toward your spouse during each activity listed under column 1.
   1 = very loving
   2 = loving
   3 = somewhat loving
   4 = slightly loving
   5 = not at all loving
10. Please list any additional people who were present during each activity listed under column 1. Identify them in terms of their relationship to you as well as by name (e.g., Son/Bob, Friend/Jim).
11. Please record any additional activities in which you and your spouse were engaged during each activity listed under column 1.

(Continued)

TABLE 6.2
(Continued)

Sample Time Diary: Day 1

1. What Were You Doing?	2. How Satisfying?	3. What Was Your Spouse Doing?	4. How Attentive?	5. Time Began	5. Time Ended	6. How Angry?	7. How Happy?	8. How Tense?	9. How Loving?	10. Who Else Was There?	11. Were You and Your Spouse Doing Anything Else?
Talking about what we would name and how we would raise our second child.	7	Talking with me.	7	12:00 a.m.	1:00 a.m.	5	2	5	2	—	Watching TV.
Sleeping.	5	Sleeping.	4	1:00 a.m.	6:30 a.m.	5	4	5	4	—	—
Getting ready for the day (showered, dressed, got material for work together).	4	Sleeping.	1	6:30 a.m.	8:30 a.m.	5	4	5	4	—	—
Kissed husband goodbye. Talked about what time I would be home, and what my day was going to be like.	6	Kissed me goodbye. Talked about what his day was going to be like and when he would be home.	6	8:30 a.m.	9:00 a.m.	5	2	5	2	—	—
Phoned husband at work. Told him I was going to the store and that I would be back at 6:00 p.m..	4	At work.	4	5:00 p.m.	5:05 p.m.	5	4	5	3	—	—
Put groceries away. Talked about my day at work.	5	Cleaning, doing dishes from last night. Talked about his day at work.	5	5:45 p.m.	6:00 p.m.	5	3	5	4	Son/Todd	Listening to news on TV.
Fixed dinner, ate dinner, talked about news on TV.	6	Set table, ate, talked with me.	5	6:00 p.m.	7:00 p.m.	5	2	5	3	Son/Todd	Watching TV.
Worked on bathroom—painting and wallpapering.	2	Painting/wallpapering bathroom.	4	7:00 p.m.	10:00 p.m.	4	5	3	5	—	Talking about new tax forms. How to fill them out.
Argued and fought about the need to buy new living room furniture, and husband's stinginess with money.	1	Argued and fought with me. Feels I spend too much money.	2	10:00 p.m.	11:00 p.m.	1	5	1	5	—	—
Being affectionate.	7	Being affectionate.	7	11:00 p.m.	12:00 a.m.	5	1	4	1	—	—

Sample Time Diary: Day 2

1. What Were You Doing?	2. How Satisfying?	3. What Was Your Spouse Doing?	4. How Attentive?	5. Time Began	5. Time Ended	6. How Angry?	7. How Happy?	8. How Tense?	9. How Loving?	10. Who Else Was There?	11. Were You and Your Spouse Doing Anything Else?
Talking about how stupid our fight was. Said I was sorry. Talked about going to my mom's tomorrow.	6	Said he was sorry. Said he wanted to watch the ball game before we went.	6	12:00 a.m.	1:00 a.m.	5	2	4	2	—	—
Sleeping.	5	Sleeping.	4	1:00 a.m.	10:30 a.m.	5	4	5	4	—	—
Getting ready for the day (showered, ironed clothes, dressed).	4	Getting ready for the day (showered, dressed).	4	10:30 a.m.	11:00 a.m.	5	4	5	3	—	Talking about what we wanted to eat for breakfast.
Eating breakfast, and talking about what we would be doing for the day.	5	Eating, talking about the day.	3	11:00 a.m.	12:00 p.m.	5	4	5	4	Son/Todd	Reading newspaper.
Washed dishes, put them away, cleaned kitchen.	4	Reading newspaper. Talking with Todd about sports.	2	12:00 p.m.	12:30 p.m.	5	4	5	4	Son/Todd	—
Cutting coupons. Putting clean clothes away. Talking to mom on phone.	4	Watching baseball with Todd.	2	12:30 p.m.	2:30 p.m.	4	5	4	5	Son/Todd	Talked about when we were going to mom's.
Went to mom's. Talking, playing cards, eating dinner.	6	Talking, playing cards. Worked on car for a little while. Eating dinner.	4	3:00 p.m.	7:00 p.m.	5	3	5	4	Son/Todd Mom/Ruth Dad/Jim	—
Went driving around looking at houses.	6	Driving & looking.	5	7:00 p.m.	8:00 p.m.	5	2	5	2	Son/Todd	Talking about the future.
Watched ice hockey on TV and the end of a movie.	5	Watching TV.	5	8:00 p.m.	12:00 a.m.	5	2	5	3	—	Talking about the game. General chit-chat. Our team lost.

(Continued)

115

TABLE 6.2
(Continued)

Time Diary: Day ___

1. What Were You Doing?	2. How Satisfying?	3. What Was Your Spouse Doing?	4. How Attentive?	5. Time Began	5. Time Ended	6. How Angry?	7. How Happy?	8. How Tense?	9. How Loving?	10. Who Else Was There?	11. Were You and Your Spouse Doing Anything Else?

lend themselves to systematic recording. For example, parents who indicate that their children are "constantly disobeying household rules" can operationally define this problem as any instance when a child deliberately behaves in a way that is inconsistent with a posted set of family rules. Parents might also record their responses to the children's behavior when they obey and disobey the rules.

In addition to functional behavioral analyses of families, it is also important to assess specific skills of individual family members and the family as a unit. These skills include communication, assertiveness, problem solving, and negotiation. A self-report instrument that assesses problem-solving attitudes and behaviors is the Family Crisis Oriented Personal Scales (F-COPES; Olson et al., 1982). The questionnaire's 29 items measure five areas: acquiring social support, reframing, seeking spiritual support, mobilizing family to acquire and accept help, and passive appraisal. Reliability data are good, although validity has not yet been demonstrated.

Whereas it is potentially useful to ask family members about their skills in these areas, because of potential biases in reporting, firsthand observations by the therapist are critical (Epstein et al., 1988). Opportunities for the therapist gathering this information are provided by asking the family to work on solving a particular problem, either one given to them or one that they choose themselves. If the family can effectively solve a problem given to them by the therapist, but cannot solve one of their own that is more emotionally laden, valuable insight has been gained.

In addition, there are coding systems to objectively rate some of these skills. Robin, Kent, O'Leary, Foster, and Prinz (1977), for example, have developed a coding system to assess problem-solving skills.

FAMILY FUNCTIONING

There are several measures that assess the overall quality of family functioning. Use of these instruments provides an overall indication of how well the family copes with its various challenges. Some of the best and most commonly used instruments are discussed next. The review focuses on measures of global family functioning and not those specific to individual dyads (e.g., parent–child relationships). In CBF terms, these instruments can be used to help family members examine their family constitution, the compatibility of their relationship scripts, and the outcomes of their problem-solving strategies. These measures can also be used to evaluate the effectiveness of CBF interventions.

The Family Assessment Device (FAD; Epstein, Baldwin, & Bishop, 1983) is a 4-point, 60-item questionnaire designed to evaluate family functioning along six dimensions: (a) problem solving, (b) communication, (c) roles, (d) affective responsiveness, (e) affective involvement, and (f) behavior control. An overall rating of general functioning is also available. The instrument is intended for administration to adults and adolescents. Items are worded so that respondents indicate their level of agreement or disagreement in terms of how closely the statement describes their family. The FAD has good internal consistency, but additional reliability and validity data are limited.

The Family Environment Scale (FES; Moos & Moos, 1986) is widely used for research purposes as a measure of the climate of the family unit. The FES contains 90 true–false items scored on 10 subscales, including cohesion, expressiveness, conflict, independence, achievement orientation, intellectual-cultural orientation, active-recreational orientation, moral-religious orientation, organization, and control.

A particularly interesting feature of the FES is that it contains three forms: (a) The "real" form measures people's perceptions of their current family environments, (b) the "ideal" form measures people's conceptions of their ideal family environments, and (c) the "expectations" form assesses expectations about how the family will be at some specified point in the future. Responses and scores from these three forms can be compared to yield valuable insight into family members' expectations and standards regarding family life. Partly because it has been used so regularly in research projects, there is considerable evidence related to psychometric properties; most of these data are supportive, although problems have been identified (Grotevant & Carlson, 1989; Nelson, 1984; Roosa & Beals, 1990) and addressed (Moos, 1990). It should also be noted that a children's version of the FES has been developed for use with 5- to 12-year-olds (Pino, Simons, & Slawinowski, 1984).

The Family Hardiness Index (FHI; McCubbin, McCubbin, & Thompson, 1987) assesses the family's ability to resist stress and to adapt to new situations. The FHI is a 4-point, 20-item Likert-type questionnaire designed to assess the family's internal strengths and durability of the family unit. Four key variables are measured: (a) commitment, (b) confidence, (c) challenge, and (d) control. Internal consistency reliability is high and some limited support for construct validity is presented in McCubbin et al. (1987).

The Family Adaptation Scale (FAS; Antonovsky & Sourani, 1988) assesses family members' satisfaction with the fit between family members and the family unit, and between the family unit and the community. The FAS is a 7-point, 11-item semantic differential questionnaire that can either be used in interview or self-report format. Limited psychometric data are available to support the instrument.

The Family Adaptability and Cohesion Evaluation Scale (FACES–III; Olson, Portner, & Lavee, 1985) is a very widely used instrument designed to measure two dimensions of family functioning: cohesion and adaptability. The instrument is based on the Circumplex Model of family functioning, which posits that there are three critical dimensions of family behavior: cohesion, adaptability, and communication. FACES–III has 20 items that family members respond to in two different ways: the way they perceive their family (real) and the way they would like their family to be (ideal). Item wording can easily be modified for use with couples. Although internal consistency is only fair, a number of studies have supported the test–retest reliability and construct validity of the measure. A limitation is that the instrument is restricted to assessing constructs from the Circumplex Model.

Some instruments have been developed to assess functioning in specific types of families. For example, Knaub and Hanna (1984) developed the Remarried Family Inventory (applicable for both parents and children) to assess family members' perceptions of the quality of their lives in their stepfamilies. To a large extent, this instrument is applicable to all families, as only a few items tap constructs unique to stepfamilies.

A potentially valuable instrument designed to assess perceptions of marital quality is Sabatelli's (1984) Marital Comparison Level Index (MCLI). The MCLI is a 7-point, 32-item Likert-type questionnaire that focuses on the contrast between marital experiences and expectations. For each item, respondents are asked how their experiences within their relationships compare with their expectations. Item responses range from "worse than I expect" to "better than I expect." Preliminary indications are that the instrument is unidimensional, internally consistent, and related to commitment levels and likelihood of perceiving the marriage as being equitable and fair. At least some of the items seem amenable to modification for applications to family life, and not just marriages. This instrument may be particularly valuable in cognitive-behavior therapy because it assesses the congruence between cognitions (i.e., expectations) and actual experiences.

CONCLUSIONS

As this chapter demonstrates, although numerous standardized instruments assess family-related cognitions, behaviors, and general functioning, further instrument development—both of existing measures and new measures—is needed because many existing instruments lack adequate psychometric properties or have not had these thoroughly tested. Furthermore, from a CBF perspective, new instruments are needed that are able to assess the various components of the family constitution, relationship script, c/b ratios, and problem-solving strategies. To the extent that these measures can be developed, tested, and used, they may aid researchers, clinicians, and educators to quickly assess these important cognitive dimensions within families.

7

COGNITIVE-BEHAVIOR FAMILY
THERAPY: AN OVERVIEW

As discussed earlier, the CBF model proposes that individuals' thoughts, feelings, and behaviors in the family setting can be understood in terms of the cognitions that they hold in their *family schema*. The cognitions in an individual's family schema include those that detail his or her understanding of the family rules, what he or she expects to give to and get from family relationships, and how healthy families operate.

The CBF model further proposes that individuals building a romantic relationship draw from their respective family schemas and, without being aware of doing so, create rules to govern their interactions. These rules, as a group, are called the *family constitution*. One useful way to understand the family constitution is to think of it as a tool that enables psychologically connected individuals to live together and meet their needs in an orderly, rule-directed way that makes household life predictable and stress levels tolerable. Of course, individuals must be able to modify the family constitution if they are to adjust to changes in the family unit, new situations, and the inevitable growth of its members. How this is to be done is also specified in the family constitution.

Cognitive-behavioral family therapy (CBFT) follows directly from these assumptions and is detailed in the next two chapters. This chapter presents the historical background of CBFT, an overview and the characteristics of this approach, the specific steps involved in CBFT, and, finally, a case illustration that highlights the key parts of the CBFT process. In chapter 8, some specific psychotherapeutic techniques are described within a CBFT framework, with the help of extensive case material.

We believe people benefit greatly by learning about the CBF model, and the teaching of it plays an important role in CBFT. Clients, who come in because of problems with behavior or with interpersonal relationships in their household, need that background so they understand why therapists focus on their thinking. They need to be taught that problems can be attacked at different levels of analysis and that some processes in interpersonal behavior are overt and others covert.

Of course, in the best of all possible circumstances, individuals would be taught lessons like these in adolescence, before they begin forming romantic relationships. Instead, in the absence of institutionalized instruction in family life in the public schools, by the time family members recognize that they have a serious family problem and need treatment, they face a challenge that is like an onion, with many issues layered upon the central difficulty. At this point, as much as they might want to solve their own problems without help, they cannot. One reason why this is so is that, given the onion-layered nature of their problems, family members, individually or as a group, lack the ability to "diagnose" the difficulties they face and to identify their underlying causes. Moreover, they lack the skill necessary to determine the kinds of adjustments that would lead them to overcome what they are facing.

Given this situation, CBFT is oriented toward helping family members both solve the problem at hand and learn about family life so they can limit the disruptiveness of problems they face in the future. Toward these ends, CBFT includes psychoeducational components during which therapists teach clients the CBF model, which provides a common language and a theory to guide them, and self-help techniques they can use to diagnose and intervene in future family problems. Before exploring CBFT in more detail, a brief sketch is given to place this method in a historical perspective.

THE BACKGROUND OF CBFT

The pioneer family therapists, who began publishing their ideas after World War II, introduced a new mental health paradigm that challenged the belief that all personal adjustment problems and psychiatric disorders stemmed from intrapsychic issues (Nichols, 1984). Instead, these early contributors proposed that some mental health difficulties resulted from the interpersonal dynamics functioning in the "identified patient's" family.

New and fundamentally different forms of treatment followed this theoretical position. Whereas the then-popular individual psychoanalytic and then-new humanistic (Carl Rogers) and Gestalt (Fritz Perls) treatment methods took an intrapsychic focus, the therapeutic approaches suggested by the works of Ackerman (1966); Bateson, Jackson, Haley, and Weakland (1956); Bell (1962); and Bowen (1961) targeted the family unit as the focus of intervention. Instead of seeking change by directly addressing the thoughts, feelings, and behaviors of the patient or client, as was done in the intrapsychic approach, these family therapists sought to alter the functioning of the family system which, in turn, affected all family members' behaviors and brought sought-after changes. Along with these early writers, many others (Boszormenyi-Nagy, Framo, Minuchin, Satir, Selvini-Palazzoli and the Milan group, Whittaker, Wynne, Zuk, etc.) have made unique contributions to the field.

The new family approaches drew from general systems theory (Von Bertalanffy, 1968), which proposed that families are themselves units and entities that are greater than the sum of their individual parts. As such, changes in one or more individuals that make up a unit will inevitably affect others in the family and the family unit itself. Although general systems theory effectively describes the family unit and the interactions within it, the theory does not inform therapists about what, where, or how to intervene to bring about desirable changes in the family system.

Each of the new family approaches and CBFT drew from general systems theory and built upon it, suggesting interventions that would be most effective in bringing about desirable changes in families. In contrast to the other approaches, CBFT directs attention to individuals' cognitions, suggesting that therapists intervene by helping family members become aware of their own family-related cognitions and how these mesh with other family members'.

The CBFT model is a hybrid that draws from both the individual/intrapsychic tradition and from general systems theory/family systems tradition. More specifically, the model assumes that what happens in family life at any given moment is shaped by many forces, including by what is happening at the intrapsychic level within individual family members as well as by a set of rules that govern the family system. The CBFT model also recognizes that these forces, plus others that shape events at a given moment, are sometimes within the conscious awareness of family members, but typically operate outside of or at a low level of awareness.

The assessment processes used in CBFT also draw from both family therapy and cognitive-behavioral therapy traditions and literatures. For example, as detailed in chapter 6, CBFT therapists, like cognitive-behavior therapists (Kuiper & MacDonald, 1983), try to identify those difficulties an individual experiences that stem from irrational or illogical thinking and design treatment programs accordingly. At the same time, CBFT therapists also study the client's family as a system, trying to identify dynamics that cause family problems and design corrective interventions for these.

CHARACTERISTICS OF CBFT

The CBFT model assumes that many emotional and adjustment problems that individuals experience can be effectively treated in the family context with interventions designed to make them more aware of their family-related cognitions and the feelings and behaviors that follow from them. CBFT further assumes, as Barton and Alexander (1981) suggested, that by improving family members' understanding of each other, they will be capable of and will find themselves experiencing more supportiveness in their interactions.

CBFT therapists are eclectic in the sense that they liberally use concepts, theory, and techniques from other approaches. However, CBFT therapists' main focus is on clients' cognitions and, more specifically, on how the cognitions affect their feelings, family problem solving, and other behaviors. Toward these ends, from the outset of treatment, CBFT therapists do the following:

1. *View clients as change agents.* CBFT therapists view themselves as facilitators who, working within their clients' value system, help them become more effective problem solvers. In this role, CBFT therapists foster their clients' skill development, sharing their expertise and empowering their clients to function more effectively.

2. *Help clients feel ownership for their treatment.* CBFT therapists explain the concept of "a psychological sense of ownership" to clients and help them take ownership for the CBFT process. Just as in the business world, families work harder for success when they "own" the work that is being done in identifying problems and in generating solutions. Further, family members who have invested themselves in, and have a sense of ownership for, problem solving will have a stake in making the solutions work and, therefore, may exert more effort.

3. *Generate realistic and hopeful expectations in clients.* CBFT therapists explain that when people facing problems are given information and support, they are empowered to find solutions and to build more effective problem-solving mechanisms into their family system. This holds especially when people are motivated enough to seek treatment to help them address their problems. Therapists share these ideas because they are central to CBFT and because they foster positive expectations that are helpful to clients (Frank & Frank, 1990; Rosenthal & Jacobson, 1966).

CBFT therapists encourage clients to feel hopeful by providing them with an overview of the treatment process and, when possible, by suggesting relatively easy steps that clients could take that might produce progress, however little.

Early on, besides working to identify clients' family-related cognitions, CBFT therapists also try to uncover cognitions clients hold about the therapy process. Most enter treatment with both realistic and unrealistic notions about therapy, what they will be asked to do, and what changes might occur in family life. Some hold cognitions that would hamper treatment, such as "nothing ever works for our family," or cognitions that would inevitably lead to disappointment, like "We should be able to overcome all our problems in one session." Once these are "out on the table," therapists and clients can address them openly and objectively.

In addressing these cognitions, therapists serve as cognitive mediators; that is, therapists explain why they have asked about these cognitions, what they think the consequences of holding particular cognitions might be, and so on. Not only do therapists model effective problem solving and teach clients by doing this, but, by sharing, they also help clients develop greater understanding and ownership of the process.

4. *Normalizing clients' difficulties in disclosing.* As in any form of therapy, some clients hesitate to disclose certain kinds of information. Recognizing this, therapists raise the issue, speaking about the confidentiality of sessions, the need for disclosure, the difficulties many children experience talking about parents in their presence, and the issue of family secrets.

After basic issues are addressed, CBFT therapists might raise other concerns: "When adults discuss their parents and childhood, they might hesitate to verbalize certain ideas. For example, you might think, 'I never became self-confident because my parents never let me take charge of anything.' As you state this you might 'get a guilty or concerned feeling,' even if your parents live thousands of miles away and you know that they will never hear about anything you utter." Therapists might add, reassuringly: "It is hard to talk about your parents even though you know it won't hurt them. But I'm sure they would want you to talk about them if they thought it would help you solve problems and become happier and healthier."

Another way therapists normalize the treatment process is by stressing that every individual who emerges from adolescence does so with a view about how family life should work that was shaped by his or her unique upbringing. No matter who their parents are or what they did, "their view" was inevitably shaped so that their family schema will have some areas of strengths and some areas of weaknesses.

5. *Reduce biases in attributions.* CBFT therapists make clients aware that they make attributions, the kinds of attributions they tend to make, and how these attributions, in turn, shape their behavior. For example, therapists teach clients about the actor–observer split (Jones & Nisbett, 1971), explaining that when an individual is the actor, he or she has access to a much more complete set of information than when he or she is the observer, and that this difference, in turn, affects the attributions the individual makes.

To illustrate, when an individual stumbles, family members will probably attribute the stumbling to a factor within the person, such as inattentiveness or clumsiness. This attributional bias is referred to as the *fundamental attribution error.* The person who stumbles, however, will more likely attribute the stumble to external factors, such as the lighting or uneven floor.

6. *Increase clients' awareness of the intricacies of communication.* Serv-

ing as a cognitive mediator, CBFT therapists help clients come to recognize the complexities of communication. They learn that (Watzlawick, Beavin, & Jackson, 1967):

a. Family members cannot not communicate. Even refusing to communicate is a message.

b. Family members' messages have report and command functions. "The time is 11 p.m." is the report aspect. The command involved is not directly verbalized in words but might be, "Turn on the television so we can watch the news." The command might be expressed by the context, tone of voice, past precedents, and so forth.

c. The command aspect of communications shapes the nature of family relationships and causes the most difficulties. People usually engage in insufficient self-reflection and metacognition to be aware of the command aspects of their exchanges and how they are shaping their relationships.

7. *Work to facilitate client progress.* CBFT therapists recognize that clients enter treatment when their c/b ratios are unacceptable (see chapter 4). Because clients want matters improved but, at the same time, experience anxiety about change, they are reassured by realistically optimistic therapists who acknowledge their concerns, actively demonstrate empathy, and have confidence in the efficacy of CBFT.

Therapists prepare clients at the outset by explaining that making changes in therapy is a challenging process and that the family members will experience ups and downs over the course of treatment. When down periods emerge, the therapists will remind clients that this was expected and they were forewarned. At such points, clients need a morale boost. Therapists can remind them that the effort they invest in fixing family problems will pay dividends for every family member and for the unit itself.

When families enter down periods, therapists may gain crucial insights into why progress slowed, perhaps identifying particular cognitions that are blocking progress. For instance, the Appletons labeled their teenage son as *lazy*. Because they view him in this way, they refrain from directly requesting him to complete household tasks. Then, when he does not do his share of chores, they grow angry and use his failure as further confirmation of his laziness. After identifying this pattern, CBFT therapists might challenge the parents' cognitions, asking them to consider what the term *laziness* explains: Was their son born lazy? Does laziness go away? Do rewards or punishment change laziness? Are there other explanations for their son's behavior? As Mr. and Mrs. Appleton answer these questions, they might develop new ways to understand their situation and approach their son.

Sometimes therapists or clients discover rules in the family's constitution that operate in ways that block treatment progress (i.e., cause *resistance*).

For example, the constitution might specify: "Don't share secrets with outsiders" or "Don't discuss Ted's drinking problem, even within the family." Other times rules can be contradictory and put family members in a bind. Consider the Appletons again who have one operating rule, "Mom is in charge of the kitchen and when she is overtaxed she can ask for help with food shopping, cooking, and cleaning" and another that says "We operate the household in a democratic, equitable way and everybody should contribute a fair share without being asked." Therapists can begin to help the family mobilize itself by pointing out, "Given this pair of rules, Mom can't talk about the problems she has been having getting help, and sister can't complain about feeling she's done more than her brother in the kitchen."

When clients have insights like this about family-related cognitions and come to new understandings, they often expect "instant changes" in their behavior patterns. Therapists teach clients to be patient, telling them that there is often a time gap between new understandings of family problems and their being able to bring about change.

In sum, CBFT therapists deal with blocked progress, or resistance, in the same ways they handle other problems: by empathetically and repeatedly asserting that family change is difficult and energy draining, by supportively working with the clients to identify cognitions that might underlie or cause the blockage, and by helping clients adopt new cognitions that will support therapeutic progress and healthier behavior patterns.

THE STEPS IN CBFT

Clients are told that although CBFT feels like a continuously unfolding process, treatment proceeds through five discrete, albeit often overlapping steps (Schwebel & Fine, 1992): (a) Step 1: rapport building and introduction to new concepts; (b) Step 2: assessment; (c) Step 3: personal application of concepts; (d) Step 4: preliminary cognitive change; and (e) Step 5: initiating behavioral change.

During all stages, CBFT therapists maintain a health-promoting atmosphere, proceeding in a planned way, modeling effective behavior, and explaining the purposes of their comments (cognitive mediation) as sessions unfold. They support clients by pointing out the inevitability of conflict in family life and the universality of the struggle to find workable solutions to the complex difficulties human beings face as they try to live together in harmony. And, last but not least, therapists explain that people in therapy are usually concerned about being criticized, embarrassed, or singled out as *the cause* of family problems. However, in CBFT no blame is leveled at individuals; the focus is on the family system and the theme is cooperative, mutually supportive problem solving. Those involved, including the therapists, will fail together as a team or, more likely, succeed together to the family's benefit.

THE FIVE-STEP PROCESS IN DETAIL

Step 1: Rapport Building and Introduction to New Concepts

While conducting first-session business (acknowledging presenting problems, rapport building, collecting relevant history, discussing office policies, etc.), CBFT therapists introduce the treatment goal of teaching clients to understand themselves and their family dynamics in new ways—ways that will foster behavioral changes, more family joy, and fewer heartaches.

Clients are told that they will be taught the CBF model and once they acquire a working knowledge of it, they will have a tool to use to better understand themselves and what is occurring in their family system. In addition, the model will provide them with a common vocabulary and way of understanding family life, both of which they will share with their therapist. Empowered in this way, they will be more effective in solving the problems they face.

During the first session, therapists introduce clients to the CBF model and concepts like the family schema, the relationship script, the PT, the family constitution, c/b analyses, and other helpful ideas, such as the notions of the family system, circular and linear causality, and feedback. As clients learn to think more actively about their family and as they integrate these concepts into their thinking, they become more aware of what occurs moment by moment in their family life. They gain a better sense of why they think, feel, and behave as they do, and they gain a better sense of what each other is thinking and feeling, partly because they have also learned to communicate more effectively.

Among the therapist's goals in Step 1 are: establish a working rapport with all family members, introduce them to CBFT and set positive expectations for treatment, have clients recognize that CBFT involves a collaboration with the therapist, and intellectually and experientially acquaint clients with the fact that cognitions affect their thoughts, feelings, and behaviors in the family setting.

Unique Challenge in Step 1. Family members entering CBFT (as well as readers) face an immediate challenge: Treatment interventions force them to think at a level at least one level deeper than that to which they are accustomed. That is, CBFT asks clients to consider what cognitive structures or family rules cause family members to behave as they do and cause the individual to react as he or she does. Through functioning at this deeper level, clients come to better understand family interactions and how cognitions (which they can change) shape how they think, feel, and behave.

The following example illustrates how CBFT therapists might teach clients to attend to deeper levels with regard to what occurs when they interact.

The Abernathys described the following conversation that unfolded during a recent dinner:

> Ronnie Ann: "Scott, is it time to bring my car in for service?"
> Scott: "I don't know. How many miles have you driven it since the last service, when I brought it in to the shop for you?"
> Ronnie Ann: "That's a good question. I never thought to look at—what d'ya call that thing—that mileage gauge on the dash."
> Scott: "Honey, just take the mileage on the odometer and subtract the mileage on the shop's sticker. You'll find the sticker inside the door jamb on the driver's side. It tells you when they last serviced the car."
> Ronnie Ann: "I'm extremely busy this week. I'm trying to bring the children in for their dental and medical check-ups before the new school year begins. And I have to take them shopping for their back-to-school clothes and supplies. I don't even have an hour to spare . . ."
> Scott (raising his voice in a firm but controlled manner): "Listen! D'ya think I'm planning on sitting on my butt this week and popping bon-bons into my mouth?"
> After Scott raised his voice, Ronnie Ann went upstairs, leaving the matter unresolved and both of them frustrated and feeling they were "in the right."

The Abernathys are bright, yet they cannot seem to solve certain types of relatively minor problems. As a result, they frequently encounter this kind of stalemate. In such cases, CBFT therapists reflect on a statement made about community psychology practice: When a problem persists in a situation, "there is some element in the social setting that blocks effective problem-solving behavior on the part of [the spouses] . . ." (Levine, 1974, p. 212). In the Abernathys' case, the element blocking their problem solving may be a lack of knowledge about what is actually happening between them.

This disagreement sounds like an argument about work loads. Hearing this exchange might tempt some therapists to help the Abernathys improve their communication and to develop the habit of stating requests to each other in a clear, direct fashion. However, in this case, such an intervention would not deal with the basic cause of the Abernathys' problem (differences in their family-related cognitions), but rather with a *symptom* (ineffective communication). To illustrate this point, the Abernathys' exchange is repeated below, but this time parenthetical material is included. This conveys the content of the Abernathys' cognitions that underlie their positions and caused their difficulties:

> Ronnie Ann: "Scott, is it time to bring my car in for service?" (Cognitions operating: From her personal theory of the ideal family [PT], "Husbands should take care of automobiles and other mechanical devices. Such behavior shows that a husband loves his wife." From her relationship script: "It is not proper for

ladies [like me] to ask over and over again for help, but ladies don't give up either. Instead drop hints and sound naive." From her c/b analyses: "Why do I always have to bug him to death to do his job.")

Scott: "I don't know. How many miles have you driven it since the last service, when I brought it in to the shop for you?" (Cognitions operating: From his view of the family constitution, "We are an equal-rights, nonsexist family. When we bought the second car we agreed that I will take care of my auto and she will take care of hers." From his relationship script: "By profession, I'm a teacher; if I give a person a fish, he eats today, if I teach him to fish, he eats forever. I could check her mileage, but I've done that repeatedly and she hasn't yet learned to check it. Now I'll simply tell her how." From his c/b cognitions, "This is downright irritating. Why should I put up with this power game Ronnie Ann's playing?")

Ronnie Ann: "That's a good question. I never thought to look at—what d'ya call that thing—that mileage gauge on the dash." (Cognitions operating: From her relationship script, "As a woman from the deep South and born in my generation, I should issue compliments freely. After all, you catch flies with honey not vinegar. If you sound really ladylike with men, they will help you. Their help proves they see you as valuable and giving the help makes them feel worthwhile too." From her c/b cognitions, "It's worth pushing this issue because if Scott takes care of getting my car serviced for me, I'll know he loves me. I could make the time to do it but what I'm really after is having Scott care for me.")

Scott: "Honey, just take the mileage on the odometer and subtract the mileage on the shop's sticker. You'll find the sticker inside the door jamb on the driver's side. It tells you when they last serviced the car." (Cognitions operating: From his view of the family constitution, "I'm busy this week, in fact, I'm way over my head. But besides, I care about her, so I'll push and teach her this basic car care skill." From his c/b cognitions, "Not only will I be relieved of this burden, but she'll feel good if she learns to do this and learns to be a more independent person.")

Ronnie Ann: "I'm extremely busy this week. I'm trying to bring the children in for their dental and medical check-ups before the new school year begins. And I have to take them shopping for their back-to-school clothes and supplies. I don't even have an hour to spare . . ." (Cognitions operating, PI: "Well, there it is, he rejected me, he won't show his caring even though I tried to get it in a tainted, roundabout way, basically begging him." From her c/b cognitions, "Well, I hope he's happy with all the goodies I give him. I better figure out another way to get some benefits, because I haven't gotten a fair share lately. It will help if he takes care of my car. Maybe I'll also see about a new outfit for the fall. . . .")

Scott (raising his voice in a firm but controlled manner): "Listen! D'ya think I'm planning on sitting on my butt this week and popping bon-bons into my mouth?" (Cognitions operating: From his c/b cognitions, "This is getting to be a pain. I better change the way things are going right now." From his problem-solving cognitions, "She'll back down and we'll have temporary peace if I let her know enough is enough.")

Viewed this way, the nature of the Abernathys' problem appears very different than it did on first blush. To effectively address the problem, the Abernathys need to go beyond debating who brought the car in last time and how they divide household responsibilities. They need to focus on their underlying cognitions and deal with the "real" reasons why this car-service issue is so important to them.

During the first session, the therapist introduced Ronnie Ann and Scott to the CBF model and then guided them through the steps of identifying and sharing their cognitions (the aforementioned parenthetical material). After this, Ronnie commented: "In the past whenever Scott and I settled disputes like the auto-service issue, I always had a residual 'bad taste' in my mouth. I guess that happened because we never got to the root of any problem." Building on this comment, the therapist explained how and why cognitions in the family schemas affected their holder's thoughts, feelings, and behaviors in the family setting.

Before completing Step 1, the Abernathys grew more comfortable working at the level of their cognitions, which involved thinking at least one step deeper than at the level to which they were accustomed. For example, the therapist had them examine each cognition that was involved in the exchange presented earlier and identify the accuracy or truth of it as well as the pros and cons of holding it. As a result, the Abernathys asked themselves, "Is it true that Scott expresses his love by doing things for Ronnie Ann? Are there other ways he expresses his love?" After determining that Scott did not view himself as expressing love by "doing things" for Ronnie Ann, the couple considered in what ways he did communicate his love. They agreed that there were too few ways outside of the bedroom and that they both wanted to work on improving their expression of loving feelings.

When they considered the pros and cons, Ronnie Ann and Scott looked at whether each cognition might be likely to cause problems for them in the future. For instance, they agreed that although Scott's "teach a person to fish" cognition was appropriate in his school, when he applied it to Ronnie Ann, it conveyed a condescending, potentially troublesome, adult-to-child message. They agreed that should either of them detect Scott treating Ronnie Ann in this "tough-love" way he treats his students, instead of in a spouselike, equitable manner, then that person will literally call, "Time out—the 'fishing cognition' is sneaking in." At that point they would stop whatever was happening and try to find another way to deal with the situation at hand.

Step 2: Assessment

The goals of the assessment process are twofold: to enable therapists to better understand the family and its members from the perspective of CBF theory and, based on this, to indicate which interventions are most likely to be helpful. Although assessment occurs throughout treatment, during Step 2 therapists and clients focus on it, identifying key cognitions in each family member's family schema and the consequences associated with holding these. They also study family dynamics that follow from these cognitions, determining the costs and benefits of these to each family member and to the effective functioning of the unit itself.

CBFT assessment techniques come from both the family therapy and cognitive-behavioral therapy literatures. As a result, during one point in a session CBFT therapists might work to identify difficulties that stem from irrational thinking whereas at another point they might be asking family members about a pattern in their family system that has counterproductive consequences for them.

Chapter 6 explains how family members use the assessment process, in conjunction with therapists, to set goals, to develop treatment strategies, and, finally, to determine whether they achieved treatment objectives. It details how therapists use various means in conducting the assessment, including interviews; paper-and-pencil measures; observations of interpersonal dynamics, household rules, and family strengths and weaknesses; and structured tasks (e.g., giving a family a task to do cooperatively) through which data are generated on specific issues.

CBFT therapists use "the healthy family member" and "the healthy family unit" as anchor points to guide them in the assessment process. For instance, they know that healthy family members hold cognitions that support other family members and themselves in seeking and achieving individual fulfillment and cognitions that help family members live in harmony (see chapter 5). CBFT therapists can compare client-family members' cognitions to these anchor points. When the therapist and clients make an assessment that these cognitions lead to counterproductive, nonsupportive, and unhealthy behaviors, they can develop a plan or intervention to deal with the issue. Ronnie Ann and Scott, for instance, agreed that her "passive way of discovering she was loved" cognition and his "teach her to fish" cognition were not healthy in the marriage and, assisted by the therapist, designed a method they thought would curtail their use of those cognitions in the marriage.

In making assessments, therapists usually focus on the functions of family members' cognitions rather than their content. Consider assessments of family constitutions, for example. The content of the rules in family constitutions and the nature of the structure they provide vary greatly in healthy family units, reflecting individuals' unique personalities, values, backgrounds, and goals. However, all health-promoting family constitutions serve the same functions. That is, they structure family life so that family members can serve the social functions society expects, interact among themselves in ways they find satisfactory, and function effectively in achieving goals and in meeting the ever-changing challenges they encounter individually and as a unit.

Besides focusing on the process by which the family unit moves toward its goals, therapists and clients also assess how family members address the interpersonal problems they inevitably face. Using discussions of past or recurrent conflicts, deduction, and whatever means work, family members consider what cognitions cause them problems and also identify the cognitions they hold regarding problem solving in the family setting. As a result of these explorations they typically look at the rules in their family constitution about problems and problem solving, and how the constitution might be edited to help them deal more effectively with persistent interpersonal conflicts.

During the consideration of problem solving, family members also are helped to consider whether they are using any FDMs. In chapter 4, FDMs were defined as specific behavior patterns that family members follow that reduce the number of incidents of expressed conflict between them, with their being only vaguely or not at all aware of this happening. In helping clients consider whether FDMs operate in their households, therapists share this clinical observation: Units that function with disengaged subsystems and rigid boundaries (between members and between the unit and the outside world) often adopt escape FDMs, whereas units with diffuse boundaries and enmeshed subsystems often practice goal-driven FDMs and multihousehold FDMs (see chapter 4). FDMs that are identified are discussed briefly at this step and treated more extensively in Step 5 of CBFT.

Unique Challenge in Step 2. During Step 2, besides gaining a better sense of the family members and of the problems they face, CBFT therapists also assess whether CBFT will work for these clients. Therapists might ask, "After X hours of treatment, how much have these clients learned?" In extreme instances, the answer to this question might be "very little," which may tell therapists that CBFT is not likely to be successful with this family. Much more likely, however, therapists will ascertain whether the level of the assistance they have thus far delivered is appropriate, needs simplification, or can be raised, meaning assistance could be provided in a more complex and speedier fashion. Consider the Hamptons who sought help for their 2-year-old marriage:

> In the first session, Kathy blamed Ed for their problems. She believed that he was angry at her most of the time and was intentionally refusing to support her emotionally. She drew these conclusions because Ed shared little and when she spoke to him, he frequently appeared uninterested and distracted. Further, she reported, at times he reacted to her with a harsh, raised voice and great anger. Ed conceptualized matters differently. Although he was dissatisfied with aspects of their marriage, he felt the problems stemmed from Kathy's "Ms. Know-It-All" attitude. He explained, "No matter what I suggest, she always has a better idea. Besides, she has problems handling angry feelings."
> As the session progressed, the Hamptons engaged in increasingly animated

exchanges. Suddenly, Kathy raised this concern: What were they going to serve Ed's parents and extended family for Christmas dinner? Kathy, hosting the family for the first time, was uncertain about what main dish to serve. She said to Ed, "I recall asking for suggestions several times and I felt defeated because you refused to give me input."

"You asked only once," Ed said, "and I recall making a couple of suggestions which you evidently ignored, probably because you thought you knew better."

After the spouses gently chided each other for wasting time on a "trivial issue," they went on seemingly determined to figure out how many times Kathy did ask Ed, who was at fault, and what menu should be planned. The therapist supported them, explaining the "dinner issue" would have value beyond their settling on whether to serve turkey or ham. It could be used as an example of the kinds of problems they encounter, and they could study it (engaging in metacognition and self-reflection) to see what principles they could abstract about their communication and problem solving.

"For example," the therapist explained, "like most people, you automatically think in terms of 'the guilty party,' when you discuss family problems." He then introduced them to the concept of circular causality and how they could apply it to the dinner issue problem.

During Step 2, the therapist assessed the extent to which Kathy and Ed had assimilated an understanding of circular causality. He asked himself, "How close are the Hamptons to the point at which, with some self-discipline, they would refrain from immediately blaming one guilty party and look at how the family system might be maintaining a problem?" He could see that the Hamptons had immediately understood the relationship between cognitions and behavior and had an intuitive sense that cognitions developed years earlier could still shape today's behavior. This assessment led the therapist, drawing from data the Hamptons had provided, to explain how their cognitions had interlocked in an unfortunate way when it came to planning Christmas dinner:

Kathy, childhood experiences taught you that parents and others "above you" are hard to please. If you fail to please them you worry that you will be rejected, "left out" or "left alone." Ed, you learned to defer to others because whatever you said as a child was contradicted or countermanded by your mother, who always told you what was right.

When you put these cognitions together, Kathy, you realize that you were trying to plan a dinner to please Ed's "hard-to-please" relatives, so you wanted to draw on Ed's knowledge. That is reasonable. But Ed, you did not want to help choose the menu because you figured your mother would criticize the choice of the main dish and, indirectly, the person who chose it. You avoided your mother's criticism by refusing to be involved in the choice. You did this, in turn, by withdrawing from Kathy. Kathy, you, however, experienced Ed's withdrawal as his "rejecting you."

The Hamptons felt this explanation was very helpful and were ready to move forward with CBFT.

Step 3: Personal Application of Concepts

Clients learn to intentionally apply CBF concepts in their family life, and in doing so, become better aware of their family schemas, their PTs, their relationship scripts, the "laws" in their family constitution, and the factors important in their c/b analyses of family membership. To assist clients in learning these, therapists use interpretive comments, lecturettes, focused questions, structured experiential learning exercises, and homework assignments to teach CBF concepts and how to apply them. Therapists also stress that few people have been taught that they ought to and how to engage in the extremely profitable activity of systematic thinking about their family life. Because most people are untrained in this area, the little thinking about their family life that they do tends to be muddled. Building on these comments, which "normalize" the kind of thinking the clients have probably done with regard to family life, therapists can be encouraging about the future. They can assure clients that as work progresses they will be taught to engage in more metacognition and self-reflection, which, in turn, will enable them to become more aware of when and how family-related cognitions are affecting family relationships.

By this point in CBFT, therapists have a sense of their clients' cognitive capabilities and what techniques will likely assist them in gaining a working ability to apply CBF concepts in their family. Drawing from their assessments of the adults (and children) participating in CBFT, therapists wanting to help clients extend their understanding in the area of c/b cognitions, for example, might choose one of the following techniques.

Lecturette. After reminding clients that all individuals conduct c/b analyses, therapists discuss the value of engaging in metacognition focused on one's c/b analyses. Next, therapists explain, family members can discuss the results of their c/b analyses and, with a modest effort, can begin to learn about other family members' costs and benefits. An example like the following can be provided:

Pam and Jamal were asked to privately conduct c/b analyses and then to share them with each other. The talk that followed led them to recognize that, without discussion, they had divided chores along traditional lines and that left both of them with unnecessary costs. Very quickly they rearranged assignments. Now Jamal cooks on weekends, and enjoys it, whereas Pam, who hated the drudgery of cooking on weekends, became the family gardener, a role that gives her the outdoor time and exercise she craves. Identifying their costs and benefits and communicating them to each other produced increased benefits and reduced costs for both of them.

Lecturette with Visual Aids.   A chart showing Maslow's (1970) hierarchy of needs (physiological needs, safety needs, belongingness and love needs, esteem needs, and self-actualization needs) can stimulate clients' thinking about the benefits they gain as a household member. Similarly, family members can use posterboard to create a list of the costs of family membership and this, in turn, can stimulate thoughtful discussion.

Depending on clients' needs, therapists may ask them to make other posterboard charts using the c/b concept. For example, they may ask family members to apply a c/b test to specific issues, like the method they use to write a budget. Or, in other circumstances, therapists might ask spouses to prepare written c/b analyses to compare choosing divorce to remaining married.

Directed Questions.   Therapists can help family members put c/b cognitions in perspective by asking questions like: "What had you expected to have at this point in your marriage?" "What do you want your marriage to be like 5 years from now?" "If a third party heard your hopes for the future, would he or she think they are realistic, or would he or she advise you to lower your expectations and set more achievable goals?"

Sometimes clients are helped greatly by the process of identifying their costs and benefits clearly enough that they can be evaluated. As Tina reported, "Once Dick and I identified our costs and benefits and said them out loud, we essentially solved our problems. What I mean is that once we recognized that our expectations of what was involved in buying and caring for our vacation property were totally unrealistic, we immediately saw that we had to change our thinking. As soon as we recognized that we would have to revamp our ideas of the costs, we got instant relief."

Structured Exercises.   Therapists can use personally prepared videotapes or popular television shows to familiarize clients with the c/b concept. For example, using directions provided by therapists, clients can watch programs and list the costs and benefits each character experiences from family membership.

This exercise helped the Jacobsons, who had been struggling over household assignments and the fact that all five children "repeatedly forgot" chores. When the therapist tried to broach this issue directly, the children quickly clouded matters, raising a litany of irrelevant side points. The therapist tried another tack; he showed them a videotape in which family members talked through how they were going to share chores and then joyfully went about accomplishing the work. Next, he had them list on a poster all the tasks and family roles (cf. Nye et al., 1976) that had to be completed in their household. Then, guided by the therapist and inspired by the film, the family members prepared a written agreement about what chores were, should be, and would be assigned to whom. The parents "okayed" the plan and, because the children had a sense of ownership for it, the plan worked and the chores were done.

Homework Assignments. Therapists can use homework to extend the "therapy hour," to reinforce teachings, or as a way to collect data for use in sessions. They can explain the role it plays to clients: "Homework gives you opportunities to practice what you learned in treatment, on your own and without assistance, and it gives us a chance to learn about your family life."

Homework can be designed to foster in clients the habit of frequently engaging in metacognition and self-reflection. For example, Mari and Mike's therapist suggested, "I'd like you to use this form next week. Before bed jot down benefits you had that day from family membership in this column, and the costs you experienced in this column." Some sessions later the therapist assigned them the task of spending 5 minutes, just before bedtime, trying to identify childhood/adolescence experiences that were still affecting their c/b cognitions. As a result of this homework Mari's recollections enabled her to discover how many of her current c/b cognitions, and thoughts, feelings, and behaviors, still bear the stamp of her family-of-origin experiences:

Mari, 37 years old, explained, "My meal schedule precisely mirrors what mother used, even down to nightly menus. Beef on Wednesday, pasta on Thursday, and fish on Friday."

"Wrong," challenged Mike, age 35 years, "Sundays are very different."

Mari, startled as if a dark secret had been revealed, paused before saying, "I blocked Sundays out of my mind. Yes, they are very different and I think I know why. I hated Mom's Sunday routine: Wake early for breakfast, rush to church, spend afternoons talking, eat dinner at 3 P.M. I hated it so much that I've avoided all of it with our kids. We have no Sunday routine. Have I thrown the baby out with the bath water? Maybe we should share a Sunday family breakfast. That would improve your c/b ratio, wouldn't it?"

"Yes," Mike said, wearing a broad smile, "I've wanted that for years." He continued reporting his discovery, "And suddenly it dawns on me. As a youngster, you learn to be like your parents in some areas and the opposite of them in others. That helps me understand your family schema and your c/b cognitions."

As this case illustrates, Step 3 provides repeated opportunities to foster clients' use of new terms and to show them the interlinking between their cognitions and how satisfied or disappointed they feel about family life, how they behave, and how family members behave toward them.

Unique Challenge in Step 3. "Improve your communication" is probably the most common suggestion marriage and family advice givers offer. Although usually well received by clients who "perk up" at the mention of this familiar issue, CBFT therapists maintain that quality communication alone is not enough; family members have to be communicating "the right stuff."

Therapists explain, "A golf pro may have a perfect swing, but he won't hit the ball very far if he has a putter in his hand. Business firms may increase productivity by improving communication between staff members but will still produce red ink if the management team fails to understand basic production strategies, marketing, or the human needs of its employees. Put another way, top-notch communication, alone, cannot guarantee prosperity. Management teams must possess skills in and communicate about essential matters; that is, they effectively analyze the situation they face and mobilize and deploy essential resources."

Similarly, although good communication can foster happiness, love, and fulfillment in family members, it only does so if the communication contains the "right" messages. That is, the communication must transmit information that helps family members develop and maintain the kinds of structures and processes that will enable individuals in the unit to meet their needs and to make progress toward their personal and family goals. Some individuals know how to engage in this kind of communication, although they may not be aware of the fact that they have this skill. Others do not, but can be taught by therapists.

Step 4: Preliminary Cognitive Changes

During this step, clients' thought processes change in two ways: First, they learn to monitor their thoughts and sound an "internal alarm" when "automatic thoughts" or any potentially dysfunctional cognitions cross their minds and, as they occur, to become aware of how they shape perceptions, thoughts, feelings, and behaviors. Second, they recognize the progress that they have made when family-related cognitions, like those described next, cross their minds and they discover that they stop themselves, link these cognitions with the thoughts, feelings, and behaviors they produce, and take action to replace these cognitions with more health-promoting ones:

1. I feel a vague distant sense of being unhappy right now sitting with my spouse. In a good relationship I expect happiness nearly all the time. That's impossible, so my cognition "sets me up" for disappointment—and then I take it out on Pat. I'm unhappy because I'm bored. If I took a walk I'd enjoy myself and feel better.

2. My cognition dictates that if a wife cares, she'll take responsibility for making me "romantic." She'd dress sexy and light candles. Because Nancy

won't do this, my expectation inevitably leads me to unhappiness. I need to replace this cognition and find new ways to get "turned on."

3. My cognitions state that other people make things happen, not me. Hence, I don't believe I have any control over problems. When Chris and I disagree, I wait for him to fix things. I need to work on giving myself permission to believe I can have an impact, to become more assertive, and to show more initiative in relationships.

4. Coming from a traditional home, my PT cognitions tell me to get my fulfillment from my marriage and children. But other PT cognitions tell me to not waste my talents and education. I'm in a bind and that's probably why I feel agitated and restless when, during dinner, everybody shares their day's adventure and all I can say is, "Today's wash is very white." I need to determine which cognition to reject and to then modify my relationship script and the family constitution accordingly.

5. Maybe from the "Brady Bunch," I learned that stepfamily members should ecstatically welcome the new arrangements and quickly come to love each other. As my counselor warned me, our stepfamily hasn't worked that way. I applied my "love conquers all" philosophy and her kids still reject me with, "Well, you're not my dad." OK, right now I can either keep my "Brady Bunch" notions and feel badly, or reject them, change my expectations and, with Beth, figure out what we need to change in the family constitution to slowly, but surely, foster caring in this home.

6. I'm upset now because the kids' curfew time is here and neither one is home. My cognitions tell me, "Children who don't respect adults never become responsible citizens. If teens respect parents, they come home before curfew and without major complaints." My kids always hassle me over curfew and return a few minutes late. If I can accept this as "healthy" independence, then it wouldn't upset me. That will be difficult to do, but it is worth a try.

As people learn to sound internal alarms and to engage in critical thinking about the consequences of holding their unique set of family-related cognitions, they often make discoveries that surprise them. For instance, Marcy, 23 years of age, came to realize how her cognitions directed her to behave in certain kinds of ways, how her pattern of behavior led others to react to her in particular ways, and how the reactions of others, in turn, created unfavorable changes in her self-view. More specifically, Marcy recognized that as a girl and teen she accurately saw herself as a bright, creative person. During those years in her household, where she was the only child, and in her small private school, where she was the brightest of the 30 students in her grade level, she was generously showered with caring and love and recognized for her many capabilities. She did not need to be assertive in these settings to gain recognition and attention. When Marcy entered college, however, the relationship script cognitions that led her to be quiet, reactive, and self-assured did not bring her the attention and recognition from fellow students and instructors to which she was accustomed.

Marcy did not engage in goal-directed thought in order to try to understand the changes she experienced in people's reactions to her and gradually drifted into viewing herself as being "not that smart and not that attractive, after all." This unhealthy change in Marcy's self-view would probably not have occurred had she been aware of her relationship script cognitions and the role they played in shaping her behavior with others. However, Marcy, like most people, has never been taught to attend to her cognitions and is generally unaware of the cognitive processes and structures she uses (Fincham, Bradbury, & Beach, 1990) and the impact these have in her relationships (Bradbury & Fincham, 1988).

Unique Challenge in Step 4.   Like Marcy, most individuals in 20th-century Western societies are handicapped by the fact that they were never formally taught to (or how to) think systematically about either their cognitions or their relationships. CBFT provides an opportunity and a structure in which clients can learn and practice an activity that is new to most of them: thinking proactively about the kind of family life they would like and engaging in lively but thoughtful dialogue with each other about their ideas.

One way therapists can prepare clients for this activity is by asking them to picture the typical engaged couple and to estimate how much time they think these partners spend, per week, considering the complexities and nitty-gritty difficulties involved in building and maintaining a marriage. Most adult clients will make a low estimate. (Those that suggest a large number can be invited to conduct an informal survey.) "Why," therapists might ask, "do you think engaged persons do so little talking about this, especially because they know divorce-rate statistics and have undoubtedly encountered some problems while courting?"

Most clients will respond by suggesting, "Engaged couples, apparently blinded by love, excitement, and nonobjective thinking, write off the statistics and aspects of their history and operate as if their love will enable them to overcome whatever develops during marriage." Therapists can explain this to those that do not already know so. Then, therapists can point out that engaged persons behave like the leaders of new settings and organizations (Sarason, 1972), conscientiously proceeding, guided by honest intentions, but deceived by hopes that lead them away from engaging in reasonable, proactive planning.

Therapists can then point out at this step in CBFT, the clients can go beyond these "blue sky traps," engage in self-reflection and metacognition, and share what they discover with each other. Such shared knowledge equips family members to engage in the kind of problem solving that leads to healthy changes in the family constitution—the kinds of modifications that lead to a more joyful family life with fewer heartaches. Put another way, metacognition, self-reflection, and family sharing can help individuals detect ineffective and counterproductive cognitions such as the following:

1. Those that are egocentric (Piaget, 1972), meaning the holder has not taken into account others' perspectives. Such cognitions cause various problems. They might lead a father to hold unrealistic expectations for and use ineffective punishments with his daughter because he fails to recognize her limited capabilities for reasoning. Or, they may lead family members to assume that others perceive, know, and feel exactly what they, themselves, do. Making this assumption, of course, discourages individuals from "bothering" to share their feelings and thoughts, causing misunderstandings.

2. Those that inadequately take into account life realities. For instance, cognitions that fail to recognize that conflict is inevitable in marriage may lead their holders to view themselves as failures when their children fight, when they have disagreements with family members, and so forth.

3. Those that are overinclusive and catastrophizing. Holders of these cognitions inevitably experience problems. Consider spouses who, after a religious intermarriage, attribute every problem to "the consequence of straying from the church" and who expect ever more severe difficulties to emerge.

In sum, during this step, therapists teach clients how to analyze their cognitions and relationships and to develop the habit of frequently doing so. As a result, clients progress in three important areas: They get better in touch with the impact that their own cognitions have on them, they learn to appreciate that each family member has cognitions and that these effect them, and they learn to identify and examine the dynamics they experience in their relationships in the family system.

Step 5: Initiating Behavioral Change

By this point in treatment, family members better understand the difficulties in solving their problems and have probably made progress in addressing them. However, in Step 5, the rate of progress accelerates substantially. The focus in CBFT turns to promoting behavioral change in individuals which, in turn, causes change in the family system.

At this step, CBFT therapists, who are eclectic, sense which treatment approaches would most likely enable family members to modify their cognitions and behaviors. They draw interventions from all literatures as well as developing their own, when necessary. For example, they use family therapy interventions, such as reframing, paradoxical directives, and sculpting; cognitive-behavioral therapy interventions, such as role playing, behavioral rehearsal, modeling, in vivo assignments, communication training, and problem-solving skill development; and behavioral marital therapy interventions, such as those described by Jacobson and Gurman (1986).

Whenever possible, therapists select interventions that help clients change their behavior and, at the same time, benefit them over the long run by bringing to light important family-related cognitions. For example, therapists may prescribe regularly scheduled family meetings. These have particular value if, first, individuals use them to discuss and find solutions to problems they are experiencing at the moment in the household and if, second, individuals use them to identify and alter (or replace) family constitution rules that have been fostering the difficulties.

Another technique with considerable value is adopted from behavioral marital therapy (Wood & Jacobson, 1985). Therapists ask individuals to list a few activities they would like each of the other family members to perform more frequently. Family members benefit in at least two ways from making such lists and from trying to meet each others' requests: They very concretely become aware of what are benefits in each other's c/b ratios while, at the same time, they improve each other's c/b ratios by providing more of what they seek in family life. Therapists may build further on this intervention, seeking to change the rules in the family constitution by asking clients to set contingencies (reinforcement or punishment) for appropriate behavior (e.g., a child cleaning her room, following a studying schedule on school nights, eating healthy meals) or to use *behavioral contracts* (Jacobson, 1984).

During CBFT, clients will raise problems for discussion that occur between sessions in their day-to-day home life. Although attending to these as important issues in and of themselves, therapists also explain that these daily problems have another kind of significance; that is, they represent the kinds of difficulties the family is prone to because of the nature of the cognitions members hold. Further, they represent a host of other difficulties that will unfold in their home in the future, unless the family makes changes. Therefore, therapists explain, while family members seek to address the problem at hand, they are also acquiring information and skills to help them avoid certain difficulties in the future (and to better manage those that do develop).

Therapists help clients address the problem at hand, understand why it evolved, and deal with what happened as it unfolded, by applying concepts from the CBF model. Using these, clients work to analyze the situation and to plan effective ways of dealing with it. Usually they reach an agreement about what the nature of the difference is and then they try to identify which cognitions in each individual are playing roles in causing and maintaining the problem.

If the problem at hand has been a recurrent one or represents a family of problems the clients have faced, and after they have some success in diagnosing and developing a plan to attack it, the therapist may be able to move the discussion to a higher conceptual level and make these points: Because the problem at hand (or the type of problem it represents) has recurred over time, there must be some factor responsible for its emerging over and over again and, there must be some obstacle that has in the past blocked family members' efforts to solve it (Levine, 1974). The therapist then congratulates the clients for perhaps "cracking the nut" and mobilizing themselves to attack and find a solution to what has been a recurrent and elusive family problem.

FDMs. During this step family members consider the c/b trade-offs involved in their use of FDMs. Therapists pose questions like: Is the price you pay to use (the identified) FDM worth the benefits it provides to family members? What kinds of conflict would emerge if you did not practice this FDM and what are alternative ways to handle it? How does the behavior involved in the FDM help family members grow and does it in any way hurt them or thwart their progress toward achieving their full potential? Does the FDM help or hamper the family unit, itself, in achieving goals the members hold for it?

During discussions of these questions, therapists might note that different types of FDMs, although serving the same purposes, have differing costs and benefits associated with them. For example, in contrast to mood-swing FDMs, both escape and goal-driven FDMs prescribe activities that might be work or hobby related and, therefore, provide benefit in terms of enjoyment or occupational advancement.

After considering questions like these, family members can make informed decisions about FDM usage. If they decide to continue with their FDMs, after the discussions they will undoubtedly feel less driven by and more comfortable with engaging in FDM-prescribed behaviors. Often, however, they find other ways to handle the issues from which FDMs had been protecting them. For example, the Wilsons, who had practiced a substance-use escape after work and before dinner, began spending this time together walking and playing basketball in their driveway.

Clients can also be alerted to the fact that, during treatment and after it, there will be times when family members will slip back into using "old cognitions" and, as a result, will practice "old behavior patterns." After forewarning clients, therapists then ask them to give each other permission to tell them when they have slipped (after Teichman, 1984).

Finally, CBFT therapists may want to again address the issue of communication and how family members can solve, or better yet, avoid common problems. Therapists remind clients that communication is not as straightforward as is suggested by this sequence: Family Member A recognizes a need and sends a message to Family Member B; the recipient, B, hears the spoken words and fully understands what A intended to convey. After CBFT therapists warn clients of the many kinds of difficulties that can emerge if they hold this erroneous view, therapists help clients acquire a more sophisticated understanding, teaching or reminding them to do the following:

1. When they spot problems occurring in their communication, call "time out," so they can determine where, in the communication process, the problem is emerging. Is it in the clarity of the messages being sent, is it in the actual hearing/listening, or is it in the understanding of the message's intended recipient?

2. Remember that people experience events differently. For example, family members may make different attributions about the same event (Jones, 1990) because they engage in a self-reference bias (seeing issues in self-centered ways) and in a self-serving bias (seeing issues in self-flattering ways).

3. Be aware of "groupthink" (Janis, 1972) and the importance of proceeding carefully when experiencing the strong feelings of solidarity that can lead family members to fall victim to the poor decisions. When the groupthink process occurs, family members convince themselves to make a particular decision, although, based on the facts, any one of them making the decision alone would have decided that the decision was unwise. For example, family members make a groupthink decision when they talk themselves into buying a fancy car they cannot afford because, they convince each other, Mom or Dad will probably get a raise soon.

4. Real world events function as stressors for family members. CBFT therapists teach clients to cope both by trying to change their environment and by modifying their family constitution and other cognitions as necessary, when faced with extrafamilial stressors like a difficult local economy or discrimination based on race, religion, ethnic background, lifestyle, illness or disability of one family member, and so forth.

5. Be aware of circular causality. Clients have more difficulty with this concept than any other in CBFT. Therapists' reminders help clients master the idea of circular causality and confront other family members who attribute blame with unidirectional cognitions like, "I only yelled at him because he yelled at me first." Reminders and pinpointed comments also help clients understand experientially why researchers have found that dissatisfied spouses express more negative affect (e.g., anger, contempt, disgust, fear, and sadness) than do happier couples (Gottman & Levenson, 1988) and why, if they successfully limit the expression of negative affect in their home, they will probably improve the level of marital satisfaction (Hahlweg et al., 1983) and the c/b ratios of all family members.

Unique Challenge in Step 5.　　Family members and therapists at this step face the task of overcoming whatever obstacles prevent effective family problem solving. As is the case with all therapeutic approaches, resistance may stand in the way of success and it may take many forms in CBFT. Obvious examples include clients who "don't have time for" or who "forget" homework and those who are tardy for or repeatedly cancel sessions. However, there are probably more subtle forms of resistance than obvious ones. More disguised versions include instances in which verbally able clients continually steer discussion during CBFT sessions toward surface-level considerations. More specifically, after repeated encouragement to do otherwise, they continually return to talk about the here and now, working toward resolving a problem at hand and only that. Their desire to address the problem at hand makes sense, because it is causing distress. However, they resist going beyond this concrete level toward deeper thinking: considering the present issue as one example of a class of problem-causing issues.

Resistance to therapy can be expected and therapists confront it as it arises. They are helped in their efforts by the fact that, except for some children and a small number of adults who were directly or subtly coaxed into treatment, most clients enter CBFT with a strong desire to make changes that will improve their quality of life. By Step 5, especially, when much change will take place, participants are generally willing to extend themselves and devote personal resources to accomplish this objective.

Therapists seek to understand why individuals' psychological defensiveness and resistance are appearing in each family at the particular time that they do. Are the counterproductive forces creeping in and hindering a family's efforts to apply CBFT learnings in sessions or at home because of the clients' hesitancy to replace "long-practiced, comfortable" patterns of interactions (with known costs) for new practices (with unknown costs)? Are they entering because one spouse worries, "I may go out of my way to make changes but I'm not certain about my mate's motivation for and ability to follow through on the other end of the bargain?" Or is the resistance emerging because clients do not yet understand or have the capabilities to make the necessary changes in their cognitions? In the latter instance, the techniques discussed in the next chapter can prove helpful to both therapists and family members. These techniques are designed to help family members learn more about the family-related cognitions that they and others hold.

8

THREE THERAPEUTIC STRATEGIES

A basic goal of CBFT is to help clients understand the concept of cognitions. Another is to help them see how they are affected by their own cognitions and by those of family members. This chapter describes three techniques we developed to help clients achieve these goals. Two of these techniques, the identification of the models of personal theory of family life and family relationships exercise (*PT exercise*) and the *psychohistory exercise*, combine elements of assessment and treatment and help clients identify and understand important family-related cognitions in new ways. The third technique, the *perspective-taking exercise*, strengthens each family member's abilities to see the world through each other's cognitions or, put another way, to view the world through each other's eyes.

In CBFT, as in other cognitive approaches (Dattillo & Padesky, 1990), before treatment begins clients are given an overview of the approach and how the interventions that will be used will fit into the process and yield benefits. This chapter describes three techniques designed to help clients understand what is in each family member's family schema, why certain cognitions are there, and the impact these cognitions have on individuals and the quality of life in the family system. In the descriptions that follow, we give some ideas about what clients can be told about these interventions and how they work. We did not include blueprints or lockstep procedures for their use, however. Experience suggests that these techniques are most effective when therapists improvise in their application, fitting them to the abilities and characteristics of the clients and to the nature of the problems at hand.

PT EXERCISE

The CBF model maintains that individuals carry with them and are guided by a set of cognitions in their PT that specify how families should ideally work, what families should ideally do for members, what individuals should ideally invest in the family, and so forth. These PT cognitions, located within the family schema (see Fig. 8.1), are of the type that Baucom and Epstein (1990) labeled as *standards*.

The PT exercise educates clients about the concept of PTs and about how PTs affect individuals' thoughts, feelings, and behaviors in the family setting. It helps family members become aware of their own PT, its contents, and how its contents affect them. It also teaches them about the contents of other family members' PT. Getting PT cognitions out in the open where they can be evaluated and shared has multiple benefits. It enables family members to better understand what influences them and how that differs from what influences other family members. Further, it typically leads them to replace the cognition that theirs is right and others' models are wrong with a cognition that recognizes each model's unique worth. Therapists might introduce the PT exercise thusly:

> The cognitions in your PT form a background fabric that shapes how you perceive and process family experiences. Your PT tells you how a family should work. For example, PT cognitions provide the basis by which individuals judge whether their marriage is working as it should, whether the children are behaving as they should, how they should fix any marital and family problems they encounter, and so forth.

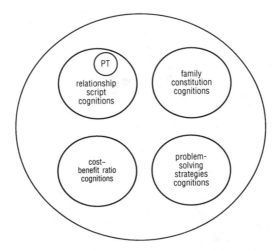

FIG. 8.1.   Family schema and the family schema subconstructs. The family schema contains all of an individual's family-related cognitions.

If you evaluate your family as approximating what your PT dictates, then you feel satisfied. If you feel your family life is not meeting your expectations, you feel less content and may act to direct it in ways your PT dictates. Ironically, most people are only vaguely or not at all aware of possessing cognitions like those in their PT, although they play a major role in shaping their everyday thoughts, feelings, and behaviors.

The PT exercise helps you get the contents of your PT out on the table, where you can evaluate your expectations and determine whether they make good sense to you. It also provides you with insight into other family members' PTs and that will help communication and problem solving.

The success of the PT exercise depends heavily on decisions therapists make at this point in deciding on the issues of focus. More specifically, after therapists write each family member's name on a chalkboard they explain, "To help you identify the contents of your PT, we'll discuss several family issues and concerns and under your name I'll write how you think happy healthy families should manage or handle these." Therapists then explain a concept or issue that is relevant to the problem the family has presented or to issues that have emerged thus far in CBFT. For example, they might ask each participant to suggest what resources he or she would ideally expect to be supplied to family members. Therapists may begin the process by indicating that *resources* available in relationships can be grouped into six classes: goods, or tangible items; information, or knowledge; love, or affection and attention; money, or other valued items; services, or help and assistance; and status, or approval, position, or recognition (Foa & Foa, 1974). After these are explained, the therapist enters what is important to each family member on the chalkboard.

Another concept useful here involves the kinds of *social support* that individuals think should be provided to family members in healthy units. Five types have been described: emotional support—family members provide each other with feelings of comfort and security, esteem support—members bolster each other's confidence; informational support—family members provide each other with advice or informational help in decision making; social integrations support—family members make each other feel part of the unit; and tangible aid support—family members provide concrete assistance (Cutrona & Russell, 1990).

After attention has been paid to concepts that promote health in family relationships, therapists might point out that some cognitions are not health promoting, perhaps illustrating this with an example showing how cognitions in the PT affect thoughts, feelings, and behavior:

As you go about your day you experience "automatic" thoughts from time to time. These situation-specific thoughts "pop" into your conscious mind as ideas or images that you may be only vaguely aware of. Yet, these automatic thoughts affect how you feel at the moment and how you behave. Consider, for example, Margo Gordon, 35 years of age, who was sitting home alone at 9:30 p.m. Her children and husband were out and she had an automatic thought when the phone rang: "Something is wrong."

The automatic thought that Margo experienced came from a deeper level within her—one that holds her underlying basic assumptions about the world in which she lives. These assumptions are stable over time and applied by her in all situations. In this case, the automatic thought indicated that a call at this hour was not business and was not from a friend or relative with whom she wanted to chat. Instead, it was unhappy news about the family.

The assumption on which the automatic thought was based followed from core beliefs in her PT that told her: "Be careful. A big and harmful mistake could occur to you or your loved ones if you for a moment let go of control in your family life." Her husband had taken the children skiing, although she had objected, and her core belief caused the "Oh my gosh!" automatic thought when she heard the sound of the ringing phone.

At this point therapists can encourage family members to identify non-health-promoting cognitions they might hold in their family models. Now or later, therapists explain that individuals begin in childhood developing the core beliefs that form the foundation for their PT. Young children do this first by observing and listening to their parents and other caretakers. At that age, they can know only one "right way" for families to operate—the way their family does. Over time, children modify their PT to some extent because of what they learn from friends, relatives, the media, and so forth. However, these modifications, like the early learnings, are made mostly outside of their awareness.

By adolescence, PTs are well formed and they strongly influence dating and marriage choices, partly because the mesh between partners' PTs plays an important role in determining how satisfied they will be as a couple. Some indication of the quality of the mesh becomes apparent during their first dates, when each person tries to lead the relationship in directions indicated appropriate by his or her PT. As the relationship develops, of course, the quality of the mesh of partners' PTs is tested in new ways.

Therapists might illustrate the issue of the mesh between PTs by sharing an example like that of Margo and Jack Gordon, who recently traveled to Atlantic City, New Jersey, for their first family vacation in many years:

The moment the Gordons checked into their hotel room, Jack wanted to go directly to the casino and the roulette wheel. His PT indicated that when a man went on a well-deserved vacation, his wife would happily follow the schedule he desired. Not only was he angered when she said "no" to the casino, but he was surprised because he did not know that her PT indicated that a mother's first duty on a vacation in a new city was to watch the children.

When she announced her plans to care for the children, Jack protested, "The casino has a free program for children. Why don't you take the kids there?"

Margo replied, "It's the kids' vacation, too, and I want them to see Board-walk, Park Place, the sand, and the ocean waves." Once they arrived in the hotel the Gordons could not seem to avoid a confrontation. Both of them were convinced that they were right and their spouse was "way off base." Much of the anger that was generated in the hotel developed because they had fallen victim to a common marital problem. Each decided the other was being unreasonable and obstinate, and it was that conclusion that fueled the fury initially sparked by their choice of an immediate destination.

In CBFT, the therapist told the Gordons that few spouses are aware of the ways that their mate's PT differs from theirs and this lack of awareness typically costs them and their relationship emotionally. As the Gordons reviewed their arrival at the hotel, they agreed that the conflict was a poor way to begin a vacation and that it could have been prevented only if they had discussed matters more thoroughly before they left home. After the Gordons made this discovery and with assistance from the therapist, they energetically shared their PT-based views of family life with each other and, in doing so, prepared themselves for the psychohistory exercise described next.

PSYCHOHISTORY EXERCISE

Clients complete the *psychohistory exercise* much like they would construct a family tree. Instead of mapping their foreparents' names and so forth, they trace the origins of their family-related cognitions into their childhood and back into their parents' and grandparents' childhoods. Involvement in this activity enables clients to discover that some cognitions are handed down from generation to generation. As the exercise unfolds, they also recognize that hand-me-down cognitions that worked to help their foreparents meet the challenges of their times may not be effective in their household in today's world

For example, the Gordons discovered that Jack's stinginess in sharing information about family finances with Margo and in handing out allowance money to the children was passed down from his grandfather, who developed the behavior and associated cognitions in the 1930s. Grandpa Gordon adopted this in his PT to help his family weather depression-related hard times. When the Gordons made this discovery they laughed with relief about the discomfort this hand-me-down practice had caused them, and Jack immediately committed himself to changing this aspect of his behavior.

The psychohistory exercise can be introduced in this way:

As you know, you acquired many of the cognitions in your family schema during childhood. Even though these have since been affected by the media and by interactions with many people, the foundation for your unique perspective still comes from your parents (or caretakers). Decades earlier, of course, your parents learned the foundations of their family schema from their parents, and so forth. In this exercise you will build a family tree of sorts (see Fig. 8.2), showing how the family-related cognitions you hold (in the forefront of your mind and in its deepest recesses) were handed down to you by your foreparents.

Clients usually react enthusiastically and therapists can immediately guide them forward in speculating about what conditions may have prevailed in the clients' families of origin during their childhood and in their foreparents' households. This discussion leads naturally into a consideration of the relationship between the conditions that may have existed in these households and particular family-related cognitions they hold. At times, therapists may want to energize the process by using an alternate approach: identifying certain thoughts, behaviors, and attitudes that they believe are pivotal in a client and asking that client to consider from whom they might have acquired these.

If clients need further assistance to conceptualize the task, therapists might ask them to compare the nature of the welcome, on average, that the following children would likely receive: a firstborn, a third baby, a girl (boy) born after the parents had already had five boys (girls), a baby conceived after parents had tried for 10 years, a baby born to parents who had recently lost their only other child, an unplanned baby born to parents with alcohol problems, a baby born to a single parent who was abandoned by her partner, and so on.

After clients respond, the therapists can ask them how they went about drawing their conclusions. Building on the clients' responses, therapists can

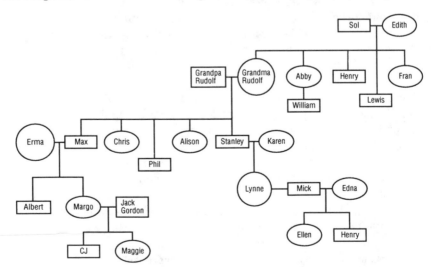

FIG. 8.2.   Margo Gordon's family tree. The Gordons and their therapist used this chart to help them "place" and "keep track" of Margo's family.

then explain how each of these circumstances might affect parents' cognitions, feelings, and behaviors and how this, in turn, would impact both the family that the baby/child experiences and the family-related cognitions that he or she would subsequently build.

As therapists guide clients through a consideration of their parents' behaviors and about the conditions in their family of origin, many clients hesitate because, at a low level of awareness, they experience a sense of guilt or disloyalty because they are talking out loud about what their parents did in child rearing. They react as if, by discussing these matters, they are hurting their parents, or at least being inconsiderate. Therapists deal with this hesitancy by indicating that people commonly have this "illogical" feeling, by suggesting to clients that their parents were probably doing the best they could for their children, and by reaffirming that therapy discussions are confidential and parents will never know about them (although they probably would be pleased that the clients are seeking help in overcoming difficulties). Once this issue is opened, clients typically smile, report being somewhat aware of the irrationality of their parent-protecting behavior, and resume tracing their psychohistory with enthusiasm.

The case of Jack and Margo Gordon shows the potential value of the psychohistory exercise and illustrates how the information it generates can be used.

During the first session of CBFT, Jack succinctly explained, "We're 14 years married, enjoy each other, love our two children, and much appreciate the split-level house we bought 30 months ago. We had a good, normal marriage and never had more than the average number of arguments until our neighbor, Nan, died and left us an $80,000 inheritance we hadn't expected. Nan was an elderly grandma-type person whom we'd cared for since we moved in."

He continued, "Although saddened by the loss of Nan, we were delighted about the money. But when the excitement passed and we started discussing how to spend the dollars, trouble found us. I wanted to use the bucks to start a business. Margo, however, wanted to build our dream house in the suburbs."

"The answer to the dilemma was obvious. We could both get our wishes if, first, I invested the money in a locksmith business. In 2 years I'd earn enough to buy Margo's dream house and more.

"Margo objected. She cringed at the idea of me starting a business, although she couldn't explain why. I thought Margo had no faith in my business sense so, I explained to her, 'Sure, beginning a business is risky, but we've been unhappy about my salary for years, and the outlook for raises at my company is not rosy.' "

"However small or big your check is," Margo responded, "we can depend on it. It arrives every other week, and I can budget with it. I make sure we have food on the table and clothes on our back. If you strike out on your own, we'll be gambling with our future. That idea gives me the willies."

"Security?" he questioned while wearing a smile. "We won't have security until we own our business. And if we're ever going to do that, we should do it now, because we're not getting any younger."

"Jack, I still can't put my finger on why the business idea scares me, but it does. And I want to spend that money creating a beautiful home for you and the kids. With the kids in school and Nan gone, I'll have plenty of time to myself," she appealed. She continued, "We've sacrificed for years, and that was fine. We wanted me to be a full-time mother and we wanted to take care of Nan. But things are different now. I'm ready to invest in us—to buy our dream house. After I decorate it you'll think our rooms came right out of *House Beautiful*. You'll be able to show it off to anybody."

Jack looked unpersuaded so she argued, "Aren't you tired of this furniture? We had this junk in our first place. Some pieces were hand-me-downs back then. You know Maggie is growing up fast. Don't you want her to have a pink, feminine room instead of the wallpaper her brother chose when her room was his?"

During the second session, Jack emphatically stated that a dream house was not his priority and that every time Margo asked about it during the past week, which was twice daily, he told her so. Margo defended herself, explaining that her persistence was unavoidable, "Every time I thought about the money I got sad and worried, 'Why won't Jack do this for me? He would if he really loved me.' "

"The money thing bothered me, too," Jack responded, acting like he was keeping score. "I figured Margo wouldn't agree to a store because of old-fashioned stubbornness."

Psychohistory: Eye Opening and Facilitating

During CBFT sessions, and with help from the data they generated during the psychohistory exercise, Margo and Jack found that the roots of part of their family problems extended back some six decades. More specifically, they learned about two predominant themes in Margo's PT cognitions that dated back three generations. These hand-me-down cognitions indicated that to have a happy family life Margo must: (a) appear to be a "perfect wife" to others, meaning that she had to keep her family well fed, clothed, and housed (preferable in an attractively decorated home) and, (b) avoid the risk of making "big mistakes." This latter cognition, of course, led her to fear the idea of Jack opening (and taking a chance in) a business.

The therapist guided Margo in reflecting upon her upbringing in her small hometown community in Ohio, and about what life was like for her as "the pastor's daughter," as she was known. When Margo found herself blocked in terms of memories, the therapist suggested that she have informal discussions with her mother and other relatives. She was fortunate enough to learn a great deal in these conversations about what occurred in her family of origin while she was growing up, and also about her parents' and grandparents' lives. By sharing in CBFT what she had learned, Margo and her family members gained insight into the patterns of family-related cognitions that were passed down to her from her foreparents. Some of these insights are detailed next.

Margo traced the origins of several important cognitions in her family schema to a 65-year-old incident that occurred when her grandparents, Mr. and Mrs. Rudolf, lived with their five children and nephew William in a small Ohio town. Back then the Rudolfs were the county's busiest hardware merchants, well known and highly respected by their neighbors. "The incident" led Margo's grandparents to live out the rest of their lives in fear of and continually taking steps to avoid making another "big mistake."

The incident that reshaped Margo's grandparents' lives as well as impacting on her parents' and her own, transpired on a balmy, thunderstorm-punctuated fall afternoon. Margo's father, Max Rudolf, then a teenager, rode as a passenger in his cousin William's car. They were having fun, talking football and girls when, suddenly, their Ford sedan skidded on the wet pavement, slid sideways off the road, and slammed, driver's side first, into the huge maple that marked the boundary of "Old Man" Smith's dairy farm.

William died instantly. Although Max was not badly hurt physically, he was deeply scarred psychologically, and would remain so for life. Max blamed himself for William's death. The only reason they were out in the storm was because Max had an examination the next day and he had forgotten his notebook in his school locker.

Although the rest of the family held together well during the funeral, Max and his mother completely collapsed, and for weeks afterward neither made much progress in the mourning process. Max's mother, in fact, remained dazed for months, muttering to herself continually about how she had violated the trust of her sister, William's mom, who had sent William to her house when she had to be hospitalized many years earlier.

Although Max and his mother were struggling to adjust, the members of the Rudolf family talked little about the tragedy and their feelings about it. However, they did pray a great deal.

The accident and its aftermath reshaped some of Max's cognitions about himself, about how he should relate to family members, and about how the world operated. He came to suffer a lifelong sentence of great guilt and low self-esteem, although this did not necessarily need to be the case. Had he seen an effective help giver, lived in a more healing family environment, or befriended the right person, he might have freed himself from this burden.

But he was not that fortunate. Instead, he forever hounded himself with the memory that before the accident his parents had countless times told him to be less forgetful and more organized. If he had heeded their advice, he would have remembered the notebook, and William would have been spared. And to make matters worse, on the fateful day he encouraged William to sneak out of the house for the excursion to the school. Had they been noticed, his pennywise mother and businessman father would have scolded Max for the waste (the unnecessary car trip) that his thoughtlessness forced.

Over the decades, Max ruminated about how his carelessness "killed" cousin William. He would think, "One careless moment, one bit of foolishness, one mistake can cost a life and change the course of everybody else's. My mistake ruined Mom by making her into a guilty worrywart. And I wrecked Dad's plans. He was grooming William and me to take over the hardware store. He believed we were the only two kids who could run it well enough to support the entire family, if the economy made that necessary."

Although Max thought about the incident as a force that intrusively drove his life against his will, it was Max, himself, who made decisions such as, "I could never run the hardware store—not without William." Although Max never became fully aware of the forces within him that led him to such conclusions, they were actually a product of his blind effort to rectify the big mistake. Specifically, instead of leading a comfortable life (taking over the hardware store), he could work hard and devote himself to a life of sacrifice and of doing good deeds.

Max began to "compensate humanity" immediately after his extended period of mourning ended. The change soon became apparent in his school work. Much to the surprise of his teachers and family, Max suddenly emerged as an outstanding student, making the honor roll, organizing and coordinating his peers in a program to help the needy, and so forth. However, Max was not driven by healthy reasons. Instead he was being driven by cognitions of which he was only vaguely aware. These said, "Be a good boy. Help others and protect yourself from making another big mistake."

In the end, Max's high school career was outstanding and he was rewarded with a partial scholarship to a fine college. However, even as Max excelled in the classroom, his mother, who now worried endlessly about nearly everything, thought to herself, "But he has no social life. His face is always in a book. Why doesn't he date some of the nice girls that keep asking me about him in the beauty parlor, at the store, and everywhere?" Mrs. Rudolf, like her son, feared another big mistake: Max's school success would lead him to a life of bachelorhood.

Max's Undergraduate Years.   Max began dating toward the end of his freshman year in college. However, one handicap he faced in this area was "a whispering voice" that haunted the corridors of his mind with, "Don't expect much of a girl, Max, you are just not that worthwhile. No successful woman would want to marry a man guilty of what you've done."

Although Max's 3.87 first-term grade point average might have boosted his self-esteem, along with his success in writing for the college newspaper, the whispering voice won out. Max's poor self-concept led him to follow the voice's directives that ordered him to date less educated women from a nearby vocational high school.

During his sophomore year, Max finished most of his general education classes and declared a double major in philosophy and ancient history. In the middle of his senior year, when it was time to apply to postgraduate institutions, Max announced his career goal. He would become a minister, one admired for his ability to save lost souls (psychologically, salving his own guilt about the auto accident).

Max thought that this choice would please his mother—he wanted to compensate her for the incident. Mother did approve of his career choice but, of course, felt Max need not repay her, the "real guilty party who failed to properly supervise Max and monitor 20-year-old William." Although Max never realized it, his mother never blamed or was angry at him for "causing" William's death. Rather she blamed herself and suffered lifelong guilt for her "failure."

Max's Divinity School Training and His Engagement.   Max graduated cum laude and was admitted to several divinity schools, including one near his hometown. After much deliberation and prayer, he chose the prestigious New Haven Divinity School. He selected this institution, located several hundred miles from his home town, not for its prestige, but because it was noted for training men of the cloth to work effectively with the most downtrodden and poor.

Soon after enrolling, Max met Erma, a high-school-educated woman who waitressed at a Greek diner near Max's rented room. Over many months the two became friends, began dating, and gradually fell in love.

After Max proposed and she happily accepted, he telegramed the good news home. His parents, however, did not immediately respond, as he expected. He figured they were displeased with his choice, a conclusion that grew stronger as time passed and nothing arrived—no congratulatory letter, no engagement present, and no invitation to bring Erma home for a visit.

Max interpreted his parents' behavior as a rejection that stemmed from his unworthiness because of the incident, and his self-concept was further damaged. Erma, who knew Max had written over time long letters describing her, also felt rejected and wondered whether she would be able to share with her in-laws the same kind of loving relationship she enjoyed with her parents. Max later learned from his siblings that Mother Rudolf was disappointed that Max had not chosen a woman "appropriate" to his position.

Erma's parents, however, were most enthusiastic. They derived great pleasure from announcing the engagement to their friends and through the newspaper. "I can't get over it," Erma's father would say, "my daughter marrying a wonderful man from New Haven Divinity."

Max's Graduation and Marriage.   Max excelled in divinity school. In fact, his instructors were so impressed that, as his graduation approached, they offered him an attractive junior faculty position. Had Max accepted the post, he and Erma could have settled into a calm, rewarding campus life. They could have rented superb faculty housing situated far enough from Erma's parents for comfort, and yet close enough for support.

Moreover, in the divinity school environment, Max could have further developed his sense of competence and independence, something that would be more difficult if he accepted another position available to him at a church located less than two dozen miles from his parents. Although Max knew the faculty position at the school was the healthier choice, he felt compelled to reject the offer because he was still holding himself hostage. That is, he could not rid himself of the irrational unconscious need that drove him to be "the good boy" who appeased his mother for William's death. To do this he needed to be physically near to her again, in case she needed help as she aged. When Max declined the faculty position and accepted the post as minister at the church near his boyhood town, Erma and his colleagues at the divinity school were disappointed, but Max's mother was elated.

Erma and her mother spent the months before Max's graduation arranging for the wedding. They chose the Sunday, 2 days before Max's graduation, as the wedding date to ease the travel burden that Max's family would otherwise face. Erma and her mother enjoyed sharing this activity and planned a lovely ceremony, reception, and weekend.

When the moment finally arrived, all the arrangements unfolded like clockwork, with one exception: Hours before the Rudolf family was to board a train in Ohio to head for New Haven, Mrs. Rudolf experienced dizzy spells. When the family physician arrived at the Rudolf home she told him, "God is punishing me, he doesn't want me to see my dear boy graduate and marry. It is too many good things at once for an undeserving woman like me."

The physician reassured Mrs. Rudolf and, after checking her symptoms, prescribed medication, drove the Rudolf family to the pharmacy, and then delivered them to the railroad station, just in time to make their train.

The trip went well. So did the graduation, wedding ceremony, and reception. After a brief honeymoon, Pastor and Mrs. Rudolf moved to their new community and church in Ohio. Time quickly proved that the Rudolfs' were well suited for each other and for the job the couple had accepted.

Erma was motivated by her PT to excel as "the minister's wife." She saw that her first task was to win acceptance by those who mattered and, in accomplishing this, she would also win approval from her new husband. Very quickly Erma emerged as a social butterfly, an active and happy participant in church activities, and a busy woman who was popular in community clubs. Though limited by their modest income, she created a beautiful home, and in it and in the church, she became known as the "hostess with the mostest." Without a doubt, Erma's charm and skills at entertaining benefited Max's career, helping him to win the minds and hearts of even the most hard-to-please congregants and community leaders.

Max, in the meantime, provided Erma with status, something her parents never achieved but had taught her to seek in marriage and family life. Erma loved hearing and telling her own parents how much the townspeople respected Max and how congregants thought of him as the most scholarly and trusted pastor the church ever had. Max also enjoyed hearing that people thought highly of him but, at the same time, he harbored fears about making a big mistake—one that would instantly ruin the fine reputation he had carefully labored to build.

Max's family life was also affected by disquieting remnants of the incident. For example, continuing guilt about the incident led Max to worry in irrational ways about trying to "please" his parents. No matter how much time he spent visiting or doing chores for them, he never felt as if he was reaching them in the way he wanted.

Erma, too, expended much effort in trying to please her in-laws. However, no matter what Erma did, no matter how hard she tried, she could not fully please Mother Rudolf or win her acceptance. Erma repeatedly failed, though she had no awareness of why this was so (because after the incident Mother Rudolf felt that Max would need a wife who could protect him from another big mistake). Mother Rudolf liked Erma as a person, but could not accept her. As a poorly educated woman from "the wrong side of the tracks," Mother Rudolf felt she did not have the wherewithal to protect Max.

Mother Rudolf's apparent refusal to accept Erma in the same way as she did her other daughters- and sons-in-law eventually became a point of friction between Max and Erma. But they could find no solutions. After struggling with continued feelings of rejection over this matter, Erma finally surrendered, although she was unaware of doing so. More specifically, Erma gave up trying to win Mother Rudolf's love. Instead, Erma unknowingly bought into Mother Rudolf's assessment and with little awareness began viewing herself as unworthy and as not deserving of others' love. When Erma felt blue (because automatic thoughts of unworthiness came to her mind), she made herself feel better by "stealing love" from Max. She did this by making a variety of demands that forced him to pay attention to her (e.g., "Honey, please get my sweater").

Soon after Erma gave up trying to win Mother Rudolf's love, she began to suffer from a medically undetectable back problem. Although the physician assured Erma that she could continue her regular routine, Erma hesitated to leave the safety of her reclining chair. That meant Max, while attending to the cooking or other chores, would have to run up stairs to get a book, her slippers, and so forth. Erma, without any awareness of doing so, was forcing Max to supply her with enough attention to compensate for Mother Rudolf's rejection.

Erma eventually recovered from her back ailment, but never again was the same spunky hostess about town who added zest to their early marital life. Not only was she somewhat less active in the church but she also was less productive around the house. In fact, at least once a week she asked Max to do this or that chore for her. Although Max almost always complied with her direct requests, he occasionally claimed to be too busy to help. After taking such action, without being aware of doing so, Max avoided the possibility of a confrontation by spending less time working at home over the next few days, and more time working late in his church office.

Ultimately, the attention Max provided Erma, in response to her demands, lost some of its value. Because Erma had to ask, it felt like "tainted love." Still, although neither one of them had a positive self-image, these were happy years for Max and Erma, probably because they so enjoyed being parents.

Max and Erma were good people, genuine and caring, and certainly the type that might win "parent-of-the-year" awards. They had healthy expectations for their children: They hoped they would be healthy, hard-working, pious, fun-loving individuals who would be caring and concerned about their fellow humans. And Max and Erma were willing to make every sacrifice necessary to help the children maximize their potential—providing musical instruments, sports lessons, sleep-away Bible camp, and so on. However, as much as they wanted to give their offspring a perfect home with every advantage possible, Max and Erma were limited by issues in their psychohistories.

Erma and Max's Children.   Albert arrived first, and brought great pleasure to Erma and Max. Late at night they would stare tenderly at him and then at each other. They would ponder out loud about how their baby, their flesh and blood, was a gift from God and a product of love. Although they fantasized about Albert becoming President Rudolf or church head someday, in reality they only wanted to raise a good boy, a happy, healthy youngster who respected authority and who would become an honest, hard-working citizen. They pledged to do everything in their power to see their wish through but, of course, forces in their psychohistories would affect their ability to give him the healthiest possible start on the road of life.

Albert, the firstborn grandson on both sides of the family, was in great demand. And Max and Erma shared Albert freely and comfortably with those interested in seeing him, with one exception: Max's parents. With them, Erma attached strings. Specifically, she "used" Albert to try to get attention from her in-laws. Suddenly, Erma had an open invitation to lunch with Mother Rudolf, as long as she brought Albert along.

From birth, Albert kept his parents busy and on edge. He ate little and slept fitfully. Before long, Erma labeled him a problem eater and a poor sleeper. Although everybody agreed that Albert was cute as a button, he did suffer from a rash that bothered him for months.

The pregnancy and Albert's problems led Erma to develop a new habit: reading. During pregnancy, Erma began devouring what she could on expectant mothers, baby care, and child rearing. In time she branched out into a program of self-education, reading popular novels, plays, books, poems, the classics, and so forth. Erma's reading had two unintended benefits. First, it pleased Max who had been hurt by his parents' complaint that he had picked a wife with a limited education. Second, by becoming well versed in a number of areas, she became an even better conversationalist, a skill both Max and she valued, and one that enhanced their efforts to hold their place in the community's hierarchy.

Albert's preschool years passed relatively smoothly and the Rudolfs' first reports received about him were encouraging. His teacher, for instance, wrote a note saying how delightful it was to teach a bright, active, and well-mannered youngster like Albert.

A few months before Albert's fifth birthday, his sister Margo joined the family. That fall Albert began experiencing a variety of difficulties in school. On his first report card his teacher commented: "Albert is bright but is often willful. He sometimes refuses to do assignments, fails to listen to instructions, and disrupts the entire class by clowning around and playing court jester. If we don't turn things around soon, I'm afraid Albert will underachieve this year and may become a serious discipline problem. Please call for an appointment."

During that year and the next, Max and Erma met often with Albert's teacher and with the principal and school counselor. Nonetheless, matters worsened and Albert's problem became the time-consuming focus of a goal-driven FDM. They tried punishment, tutors, and other interventions, but the only action that seemed to help was having Max and/or Erma sit down and work with Albert every evening. They would talk over the school day, review academic lessons sent by the teacher, read to Albert, and, finally, sit on the bench with him to make sure he practiced his piano lessons.

Meanwhile, the parent who was not with Albert would attend to Margo. When Albert's nightly routine was finally finished, it would be late. Erma would have to hurry the children in their washing and preparing for bed while Max would unload his briefcase and try to complete his day's work.

Some months after Margo's third birthday, heartache struck the Rudolfs. Erma, driving home from a church conference 75 miles away, encountered fog and collided, nearly head-on, with a tractor-trailer truck. To avoid that accident, she steered the car to the right but ran off the road and into a ditch. Although she wrenched her back and broke her arm, the greatest damage was psychological.

Although they did not recognize it as such, the accident marked a milestone in Max and Erma's marriage, changing it forever. The near calamity scared Erma and made her face for the first time thoughts of her own mortality. Max's reactions were equally strong. He shuddered to think that he almost lost Erma. The near calamity, of course, also reminded Max of the incident with William so many years earlier.

During Erma's recovery, Max willingly served as her Man Friday, doing whatever was necessary to keep the household functioning. However, as the weeks passed and spring approached, Max's calendar tightened. He asked Erma to resume driving—with short trips, like the 10-block jaunt to pick the children up at day care. Erma declined, explaining that she was too afraid, and, in fact, planned to let her driver's license expire.

Over the next years, Max occasionally suggested driving again to Erma, but he never insisted. And Erma never volunteered. As a result, Max had to juggle his schedule so he could chauffeur the children and transport Erma to church meetings, school events, beauty parlor appointments, shopping, and so forth. Although Erma's friends pitched in and Erma gave up some club activities and organizational memberships, Max bore the greatest burden. Although he recognized that the extra hours of driving were harming his career, he faithfully drove Erma from place to place, responding to his relationship-script dictated need "to be good and take care of others (as he should have done for William)."

Margo and Albert Growing Up. Although Margo never possessed Albert's natural charm and sparkle, she showed herself over the years to be a caring individual who was quiet, sweet, dependable, and average. Margo's average grades, her pleasant-enough personality, and the fact that she had a few good friends satisfied her but greatly disappointed Erma and Max (who tried to conceal these feelings). They were, after all, "on a mission" and had hoped that at least one child would make a splash in the world so visibly that Max's parents would be "wowed" by Erma's mothering.

Throughout her youth, Margo contrasted most sharply with Albert in temperament and personality. When Albert walked into the room, everybody present knew he had arrived. Margo, in contrast, could walk in and out almost unnoticed. Whereas Albert charged through the world headfirst and "kept the pot boiling," whatever he was doing, Margo tiptoed around, seeking what she desired in a quiet, determined manner.

Although Erma and Max explained the differences between their children in terms of inborn temperaments, learning played some role, too. Margo undoubtedly learned by observation, and without awareness, that Albert's headfirst approach caused him problems. She saw that Albert, more often than not, was beaten down as he battled his way through life. Margo, without being aware of it, learned to avoid Albert-style confrontations that might put her at risk of losing parental love.

Instead, Margo acquired a distinctive and quiet, yet effective take-care-of-others approach that won Max and Erma's praise. In fact, the more havoc Albert raised and the more agony Max and Erma had to suffer to bail him out of trouble, the more effective Margo became in getting attention and meeting her needs by giving in to Albert, by calming down Mom and Dad when they became upset with him or with each other, and by functioning as a "junior" mother.

During Albert's high school years, the stage on which the family members' dramas were played out changed, but the themes remained the same. Albert failed English during the first term of his sophomore year and was not allowed to play football. Angered by this, he cheated on the next English test and was caught in the act. Because he refused to return the test to the teacher and instead starting shouting out answers, he was suspended for 3 days.

Max and Erma, after openly expressing concern about Albert returning to the school and privately worrying about the damage he was doing to their family's reputation, decided to transfer Albert to a nearby private school. Albert begrudgingly agreed. During his several-year tenure at this school he was suspended for drinking on the school grounds, got in trouble for impregnating his girlfriends, and was without insurance because he wrecked the car he had weaseled from his parents by promising to no longer date girls of a different religion. During these difficult times Pastor Rudolf often repeated to himself and in his sermons, "Little children mean little problems, bigger children mean bigger problems."

Margo had personal problems too but hers were less apparent to others. In contrast to Albert, who was disturbing at home and school and who, therefore, received much attention, Margo was disturbed (rather than disturbing) at times, but her episodes of upset mostly went unnoticed by the adults in her life. That was partly because she chose to suffer privately, so as to not disturb others.

Margo's lack of self-confidence and concern about taking care of family members affected her school performance to the point that she did not fulfill her academic potential. Her grades dropped once during her high school sophomore year because Albert, who had been living in his college dorm, moved home because of academic difficulties. Her grades improved the next year, when Albert returned to the dorm, but not to the level they had been.

Because of her weak high school record, Margo did not win a scholarship at her first-choice college. Instead, she decided to live at home and commute to a nearby school. Although this arrangement limited Margo's social life and caused Erma and Max worry because she seldom dated, Margo assured them that she was happy. During her junior year, she accepted a summer management-trainee position in a large retail chain headquartered nearby. In this position she met many single men, including Jack Gordon who was to become her husband.

Closure on Margo and Jack's CBFT Sessions.   As they thought about their life together in CBFT, Margo and Jack came to recognize, with much surprise, that over the 14 years since their wedding they, as a couple, did not face life's challenges with the same teamwork that had earlier characterized them as a couple. During the years of marriage, the dynamics between them had changed. They still loved each other, certainly, but now they had more heartaches and less fun together. They wanted to change this fact and have more fun and fewer heartaches.

As the impact of her psychohistory began to emerge during CBFT, Margo came to realize why she had acquired certain cognitions in her family schema and, more specifically, in her PT. For instance, she saw that her fear of letting Jack start his own business stemmed from the cognition that a big mistake would befall them if they took such a risk. She saw also why it was so important to her to spend the money left to them by Nan to buy and decorate a house that the family could be proud of. With assistance from the therapist, Margo and Jack began understanding themselves in new ways. This, in turn, led to behavioral changes. Margo reported, "Last night when Jack was sitting on the couch watching television, I decided to stretch out with my head nestled against Jack's chest and arm. This is how we use to watch television together when we were dating. During the first advertisement, I asked him for a kiss."

During CBFT the therapist helped the Gordons with the perspective-taking exercise, an intervention that is described next.

PERSPECTIVE-TAKING EXERCISE

The *perspective-taking exercise* has lessons for speakers and listeners. It teaches speakers, while formulating how they will express what is on their mind, to consider how their listeners view the world. Similarly, it teaches listeners that they can enhance the likelihood of understanding a speaker's message as it was intended, if they take into account the communicator's perspective.

Because the concept of *perspective taking* is difficult and outside the world of direct experience of most clients, therapists take time to explain it. They might begin by revealing that perspective taking involves going beyond one's own perceptions and seeing the world in other, alternative ways. Doing this is challenging, therapists might add, and history is replete with examples of well-intentioned people who failed. For example, scientists are often deceived by their own perceptions, even after making careful observations and reasoned-out conclusions. Consider those who some centuries ago believed that the sun and the stars revolved around the earth. They concluded this because, from their perspective from earth, this was the "truth" they perceived when they looked into the sky. Today we understand why scientists made that error and, because we have advanced to the point of being able to take other perspectives, we recognize the truth even if it still appears to us that the sun and stars revolve around our planet.

Not only can observers be deceived in drawing conclusions from their perceptions of the physical environment, but their own feelings at the moment can lead them to make errors about the minds, the hopes, and the wants of other people. Leading public figures around the turn and early part of the 20th century made comments that illustrate this point:

1. "Anything that can be invented has already been invented," concluded Charles H. Duell, Director of the U.S. Patent Office, 1899.
2. "Sensible and responsible women do not want to vote," explained former President Grover Cleveland, 1905.
3. "Who the hell wants to hear actors talk?" argued Harry M. Warner, Warner Brothers Pictures, 1927.

At this point therapists might state:

The ability to take the perspective of others is a skill. Learning it is a challenging, yet achievable undertaking, at least to the extent necessary to improve interpersonal communication. The biggest task is learning to hold yourself back for a moment so that you can reach beyond your own perspective—which is immediately available to you. By holding back automatic reactions, you are able to spend an instant taking into account another person's perspective. This helps you both as a sender and receiver of communications.

For instance, you may receive messages from your children punctuated with comments like, "Why can't you ever see it my way," or, "Don't you see, I don't care if you loved clothes like this when you were my age. Kids don't wear this junk today and if you make me wear this to school everybody will laugh." Basically, these youthful pleadings are making this request, "Please understand the world that I experience—understand how embarrassing it would be for me to be caught wearing this old-fashioned piece of apparel."

As a sender, perspective-taking skills help you better gauge your effectiveness in getting your point across. Those without exceptionally well-developed skills tend to overestimate their effectiveness. For example, one evening Margo, in an irritated, demanding voice, questioned, "Why don't you do the dishes tonight?" Margo intended to and thought she sent this message: "I've worked all day while you golfed and watched ball games. I've gotta get up earlier than you tomorrow morning and I'm tired. Please do the dishes—that's only fair." Because Margo assumed that Jack understood her message, she went to bed and was surprised and angry the next morning when she found the dishes piled in the sink, exactly where she had left them.

Margo's perspective-taking abilities failed her. She thought Jack would understand that she wanted "repayment" for her hard work in the form of washed dishes. She would have liked to have accomplished what compatible computers do with the use of modems or diskettes; that is, to transfer her thoughts exactly as they are filed in her mind directly into her husband's mind.

To help clients be more effective in transfers like these, CBFT therapists, besides teaching perspective taking, assess clients' communication skill needs and provide instruction, as needed, in active listening, reflection, the use of nonverbal communication, and the use of questions to determine whether messages were received as sent (e.g., Ivey & Authier, 1978; Kleinke, 1986).

Different Perspectives of Family Members: Joy or Grief?

Individuals' family schemas and PTs shape their perspectives of family life, indicating what is important, how spouses and children should interact, how and when caring should be expressed, and so forth. Although the family-related cognitions of family members are more alike than those of a group of randomly selected individuals, important differences always exist.

These differences stem from many factors: individuals' family positions (parent or child), roles, ages, genders, upbringings, temperaments, personalities, and so on. Whereas much time is spent in CBFT discovering how differences in perspectives cause problems, the favorable effects they have on family life are also noted. They stimulate interesting conversation, create variety in the household chores for which individuals want responsibility, and produce unanticipated outcomes like this:

> The Gordons had nearly completed their 350-mile Thanksgiving holiday trip and were cruising toward home on an interstate highway when, at 3:30 a.m., misfortune struck. Their car's muffler broke from its bracket. Besides making awful noises, it spewed an intermittent stream of Fourth-of-July-like sparklers as it bounced rhythmically along the pavement.
>
> "Don't worry," Jack said, calming the children who had been unpleasantly roused from deep sleep. Although they almost immediately came to an exit, their luck ended there. The gas station and restaurant located at the end of the exit ramp were closed and no signs of life were in sight.
>
> Jack checked under the car and then read the "hours open" sign posted at the filling station. "Darn it," he reported. "Our muffler's broken and they don't open 'til 6 a.m. Guess we'll have to sleep in the car," he muttered to tired passengers who dreamt of their bed at home, less than an hour down the road.
>
> "I'm hungry and I'm cold, I'm hungry and I'm cold," Maggie proclaimed.
>
> "Nothing's open," Margo explained, "and we can't run the car heater because of the danger of carbon-monoxide poisoning."
>
> Conditions were ripe to dampen their holiday spirits especially after Maggie reminded everybody of a thriller movie they had seen recently, and of the fact that the film's murder victims were stranded at a highway exit.
>
> After joking about how movies exaggerate, Margo distributed one hard candy per person, from the reserves squirreled away in her purse. And for warmth, everybody improvised, covering themselves with what happened to be in the car.
>
> C.J. also attacked the grim atmosphere that had momentarily pervaded, calling attention to himself. He claimed, "It's fun to be stuck. And I'm sure warm enough." When everybody turned to find out why he, alone, was warm, they

discovered he had donned socks on his hands and a book on his head. Jack laughed a big, hearty, contagious laugh, and soon everybody else chimed in.

Because C.J. expressed his unique perspective on the family's fate, he helped everybody feel a whole lot better. Once they shared a laugh they knew they could huddle together and weather the storm that would surely end at daybreak.

Often, of course, the differing perspectives of family members have the opposite effect, leading to misunderstandings, conflict, and interpersonal problems. All family members some of the time and many family members much of the time have difficulty in taking the perspective of others or, more symbolically, cannot or do not "get into the shoes" of other family members in order to better understand their experiences.

Consider the differences in perspectives of Margo and Maggie, age 14 years, and how these could potentially turn a special evening into a family disaster. Unspoken yet important thoughts (indicative of their perspective) of each of them are given in parentheses.

Maggie: "Do you like this dress that I found at the mall today?"

Margo: "You look irresistibly gorgeous, pumpkin."

Maggie: "Perry will be here to pick me up in a few minutes. I talked things over with Dad and he told me to ask you about my curfew."

Margo: "He did? Well, because this is your first real date, pumpkin, I'd like you home early, right after the dance is over—11:00." (I remember my first dates and I know what boys were like. Perry won't be any different. I don't want any boy to mess up my pumpkin's first date by taking advantage of her.)

Maggie: "Why do I have to come home that early . . . right after the dance is over?" (I'll miss the fun at the Malt Shoppe. And Perry will be angry about me leaving early and will never ask me out again. And what'll Marge and Liz think? They can stay out much later with their dates.)

In less than a minute, the conversation had reached a pivotal point and threatened to turn sour. From here they could reach a happy resolution of their different perspectives, a submissive agreement by Maggie, an angry impasse, and so on. Of the uncountable number of directions their interchange could take, the odds are that one or both of them will eventually feel unhappy, unless their talk moves in a direction that allows them to better understand each other's perspective.

To this point, neither person has verbalized what underlies her wishes about curfew, and neither one was effective in reading and being sensitive to the other's. Maggie did not recognize that her mother: (a) expected Perry, a boy she never met, to try to "get frisky," and (b) concluded she could not take care of herself. Maggie wondered whether her mother was angry because she had spent over $200 for the outfit she was wearing.

Margo had shown no insight into Maggie's perspective, and vice versa. Had Maggie verbalized her concerns, helping her mother see that the importance of this date, as she, Maggie, saw it, her mother might have responded differently. And if Margo, as an adult and parent, had expressed more about how she saw things, they might have taken each other's concerns into account and had this conversation:

> Margo: "Well, I was figuring it would be better if you came home on the earlier side, but now I see that this is a special night for you. And for me too. I hope it'll be fantastic and that things will go perfectly for you. What would you do if you didn't have an 11:00 curfew? Do you expect to be with Perry and your girlfriends and their dates after the dance?"
>
> Maggie: "Yes, that's what I'm figuring. The girls and I are doing all the planning."
>
> Margo: "Did you girls decide what you want to do after the dance and about what time you might plan to get home?"
>
> Maggie: "Yes, a bunch of us talked a lot about this. We agreed to leave the dance at 10:15. Then we'd go to the Malt Shoppe, have shakes, and stay there for about an hour. Then Mr. Stone is going to pick up Marge, Jeff, Perry, and me and bring us home. The others have their own rides. If we left there by 11:30, I'd be in by midnight."
>
> Margo: "We want to know when to expect you and what your plans are, not because of mistrust. We want to know so we won't be worried. This is new to Dad and me. We still think of you as a youngster we have to protect, even though we know you think you can do a good job of taking care of yourself. I worry about how Perry might act; I don't even know him."
>
> Maggie: "You don't have to worry. I'll take care of myself superbly. Remember, you and Dad taught me how! I'm glad you care and worry because that means you love me. But I can take care of myself with any date, because I'm a responsible person."

Had this conversation taken place, both Maggie and Margo would have better enjoyed the evening, an important milestone in their lives. In CBFT, Maggie and her family were taught to take into account the perspectives of other family members and, when the need develops, to stop the flow of the content of their conversations and to focus on the underlying perspectives of the discussants.

Another important CBFT lesson is teaching parents and teenagers to use care in making assumptions about young children's perspectives. Those who know little about the development of thinking ability in children are particularly at risk. They tend to assume that their youngsters' minds are more like adults' than they actually are, and this often causes difficulties.

Such problems are most likely to develop when children, particularly bright ones, begin to speak well. Once youngsters being putting together sentences and demonstrating a good vocabulary, parents have seemingly obvious "evidence" that the child's mind and potential to think are like their own. At this point, parents often misread their children's perspective and ask them to do more than they are capable of.

Margo shared an example of this, discussing an incident that took place some years ago when Billy, 4 years of age, was playing with her son, C.J., also 4 years old, in the family room. Although the episode occurred years before, it was fresh in Margo's mind:

> I was working in the kitchen when I heard Billy scream, "Give me that! Give me that!" I went into the family room and saw Billy trying to tug a big Tonka dump truck from C.J.
>
> "You need to take turns because you both want to play with the same toy," I told the children. "Because C.J. has been playing with it, he will have 1 more minute in his first turn. Then Billy, who is your guest, C.J., will have the first 5-minute turn."
>
> I went back into the kitchen to finish what I was cooking. After a few minutes I heard Billy scream, "Give it to me! It's my turn!"
>
> I went back to the family room and Billy wept, "I didn't get a turn. C.J. won't share."
>
> C.J. likes Billy and was not being hurtful. But the task of sharing his favorite toy was as yet beyond his capabilities, especially without supervision from his mother. C.J. lacked the abilities to take another's perspective, to reason what Billy was thinking, and to balance his needs with whatever he thought Billy was thinking. In fact, when Billy was not verbally complaining, C.J. might have, without much awareness, reasoned thusly, "I, C.J., really want to play with the truck. Billy must know that because I feel it so strongly. Because I want to play with the truck he too probably wants me to play with it." C.J. was simply unable to take Billy's perspective because his mind had not yet developed the ability to handle the thinking necessary for this task.
>
> After Billy complained about C.J. the second time, Margo criticized C.J., "What kind of host are you? You're selfish. You'll never have good friends." Later that day, with the entire family present, Margo reviewed C.J.'s "selfish behavior." Jack said that the failure at turn taking reminded him of last weekend when C.J. didn't share candy with his sister.

This example illustrates how a child, with limited perspective-taking ability, is often unable to carry out certain directives. When parents do not understand the reason why the child fails to follow their instructions, they may make negative attributions about the "failure." For example, they may conclude that the child did not follow their directive because of stubbornness, contrariness, or dullness, when the real "cause" was that the child has not yet developed cognitively to the point of being able to adequately handle the mental work required for the prescribed task. Of course, the parents' attributions then shape their behavior toward the child which, in turn, may affect the child's self-view, behavior, and so forth.

Ironically, C.J.'s inability to take Billy's perspective "caused him" to disobey his mother. Although the problem appeared to be C.J.'s fault, it would have been quickly remedied had Margo accurately read C.J.'s perspective. To illustrate, Margo would have never asked 4-year-old C.J. to carry a 100-lb load of bricks down the street. She is protected from this mistake because by looking at her youngster's body, she can effectively assess his physical strength. Until she is taught about child development principles and perspective-taking skills, she will have no such protection with regard to C.J.'s intellectual capabilities.

Enriching Family Members' Perspective-Taking Skills

Life experiences help individuals acquire perspective-taking skills. For example, youngsters gain insight into their mother's perspective when she pulls a toy away from them. They gain a deeper insight, however, if she provides cognitive mediation (see chapter 2) at the same time: "I'm taking this toy away because you haven't shared it fairly with your sister." When caretakers, teachers, and others make comments such as these, they help children glimpse the world through the eyes of others. These comments also can help teach children to engage in the kind of metacognition that takes other persons' perspectives into account.

Teaching Children Perspective-Taking Skills

Newborns are not at all aware that the nipple in their mouth is part of their mother's body. Slowly, and step by step, infants learn from their senses and construct mental structures that help them transact more successfully in the environment (Piaget, 1972). Even though children acquire increasingly complex cognitive abilities during childhood, throughout this period their thinking is limited to what is concrete for them (Piaget, 1972). In other words, until they become teenagers and reach what Piaget called the stage of *formal operations*, they cannot effectively reason through abstract problems. That means no matter what effort is invested, certain kinds of mathematics and science are beyond them, as are the highest levels of moral reasoning and perspective taking.

Given this, CBFT therapists use concrete, age-appropriate exercises to assist children in developing and sharpening perspective-taking skills and to foster the habit of using them. The basic method is this: Child A observes data available from Person B and tries to get into Person B's shoes. (Therapists may literally ask the children to stand in Person A's shoes for a moment.) Child A then makes educated guesses about Person B's perspective, verbalizes them, and gets feedback from Person B, indicating whether the educated guesses were on target or, if not, in what way they missed. Therapists may also ask Person B to try to understand Child A's perspective. Other steps used in teaching children perspective-taking skills are described next.

Step 1. As illustrated in the following, by using concrete, tangible materials, children can be taught the meaning of the term *perspective taking*:

At one point C.J. Gordon, then 9 years old, was having difficulty with his peers. At least once a week he became involved in name calling or physical squabbles with classmates, sometimes on the playground, sometimes in school, and sometimes on the bus.

To lead into perspective-taking exercises, among other reasons, the therapist asked C.J. in a kind and supportive way, how he thought he would feel if a classmate called him *stupid*, a label he had regularly applied to several classmates.

"That wouldn't happen," C.J. replied with satisfaction in his voice.

"Why?" quizzed the therapist.

"First of all, I'm not stupid. Second, everybody knows I'd cream anybody who called me that."

At this point, the therapist pulled a Baby Ruth candy bar from his desk. Holding it at the bottom, and with the brand name facing C.J., the therapist asked, "What do you see?"

"A Baby Ruth," the boy said.

"Do I see the front of the candy bar wrapper?"

"No," he replied.

"Describe what you see. Tell me everything that you see on the wrapper that you think I can't see."

After C.J. answered, the therapist asked additional questions, "How do you know what I see? How do you know what I don't see? Why do you and I see different things?"

Next, the therapist rotated the candy bar so that the name faced away from C.J. After several more questions were asked and answered, the therapist explained the concept of perspective taking in concrete terms and rewarded C.J. with the candy bar. Then, the therapist and C.J. applied the idea of perspective and perspective taking to the other children in school and how they might feel about being called names.

Step 2. Children with some understanding of the concept of perspective taking can be posed with relatively simple, concrete tasks that help strengthen their understandings and sharpen their skills. For example, the therapist, C.J., and his family examined a striking painting and then a photograph long enough so that the image and content could soak in. Then, each person took the artist's perspective—suggesting what the artist was trying to communicate when creating the work and what the artist was feeling and thinking. After each person shared his or her conclusions, the therapist led a discussion of their observations and the perspective-taking process.

For homework, the Gordons listened to musical compositions and tried to decide what the artist was experiencing when creating the work. Family members hypothesized what the artist was trying to communicate with the rhythm, the melody, the instruments used, the lyrics, and so forth. After the participants shared their conclusions, the family discussed their observations and the perspective-taking process.

They also observed a toddler exploring his environment. To get a concrete sense of how this youngster viewed the world, each family member got down to his level by kneeling or squatting. They moved forward, from knee to knee, trying to imagine the unstable legs of a toddler and experiencing the "shakiness" of locomotion during this stage of life. They looked up to see people and furniture towering above them. After getting a sense of what the child's view was, Jack lifted the children on his back and took a few steps forward, giving them concrete experience with the adult's perspective.

Step 3.   Younger children typically assume, without thinking about it, that everybody else knows everything that they know. For example, a first grader returns from school and describes a classroom incident as if his listeners were at school and witnessed the events he did. One way to teach children how to avoid this type of mistake is to foster in them the habit of metacognition. During metacognition, children can consider what information they need to share in order to effectively convey a thought or idea.

Many types of lessons can be fashioned to intentionally advance children's development in this area. For instance, therapists can teach parents to read stories to their children and to stop at various points to ask the youngsters which characters know what information. Videotaped television programs and movies also can be used for this purpose, and can be reshown to aid in checking conclusions.

A straightforward question and answer format can also be useful in teaching children how to better communicate their perspective. For example, a father can say, "You know, I've been thinking about your teacher and wondering what she's really like. Could you tell me?"

When the youngster finishes her report, father can offer praise and then ask for more information, share what conclusions he drew from her comments, or explain what formerly held assumptions had been corrected by her report. All three responses show the child that people know different information and have different perspectives.

Similar dialogues can address what the teacher does at various points of day, how she talks to the children, how the child really feels about her, what qualities the child likes in the teacher, and so on. Or, the dialogues can involve other themes, such as the child's friends, favorite activities/games/toys, happiest or funniest recollections, and so forth. In these interactions parents also learn a great deal about children's perspectives. This is illustrated in the following example.

Four-year-old Ellen was visiting the Gordons and, in answering a question, told Uncle Jack and Aunt Margo that, "from now on until I'm a mommy, I want to go to sleep with my light on."

Uncle Jack explained that burning the light all night would make it hard for her to sleep and would waste electricity. "After all," he reasoned, "nobody needs to use light to see after they go to sleep. Their eyes are closed."

Ellen countered by explaining, "I need light 'cause I sleep with my eyes open."

Uncle Jack fought a temptation to laugh. Ellen's look of conviction told him that she was not being playful or using a bedtime-delaying tactic, but rather seriously believed that she slept with her eyes open.

Uncle Jack and Aunt Margo tried to understand Ellen's perspective by engaging in detectivelike work. They sought to determine why Ellen would want the lights left on by asking themselves questions like: What experiences and/or reasoning would lead Ellen to conclude she sleeps with open eyes? What problem would be solved by having lights on? Did Ellen believe that with her eyes open and the lights on no "bad guys" would come?

Suddenly, a possibility dawned on them: nighttime dreams. Did she believe she slept with her eyes open because she saw images during dreams? Did she believe that lights would keep away bad characters that sometimes inhabited her dreams? Once Margo and Jack asked these questions, it occurred to them to call Ellen's parents and, from them, they learned that Ellen had been awakened during the past few nights by frightening dreams.

When it was time for Ellen to go to bed that night, Margo and Jack made an important decision. Instead of trying to impose the adult perspective on Ellen (you don't sleep with your eyes open), they accepted hers. They installed a nightlight, which made Ellen comfortable and enabled her to sleep peacefully through the night.

By knowing and working from Ellen's perspective, they avoided other actions that might have caused problems, then or later: (a) getting angry with Ellen for insisting on a light, thereby setting the stage for a distressing night, (b) trying to convince Ellen that she slept with her eyes closed and, at the same time, giving her data that devalued her observation process and reasoning, and (c) telling Ellen that her idea was silly, thereby causing self-doubts and, perhaps, fear that her future concerns will not be taken seriously.

CBFT therapists tell clients that, even with help, children's perspective-taking skills grow slowly because progress is limited by the children's developmental level (which, in turn, is likely related to brain development). Nonetheless, parents often ask, "How fast can you push this growth?" Piaget (personal communication, May 1967) often jested about this question, which he called the "American question," so named because Americans asked it much more frequently than any other nationals.

Developing Perspective-Taking Skills with a Spouse

It is far easier for spouses to work cooperatively to sharpen their perspective-taking skills than it is for them to help their children develop in this area. Spouses are advantaged by their better developed intellectual capabilities and vocabulary, and by their potential to assess and understand how another adult thinks. A three-step agenda that spouses can use over and over again to build their perspective-taking skills is described next.

The goal of Step 1 is for the spouses to gain insight into each other's perspective. To accomplish this, the spouses open their family schema cognitions to their partner, answering a set of questions either they or their therapists have written. The questions used in Step 1 run the gamut, covering issues that include how they view their: marriage, use of leisure, evenings at home, bedtime activities, roles in the marriage, interactions with the children, problems with the children, social life, relationships with the extended family, budget, way of sharing work and dividing resources, and so forth. Therapists sometimes ask couples to use questions from quizzes printed in newspapers and magazines as stimulus material or to spend a week collecting stimulus questions that come to mind during the course of their day-to-day activities.

During Step 1, each question is answered by each spouse, providing the partner with insight into his or her perspective. While sharing answers, spouses sometimes find it useful to call time out. During time out, an individual may ask additional questions or try to rephrase previously made statements to achieve a greater clarification of what the spouse is intending to communicate.

After the list of questions has been answered by both partners, the couple begins Step 2. They return to the first question and each explains how his or her spouse's answer differed from what was expected.

When they again complete the list, they begin Step 3. Here the spouses have two goals. First, they analyze the discrepancies between how their spouse answered the questions and what they expected, trying to determine if any patterns exist. For example, after hearing Margo's answers on several money-related questions, Jack discovered that he had been greatly underestimating her concern over their financial state. Second, they try to identify blind areas, that is, areas in which they do not know enough information about their spouse's thoughts and feelings to be able to be effective in perspective taking.

When blind areas are identified, spouses will in all probability discover that in the past they filled in these gaps with inaccurate assumptions. For instance, during this exercise Jack learned of Margo's views about C.J. playing Little League football. He had had a blind spot in this area and had simply assumed that she felt the same way that he did; football builds character, so of course C.J. will play. Margo, instead, fearing that C.J. might get injured, was opposed to his playing and resented the fact that Jack went ahead and enrolled C.J. without consulting her. Because of a blind spot, however, he had assumed no discussion was necessary.

As the Little League football example shows, spouses gain new insights during this exercise. However, for every question they answer about each other's perspectives, a new one almost inevitably arises. Nonetheless, as clients become more aware of their perspective and those of other family members, they are empowered to be more effective problem solvers in the family setting. They also discover that huge differences in perspectives can exist among family members who love each other and that although their mate's and children's PTs are different from their own, they are equally valid.

9

FAMILY LIFE EDUCATION

Counseling and psychotherapeutic interventions generally are designed to help dysfunctional families function more effectively. By contrast, the purposes of family life education are to prevent family units from developing serious difficulties and to promote adaptive, health-promoting functioning through the dissemination of information related to family life. Thus, all families, not just those experiencing problems, may benefit from family life education. Information can be shared in a variety of settings (e.g., churches, schools, community centers, universities), using a variety of formats (e.g., lectures, discussions, workshops), and with different age groups (e.g., children, adolescents, adults).

There was a recent effort to conceptually specify the nature of what is taught under the rubric of family life education (Thomas & Arcus, 1992). Traditionally, it devotes some attention to cognitive processes (e.g., value clarification) and how they affect the relationships of family members (Nelson-Jones, 1990). In this chapter, we discuss how the cognitive-behavioral model (CBF) can be used to enhance family life education. Our goal is not to be exhaustive; rather, our focus is to show how the theoretical notions presented earlier in the book can be fruitfully applied in educational work with families. To accomplish this purpose, some background on family life education is initially provided. Building on this foundation, ideas are presented for using the CBF model in family education programs. Next, the important issues of ethics and evaluation of family education programs are discussed. Finally, examples are provided to show the range of possible educational activities.

TRADITIONAL FAMILY LIFE EDUCATION

Arcus (1987), based on work by the National Council on Family Relations Committee on Standards and Criteria for Certification of Family Life Educators, presented a model called the Framework for Life-Span Family Life Education. According to Arcus (1990), the goals for participants in family life education are to: (a) gain knowledge about concepts and principles relevant to family living, (b) explore personal attitudes and values, and understand and accept the attitudes and values of others, and (c) develop interpersonal skills that contribute to family well-being.

The model describes the following topic areas: human development and sexuality, interpersonal relationships, family interaction, family resource management, education about parenthood, ethics, and family and society. For each of these topic areas, key concepts are listed separately for children, adolescents, and adults.

For example, for the topic of interpersonal relationships, key concepts include: (a) for children: building self-esteem, communicating with others, sharing time, friends, and possessions, and acting with consideration for self and others; (b) for adolescents: dealing with success and failure, assessing compatibility in interpersonal relationships, respecting self and others, and accepting responsibility for one's actions; and (c) for adults: establishing personal autonomy, exercising initiative in relationships, creating and maintaining a family of one's own, and communicating effectively. As these illustrations demonstrate, although the concepts are similar for children, adolescents, and adults, they are tailored to the cognitive capabilities and social maturity of those in the particular age group.

The Framework for Life-Span Family Life Education model emphasizes the content of the material to be presented. Thus, most of the topics are covered by presenting straightforward, perhaps empirically derived information about the various aspects of family life. Strengths of this model are that: (a) It includes a broad definition of family life education, (b) it stresses that education about families is relevant to individuals of all ages, (c) it recognizes that the content of the material and the manner in which it is presented will differ across age groups, and (d) it encompasses many aspects of learning, including knowledge, attitudes, and skills.

Whereas the information conveyed in these lessons is very useful for family members and can help them find more satisfaction in their family life, we believe that education programs can provide a great deal more to participants. First, the content suggested by the model does not include many of the cognitive phenomena discussed earlier in the book. For example, whereas material regarding roles is included, there is no specific mention of the cognitions involved in role expectations, role standards, and role assumptions, and how these affect individuals' thoughts, feelings, and behaviors.

Second, the model could be interpreted as making the assumption that individuals are passive recipients of information gathered and integrated by experts, rather than active processors of information about family life.

Recognizing that earlier models and approaches to family life education have and will continue to play an important role in teaching individuals about family life, we believe, however, that the CBF perspective adds an important element to them. More specifically, we believe that many currently used programs could be enriched by adding to them the cognitive-behavioral perspective discussed in this book. Such offerings would provide a unique and personally involving approach to family life education.

COGNITIVE-BEHAVIORAL FAMILY EDUCATION

In chapters 3 and 4, we argued that individuals often have a very limited awareness and understanding of the cognitions in their family schemas. Although individuals have cognitions within their personal theories (PTs), relationship scripts, family constitutions, cost–benefit ratios, and problem-solving strategies, they typically are unaware of the presence and the importance of these cognitions.

As a result, to acquaint family members with the CBF model, family life education begins with an explanation of two key facets of family life: (a) how individuals gain knowledge about their family lives and how they negotiate and problem solve when difficulties arise (i.e., the process of how individuals acquire and use cognitions), and (b) adaptive, balanced, and reasonable cognitions about different aspects of family life (i.e., the content of healthy cognitions). The first facet is concerned with teaching family members about how they come to hold the family-related cognitions that they do and how these cognitions can be changed, if that would be beneficial. The second facet addresses information related to cognitions that may be adaptive and helpful for them to have as they adjust to their family lives over the life span.

Process of Acquiring and Using Cognitions

This facet of family education addresses how individuals use their cognitions to make sense out of their family-related experiences. After outlining the CBF model, which gives learners a lattice on which to build their understandings of themselves as family members, our focus is on two areas: maladaptive/irrational thinking and perspective taking.

Maladaptive and Irrational Thinking. This area was initially explored by cognitive-behavioral therapists who worked with individuals. Beck et al. (1979) identified several types of "cognitive errors." *Arbitrary inference* refers to the process of drawing a specific conclusion in the absence of supportive evidence or when the evidence is contrary to the conclusion. *Selective abstraction* consists of focusing on a detail taken out of context, ignoring other more important features of the situation, and coming to a conclusion on the basis of this fragment. *Overgeneralization* refers to the pattern of drawing a general rule or conclusion on the basis of one or more isolated incidents and applying the conclusion to both related and unrelated situations. *Magnification and minimization* are reflected in distortions in evaluating the significance or magnitude of an event. *Personalization* refers to a person's tendency to relate events to him- or herself when there is no empirical evidence for making such a connection. *Dichotomous thinking* is reflected in the tendency to place experiences in one of two opposite categories (e.g., good or bad, healthy or unhealthy) without recognizing gradations between these two extremes. Note that these cognitive errors refer to the process of interpreting one's environment and not to specific factual errors in beliefs.

Similarly, Ellis (1984) argued that individuals cause themselves to be disturbed by making numerous types of illogical assumptions. He claimed that individuals tend to make rigid, absolutistic evaluations of the events in their lives and these evaluations are couched in the form of dogmatic "musts," "shoulds," "oughts," "have to's," and "got to's." For example, many individuals form the beliefs that "I must be liked by everyone or I am completely unworthy" and "I must never make a mistake, or I will be completely incompetent." These beliefs are considered irrational and they typically impede individuals in their pursuit of life satisfaction.

When family members regularly engage in this kind of illogical evaluation they may be said to be engaged in "awfulizing," which occurs when an event is rated as 100% bad; "I can't stand-it-itis," which means that individuals believe that they cannot experience virtually any happiness at all, under any conditions, if an event that must not happen actually occurs or threatens to occur; or "damnation," which is a tendency for individuals to rate themselves and other people as undeserving if the self or another does something that they must not do or fail to do something that they must do. When individuals apply these types of shoulds, musts, and have to's in their family life, it has implications for how they will think, feel, and behave which, of course, will affect the experiences and/or the development of their family members.

Another way Beck et al.'s (1979) and Ellis' (1984) positions can be easily explained to and understood by learners in family education programs is if they are put in terms of CBF concepts. For example, Ellis' notions suggest that some individuals' cost–benefit (c/b) cognitions are based on unrealistic (or impossible to achieve) standards. When individuals have unrealistic standards, they are likely to have unacceptable c/b ratios and, more important, are likely to continue to have unacceptable ratios despite continual efforts to improve them.

Similarly, although the notions of cognitive errors and irrational thinking were developed in an individual context, they can be understood in the family context in terms of CBF concepts. For example, individuals' family schemas may lead them to apply irrational beliefs not only to themselves, but also to their relationships within the entire family. Their cognitions might dictate that "Families are supposed to be happy all of the time" and "Mothers should always be nurturant." They are irrational because of the implication that these states should always be present. Further, the latter belief may be maladaptive, because not all mothers' relationship scripts lead them to be nurturant and there may be many different successful roles that mothers may adopt.

Used together in family education, Beck et al.'s (1979) and Ellis' (1984) work presented and organized in terms of the CBF model (or in other ways) can be of great value to learners. This material can help them become more satisfied with their lives by assisting them in coming to view their life situations in a more realistic, flexible, and accurate manner. In this connection, Beck et al. suggested that individuals empirically test their beliefs about themselves, their futures, and their environments by actually devising experiments to determine if these beliefs are accurate. Likewise, according to Ellis' perspective, musts and shoulds are always maladaptive and so such beliefs need no empirical testing before they are modified. Their work is consistent with the claim that family educators might fruitfully teach that individuals having realistic expectations, assumptions, and standards may function more adaptively than those who make cognitive errors or hold irrational beliefs.

Perspective-Taking Skills. As discussed in chapter 8, a skill that is often poorly developed and inadequately used among family members is the ability to take the perspective of others. Particularly during periods of conflict, but also at other times, it is critical that individuals attempt to understand other family members' behavior from their perspective. Children, of course, are limited by their own developmental abilities in being able to exercise this skill, but can understand some simple notions, such as that people differ in how they view a situation and that it is possible that these different views are neither right nor wrong.

Chapter 8 presents several techniques that CBF therapists can employ to help clients learn the value of and enhance their ability to use perspective-taking skills. Similarly, although family educators do not have as much personal contact with program recipients as therapists do with their clients, family educators can help individuals improve their perspective-taking abilities. First, family educators can help individuals recognize the importance of perspective taking. Once this is accomplished, the next stage in the process— checking out whether one's perceptions are accurate—can be presented and taught. The main educational point to be stressed is that the process of perspective taking is not complete until all individuals involved in the particular situation have an empirically validated understanding of the others' views.

Family educators can also use the notion of perspective taking to help them teach important basic skills necessary for successful family functioning. As discussed in chapter 7, some of these behavioral skills are communication, problem solving, assertiveness, and negotiation. These skills can be taught separately or as part of comprehensive skill-training programs. Because comprehensive and thorough descriptions of training programs in these areas have been described elsewhere (see Egan, 1986; Ivey & Simek-Downing, 1980), the goal here is to explain how the teaching of these skills can be enhanced by the development of perspective-taking abilities.

In CBF skill training, individuals are taught not only the behavioral skills that are associated with problem solving, assertiveness, communication, and negotiation, but are also taught to consider both their own cognitions and those of others involved in the interaction. As discussed in considerable depth in chapter 8, rather than just learning the skills, the CBF approach encourages individuals also to step back and examine their own and others' cognitions in the situation. For example, a mother who wishes to have more time to herself outside of the home might learn how to express assertively her needs and desires to her husband. In addition, however, the CBF approach argues that she would benefit from being aware of her own cognitions regarding her needs and her husband's behavior, as well as her husband's thoughts and feelings regarding their allocation of time outside of the home without the children.

Content of Family Education

This facet focuses on what can be taught to family members about the concept of family-related cognitions and, further, about those that they hold. For example, learners can be taught that some cognitions can be maladaptive for those who hold them, such as beliefs that are generally inaccurate and set up unreasonably high expectations about family life. One way that family members can be taught these lessons is through the use of material focusing on common misconceptions and the cognitions that underlie them.

Larson (1988) developed a 20-item Marriage Quiz to measure the extent to which individuals believe in "myths" about marriage and family relations. These myths were developed by reviewing the literature on myths about marriage, generating a list of myths, and having these myths reviewed by four university professors. The specific myths are listed in Table 9.1, along with the "correct" answers. For example, one myth is "In most marriages, having a child improves marital satisfaction for both spouses." Because empirical findings suggest that this statement is false, a true response indicates that an individual has adopted an inaccurate belief.

TABLE 9.1
Items from the Marriage Quiz

---

1. A husband's marital satisfaction is usually lower if his wife is employed full time than if she is a full-time homemaker. (correct answer is false)
2. Today most young single, never-married people will eventually get married. (correct answer is true)
3. In most marriages, having a child improves marital satisfaction for both spouses. (correct answer is false)
4. The best single predictor of overall marital satisfaction is the quality of a couple's sex life. (correct answer is false)
5. The divorce rate in America increased from 1960 to 1980. (correct answer is true)
6. A greater percentage of wives are in the work force today than in 1970. (correct answer is true)
7. Marital satisfaction for a wife is usually lower if she is employed full time than if she is a full-time homemaker. (correct answer is false)
8. If my spouse loves me, he/she should instinctively know what I want and need to be happy. (correct answer is false)
9. In a marriage in which the wife is employed full time, the husband usually assumes an equal share of the housekeeping. (correct answer is false)
10. For most couples, marital satisfaction gradually increases from the first year of marriage through the child-bearing years, the teen years, the empty nest period, and retirement. (correct answer is false)
11. No matter how I behave, my spouse should love me simply because he/she *is* my spouse. (correct answer is false)
12. One of the most frequent marital problems is poor communication. (correct answer is true)
13. Husbands usually make more lifestyle adjustments in marriage than wives. (correct answer is false)
14. Couples who cohabitated before marriage usually report greater marital satisfaction than couples who did not. (correct answer is false)
15. I can change my spouse by pointing out his/her inadequacies, errors, etc. (correct answer is false)
16. Couples who marry when one or both partners are under the age of 18 have more chance of eventually divorcing than those who marry when they are older. (correct answer is true)
17. Either my spouse loves me or does not love me; nothing I do will affect the way my spouse feels about me. (correct answer is false)
18. The more a spouse discloses positive and negative information to his/her partner, the greater the marital satisfaction of both partners. (correct answer is false)
19. I must feel better about my partner before I can change my behavior toward him/her. (correct answer is false)
20. Maintaining romantic love is *the key* to marital happiness over the life span for most couples. (correct answer is false)

Note. Items with "false" as the correct answer are common myths; the other items are fillers. From Larson (1988). Copyright (1988) by the National Council on Family Relations. Reprinted by permission.

Larson's (1988) work is helpful to family educators wanting to integrate components of the CBF model in their programs. As he suggests, the Marriage Quiz can serve as a stimulus for group discussion and for the clarification of misconceptions. When items are "missed," individuals can be challenged about their belief and empirical evidence can be reviewed that suggests the belief is inaccurate. Further, because reliable empirical findings provide the support for any development of a list of myths, professionals who engage in family education activities can develop their own list of empirically established myths specifically suited for the students they teach and can share these with those they teach over the years. For example, educators working with engaged couples, church members, or those married for dozens of years, can obtain data from these specific groups and then put that information to use in their next programs.

Another example of how family members can be taught about myths comes from the stepfamily literature. Researchers have identified commonly held expectations that are inconsistent with the realities of daily living in stepfamilies (Leslie & Epstein, 1988). Visher and Visher (1988) reported that stepparents often have unrealistic expectations ("stepfamily myths") of themselves and their new families, including the beliefs that stepfamilies are functionally equivalent to first-marriage families, that stepfamily adjustment will be attained quickly, and that loving and caring will develop instantly between stepfamily members. These are considered unrealistic because stepfamilies are not functionally equivalent to first-marriage families, stepfamily adjustment does not occur quickly for most stepfamily members (Papernow, 1984), and loving and caring typically do not develop immediately between stepparents and stepchildren.

Holding beliefs like these in their family schemas leads stepparents to have the expectations and to exhibit the behaviors characteristic of first-marriage families. This, in turn, typically leads to frustration when the expectations are not met (Leslie & Epstein, 1988). Further, individuals with high expectations sometimes make overly vigorous attempts to meet their lofty goals and this may, paradoxically, make matters worse. For example, a stepfather whose relationship script and PT indicate that he should immediately love his stepdaughter and yet finds himself frequently becoming angry with her may vigorously try to find a way to improve the relationship. This effort may appear "forced" and, furthermore, the stepdaughter may not be emotionally prepared to deal with his assertive efforts and to have positive interactions with him. Thus, the child, following the dictates of her PT, may withdraw and the relationship may be even less positive than before the stepfather initiated his unsuccessful efforts. Indeed, Kurdek and Fine's (1991) study of stepfather families showed that the holding of unrealistic expectations was related to lower satisfaction with family/marital/personal life for biological mothers in stepfather families and lower satisfaction with parenting for stepfathers.

Another implication of Kurdek and Fine's (1991) study is that stepfamily members who have expectations that are consistent with the realities of daily living in stepfather families adjust more effectively than those who do not. Such expectations include the following: Adjustment in stepfamilies is a gradual and slow process, caring and warm feelings toward stepkin take time to develop, stepfamilies are qualitatively different (neither better nor worse) than first-marriage families, and working hard on developing relationships with stepkin does not necessarily lead to immediate improvements in intimacy (Visher & Visher, 1988). One implication of these findings for those conducting education programs for families in transition is this: Stepfamily members taught to hold cognitions consistent with this research would appear to be better positioned for the adjustment process than those who are not.

Principles for Presenting Family Educational Material

Cognitive-behavioral educational presentations vary along a number of dimensions, including the length of the session(s), the relative proportion of didactic and experiential material, the setting, and the audience. Presentations of the CBF model can be very flexibly developed and specifically tailored to meet the needs required by the type of audience, the amount of time available, the desired mix of didactic and experiential material, and the topic to be addressed.

More important than these structural details, however, are principles that should be followed in choosing content so as to maximize the educational benefit to participants. These are:

1. The material covered should meet their stated needs and be of interest to participants. To fulfill this principle, a careful review of the audience's goals should be conducted prior to the presentation. In addition, it is often helpful to ask participants at the beginning of the session what material they would like covered. Of course, after such information is sought, presenters should make their best efforts to address the issues of interest identified by the participants. Educators often face the situation in which learners state an interest in a particular topic, such as improved communication, when experience tells the educators that other material should have a higher priority. In such cases, educators can find creative and persuasive solutions to the dilemma.

2. CBF material addresses areas that individuals usually think little about and, therefore, it often takes some effort on the part of instructors to present the content in a manner that is understandable to participants. Certainly, when teaching children, presenters have to use simple and concrete language and many examples. Even adults vary in their level of understanding and presenters have to plan to the skill levels of those expected in the particular audience.

3. We believe that learning is best accomplished when participants are encouraged to participate actively in the form of asking questions, making comments, performing exercises, and applying material to their lives. There are certainly times when didactic presentations are useful and necessary, but, eventually, interaction between the presenter and the audience is invaluable. This principle highlights our value that learning about and changing one's

own family schemas are enhanced when participants are encouraged to think critically about concepts, put their ideas into words, and receive feedback from the presenter and other participants.

4. We also believe that the kind of learning involved in integrating the CBF model in individuals' lives occurs most effectively when abstract material is applied to the individuals' own lives. For example, if the topic covered is marriage, then individuals at some point in the presentation should be given an opportunity to, either in large or small groups, in couples, and/or privately on paper, reflect on and verbalize how the material covered relates to their own intimate relationship.

5. We believe that learning is enhanced and is more likely to be maintained when participants are encouraged to engage in out-of-session activities. For example, if there is more than one session, participants can be asked to complete homework assignments between sessions. In addition, we encourage scheduling follow-up or "booster" sessions after educational programs are completed to maximize the maintenance of gains. For example, Schwebel et al. (1988), in their educational program designed to help divorced, non-custodial fathers communicate more effectively with their children, reassembled the group approximately 3 months after completion of seven sessions. Put another way, learning to apply CBF model concepts in one's family life involves changing old habits, many of which individuals were unaware of having. Therefore, maximizing the learning yield from available sessions and providing back-home support for new learnings can be a great benefit.

EVALUATION OF EDUCATIONAL PROGRAMS

As is the case with all forms of intervention, the continued improvement of family education programs depends ultimately on evaluations of their effectiveness. If evaluation data are collected appropriately, they can provide information that family educators can use to refine their programs. Once improvements are made, of course, evaluation data can indicate whether the desired effects were achieved.

The nature and comprehensiveness of program evaluations can vary tremendously. At the very least, after individuals have participated in the program (i.e., a posttest design), useful feedback can be gathered by asking participants whether the presentation was well organized, clear, interesting, informative, and useful. A stronger evaluation strategy consists of testing subjects' knowledge of a particular topic or some measure of their well-being before and after they participate in the program (i.e., a pretest–posttest design). This approach, although more costly and difficult to use, allows one to determine the extent to which participants changed from before to after the program.

An even stronger evaluation strategy involves the use of a control group of individuals who do not participate in the educational program (i.e., pretest–posttest with control group design). If program participants improve (from before to after the intervention) to a greater extent than those who do not participate in the program, then one can conclude that participation in the program was at least one factor that led to the observed improvement in well-being.

Obviously, the more detailed and comprehensive the evaluation strategy, the more resources are needed to implement it. Thus, it is not surprising that few programs have been able to conduct thorough evaluations (Small, 1990). To help family educators allocate precious evaluation resources in an efficient manner, Small made several suggestions, including recognizing which programs lend themselves to evaluation and planning the evaluation strategy before the program begins.

ETHICS OF FAMILY EDUCATION PROGRAMS

Ethical codes have been developed for mental health practitioners engaged in a variety of professional activities (e.g., the revised code published by the American Psychological Association, 1992). The primary focus of these ethical codes has been on psychotherapy, counseling, and assessment. Relatively less attention has been devoted to the ethics involved in teaching and education, including the area of family education.

Leigh, Loewen, and Lester (1986) recommended that family life educators follow a proposed code of ethics. They suggested that professionals engaged in family life education act responsibly toward participants, inform participants about program values, risks, and benefits prior to consent, show respect for individual rights and confidentiality, demonstrate integrity and honesty when interacting with the public, behave responsibly with respect to dealing with their own and others' values and possible influence, be competent, be committed to continued professional development, and show concern for how interventions affect participants and their families. They also should be prepared to make referrals to other professionals and agencies when appropriate. These recommendations are consistent with guidelines in the ethical codes developed by such professional organizations as the American Psychological Association, American Association of Counseling and Development, American Association of Marital and Family Therapy, and the American Psychiatric Association.

We concur with Leigh et al.'s (1986) recommendations. Furthermore, because unique ethical issues arise in implementing family education programs, we suggest that family educators continue to develop ethical standards for their professional activities (see also Brock, 1993). For example, family educators using aspects of the CBF model may face situations in which clients are divulging personal information. They may be sharing this with those in their family unit, strangers, or members of the community who are also in the class, perhaps posing the problem of at what point should the instructors intervene in order to protect the person revealing the information, members of his or her family, and others in attendance. Obviously, family educators will be most helpful to those they serve if they evaluate their performance not only in terms of the effectiveness of their interventions, but also with respect to adherence to their ethical standards.

EXAMPLES OF FAMILY EDUCATION PROGRAMS THAT ARE CONSISTENT WITH A COGNITIVE-BEHAVIORAL PERSPECTIVE

Although the family education programs discussed in this section were not developed to be consistent with the CBF model, they have program components that make them compatible. The three programs presented here address families in three different stages of the family life cycle: before marriage, following divorce, and following remarriage. Although these programs are targeted to individuals who are experiencing major family-related transitions, not all family education programs are intended for individuals who are undergoing change and/or stressful experiences.

Prevention and Relationship Enhancement Program. Renick, Blumberg, and Markman (1992) described the Prevention and Relationship Enhancement Program (PREP) as an educational program designed to prevent later marital distress and divorce among premarital couples. The program is based on the notion of primary prevention, proposing that the probability of serious problems developing later can be lowered by teaching individuals skills that will help them in problem solving and that will facilitate their building satisfactory marriages.

Two formats are currently used—one that involves six weekly sessions for 2 to 2½ hours for groups of four to eight couples and another that involves 20–40 couples who convene for a single weekend. Topics covered include communication skills, expectations about communication and relationships in general, hidden agendas or expectations and how they relate to communication processes and problems, the role of fun in successful relationships, problem solving, ways to increase commitment and intimacy, spiritual values and beliefs that foster healthy relationships, and communication about physical intimacy. In terms of CBF constructs, PREP—particularly those aspects focusing on expectations and beliefs—addresses problem-solving strategies, relationship script cognitions, and, to some extent, cost–benefit (c/b) analyses. A number of evaluation studies have supported the effectiveness of the PREP program in enhancing the long-term quality of marital relationships (Markman, Floyd, Stanley, & Storaasli, 1988).

Orientation for Divorcing Parents. Buehler, Betz, Ryan, Legg, and Trotter (1992) described and evaluated the Orientation for Divorcing Parents (ODP) program. The program is designed to minimize divorce-related difficulties by helping participants identify potential problems, increase their awareness of adaptive ways to cope with divorce, foster a sense of self-efficacy, learn skills to cope with divorce, and mobilize existing resources so that they are not overwhelmed by divorce-related stressors.

The program consists of five weekly, 2-hour sessions. Material is presented in a variety of modalities, including lecturettes, role plays, and discussion. Topics covered in the sessions include parents' adjustment, common responses that children have to divorce, legal aspects of divorce, relationships with ex-spouses, and parent–child relationships.

Although the ODP program does not specifically include material related to divorce-related cognitions, the information related to typical reactions to divorce helps participants develop realistic assumptions, expectations, and standards for what they can expect from themselves and their children following divorce. In CBF terms, subconstructs that are targeted include relationship scripts, problem-solving strategies, and, to some extent, c/b ratios.

Personal Reflections. Kaplan and Hennon (1992) developed the Personal Reflections program for education regarding remarriage. Their program is designed to help couples learn about their role expectations, role compatibilities, potential role strains, and possible stresses that often occur in remarriages.

The Personal Reflections program is designed to meet three times per week for a total of approximately 8 hours. Topics covered (with the related CBF construct[s] identified in parentheses) include the importance of remarriage scripts (relationship scripts), roles in remarried families (relationship scripts, family constitution), expectations for roles (relationship scripts, family constitution), the importance of congruent expectations (family constitution, problem-solving strategies), and negotiation (problem-solving strategies). These topics are covered in both a didactic and experiential manner, with members of participating couples discussing and clarifying their beliefs and expectations in the relevant areas.

This program addresses both the process of how individuals gain information about stepfamily functioning and the content of some of the commonly encountered issues and problems facing remarried couples. Although its effectiveness has yet to be empirically demonstrated, Kaplan and Hennon (1992) provided a number of suggestions for how program evaluations can be conducted.

In conclusion, these three programs highlight the range of possibilities that characterize family education. Although the specific content of these programs varies somewhat, they share an emphasis on both didactic and experiential learning, the development of relationship-enhancing skills, and an exploration of expectations regarding family life. Whereas the programs were not developed within a CBF framework, they are compatible with this approach. Clearly, there is a need to develop family educational programs that are specifically derived from the CBF model.

10

RESEARCH

This chapter provides an agenda for future research designed to further understanding of family life and how to improve it. In addition to a discussion of methodologies that are likely to be fruitful in cognitive-behavioral family research, specific recommendations are offered about some of the content areas that warrant future research.

The first section of this chapter reviews methodologies that have been used to study cognitions in families and suggests some new approaches to this growing field. The second section describes research areas that are likely to yield valuable information about families. A concluding section discusses how the relations between researchers and clinicians can become more cooperative and mutually beneficial than they presently are.

METHODOLOGIES TO STUDY COGNITIONS
IN FAMILIES

There are several ways that researchers have studied cognitions. These can be categorized according to whether researchers investigated general cognitions or whether they assessed cognitions in the context of specific behavioral interactions.

General Cognitions About Specific Persons or Relationships

One way to investigate cognitions is to study general cognitions that individuals hold toward specific persons or relationships. For example, to determine whether individuals' standards and assumptions for parental behavior varied for different types of parents, Schwebel, Fine, and Renner (1991) developed a questionnaire that asked subjects to respond on several dimensions to a series of 16 scenarios depicting situations calling for parental behavior. On the biological parent version of the instrument, biological parents were included in the scenarios; on the stepparent version, stepparents were included; and, on the adoptive parent version, adoptive parents were included. In each scenario, subjects were asked to what extent they thought that the (step)parents would engage in predesignated parental behavior (i.e., assumptions) and the extent to which they thought (step)parents should engage in the parental behavior (i.e., standards).

As hypothesized, Schwebel et al. (1991) found that, in contrast to perceptions of biological and adoptive parents, there was greater variability in perceptions of how stepparents would and should behave. In addition, they found that stepparents were perceived as being less likely to act in a parental manner and as being less obligated to do so than were biological and adoptive parents. These results suggest that there is less clarity about the stepparent role than there is for biological and adoptive parents and that stepparents are not expected to act in a parental manner to the same degree as other parents. Thus, this procedure is useful in assessing general assumptions of how parents typically behave and standards for how parents should behave. Results generated from studies that use this method may illuminate the cognitions that family members have related to parental behavior, identify possible inconsistencies in cognitions across family members, and reveal potential family problems that may arise from these inconsistent parenting cognitions. Of course, the same type of method can be used to investigate expectancies of other roles, and the roles expected by respondents from various ethnic and socioeconomic groups.

As another illustration, Fincham, Beach, and Nelson (1987) developed the Marital Attribution Style Questionnaire (MAST) to assess attributions for hypothetical spouse behaviors. This scale lists 12 spouse behaviors (6 positive and 6 negative) that represent behaviors often found in checklists used by behavioral marital therapists. For each hypothetical behavior, the spouse is asked to record one major cause of the action. Causal attributions are obtained by asking the subject to rate the cause in terms of three dimensions: whether the cause reflected something about the spouse as opposed to something about oneself (i.e., internal vs. external), whether the cause is likely to be present when the behavior occurs in the future (i.e., stable vs. unstable), and whether the cause was specific to the behavior as opposed to whether the cause affected many areas of the marriage (i.e., specific vs. global). Responses to these attributions are made on 7-point rating scales.

Similar methods have been used to study the cognitions individuals hold regarding specific family roles and family relationships. As described earlier in the assessment chapter, there are several instruments that assess expectations and beliefs regarding one's spouse, marriage, and family. We believe that these instruments have value in giving researchers relatively unobtrusive and quick measures of various cognitions. Their primary limitation is that they rely on self-report, which may be vulnerable to response biases.

Cognitions That Occur During Behavioral Interactions

As opposed to methods that assess the general cognitions individuals hold about roles or relationships, some techniques attempt to identify the cognitions that guide individuals as they are in the midst of specific behavioral interactions. Fletcher and Kininmonth (1991) provided a useful review of how cognitions can be assessed during the unfolding of dyadic interpersonal interactions. They suggested that there are three methodological approaches to assessing the cognitions that affect individuals before, during, or after dyadic interactions occur.

The first method of assessing cognitions measures cognitions, such as attributions or expectations, regarding an identified problem that is to be discussed or a particular interaction that will occur. Typically, questionnaires are used to collect data. For example, in a series of studies that used measures of attributions for negative spouse behaviors and marital difficulties, Fincham and Bradbury (1988) found that positive attributional patterns (e.g., internal attributions for positive behavior and external attributions for negative behavior) for specific relationship problems were positively correlated with positive behavior and negatively correlated with negative behavior performed during discussion of these same problems.

Another example of this method is drawn from Bradbury (1990), who assessed the impact of holding prior cognitions on the behaviors and affects of 47 married couples during discussions of their marital problems. The results, although complex, showed the impact prior cognitions have. Specifically, the findings generally indicated that: (a) Subjects who produced more positive attributions for a problem were more effective problem solvers and made fewer negative emotional displays, (b) spouses who judged the problem as more readily solvable produced more effective problem-solving behavior and fewer negative emotional displays, and (c) those who had more positive expectations for the discussion displayed more effective problem-solving behavior and less anger and contempt.

The second methodological approach of assessing specific cognitions that affect individuals before, during, or after dyadic interactions occur focuses on behavioral intentions underlying specific behaviors. The "talk-table" technique (Gottman et al., 1976) exemplifies this approach. The talk-table is a double-sloping table with switches that enable each partner to indicate who has the floor at any given time. Each partner rates each verbal message on a positive–negative dimension in terms of its intended effect (if the message was sent) or its perceived effect (if the message was received). The ratings are made on a set of buttons that are hidden from the partner. In the original Gottman et al. study, happily married spouses judged the impact of their spouses' messages more positively than did distressed spouses. This procedure has been used in numerous studies and it has provided information to show that the attributions that partners make during actual interactions are related to their marital satisfaction.

The third approach to the assessment of specific cognitions that are affecting individuals during dyadic interactions typically involves asking partners to remember their cognitions while they watch videotaped recordings of their own behavioral interactions. Specific cognitions that relate to particular events can be recorded from either or both spouses, or, alternatively, global thoughts and feelings about the entire sequence of interaction can be gathered. For example, Gaelick, Bodenhausen, and Wyer (1985) required married couples to watch selected videotaped segments of interactions. Each partner independently reviewed tapes of a 10-minute problem discussion and selected three verbal statements that they considered to have important effects on the interaction. Subjects rated the statements they selected and those chosen by their partners on several dimensions, including the emotional flavor of the message, the feelings that the communicator intended to send, and the recipient's perception of the communicator's feelings.

Gaelick et al. (1985) found that partners believed that there was substantial similarity between their own feelings and those they attributed to their partners for each behavior, regardless of whether or not they were the speaker or the listener. However, correlations across couples for each behavior on the relevant ratings (e.g., the correlation between the husband's self-rated feelings and the feelings the wife attributed to him for the same behavior) were nonsignificant for emotionally positive messages, but moderate for emotionally negative behaviors. These findings suggest that negative behaviors appear to play a more important role in dyadic interaction than do positive behaviors.

The primary disadvantage of this approach—and other self-report methods—is that there is no assurance that the cognitions reported in response to questions are the same as those that occur in the absence of the probes. One strategy that has been used to address this difficulty was developed by Ickes, Robertson, Tooke, and Teng (1986). These investigators had partners independently watch videotaped interaction sequences, stop the tape whenever they could remember having specific thoughts or feelings, and record them. Fletcher and Fitness (1990) used a modification of this technique: Rather than writing down their recalled thoughts and feelings, subjects verbally stated them and these were audiotaped.

There are two central problems with many research strategies widely used at present. First, cognitions reported after the event actually occurred may not correspond to those that arose in the individual while the interaction took place. However, the methodologies used by Ickes et al. (1986) and Fletcher and Fitness (1990) are dramatic improvements in that they access cognitive activity very close to when it actually occurs in the context of dyadic interactions.

A second methodological problem with most of these research strategies is that only consciously experienced and noticed cognitions can be reported. Unconscious mental activity and rapidly occurring cognitions are not amenable to self-report procedures. This is a major research limitation because, as we have suggested throughout this book, many important cognitions (e.g., in the PT, relationship script, and family constitution) exist outside of conscious awareness or at a very low level of awareness.

Future Methodological Directions

We believe that both approaches—assessing general cognitions about roles and relationships and assessing specific cognitions in the context of behavioral interactions—provide useful and complementary information. With respect to the latter methodological approach, future research might include combinations of already existing strategies. For example, couples and family members could be asked to discuss a commonly addressed issue in the family, one that has led to conflict in the past or one that requires some resolution, and could be interrupted at times during the course of the interaction to reveal privately their cognitions at that moment. These interactions could be videotaped to allow subjects to react to their cognitions and behaviors a short time later.

Using the same procedure, participants could be asked to reveal independently the rules (i.e., family constitution) that appear to govern the family interactions during the discussion. This would permit researchers to assess not only each individual's perceptions, but also the degree of consistency in perceptions of family rules and norms. We consider probing for cognitions during a family interaction and assessing perceptions of the interaction after it occurs, to be a promising methodological procedure.

EMERGING RESEARCH AREAS

The theoretical notions in the CBF model presented earlier in this volume require additional empirical verification. For example, with the family constitution construct, research is needed to explore the extent to which family members actually have the same understandings about the rules and procedures that are followed in their families. Other important questions include:

How do families differ in the content of their constitutions? How do family constitutions change over time? What types of constitutions are most adaptive? What family to family differences exist in how their family constitution rules are enforced?

Similarly, research could explore the types of relationship scripts that family members possess. How does gender-role identification relate to relationship scripts? How do relationship scripts develop from families of origin? How does dyadic satisfaction in romantic relationships and marriages relate to the similarity or compatibility of scripts? How are scripts modified over time? Are some types of scripts more adaptive than others, or are certain combinations of scripts most adaptive for couples? How do relationship scripts of families in various countries differ from those of their counterparts in the United States and Canada?

There are also numerous research questions related to cost–benefit (c/b) ratios. How do individuals compute their c/b ratios? How do individuals determine what constitutes an acceptable c/b ratio? Do acceptable c/b ratios change over time? How unacceptable does a c/b ratio need to be before the individual takes action to improve it? When a c/b ratio is unacceptable, what are the typical steps that individuals take to improve it? Are some of these efforts more helpful than others?

With respect to problem-solving strategies, what kinds of problem resolution strategies do family members typically use? Are consciously used strategies more effective than automatic ones that occur outside of conscious awareness? To what extent can children of varying ages provide input into the problem-solving process?

The family defense mechanism construct could be evaluated in several ways. What types of families use each kind of FDM? Do fathers, mothers, and children differ in the behavior prescribed to them by FDMs? Are some family defense mechanisms more destructive than others? When family members learn to use more direct and conscious strategies for resolving family conflict, does their overall level of functioning improve?

Many other issues important to the CBF model and, in general, to the application of cognitive-behavioral theory to family life need to be studied as well. Significant questions include among others: How do individuals draw upon and use their cognitions during family interactions, especially those that they are only vaguely or not at all aware of having? How can the interlocking cognitions individuals hold be understood and described in terms of systems theory and family homeostasis? How do changes naturally occur in individuals' cognitions and family systems over the short and long run?

Other kinds of basic, applied research goals include: determining the extent to which individuals are aware of the specific and general cognitions they hold regarding family roles and interactions; developing and evaluating means to make them more aware of their cognitions; and assessing how, if at all, with greater awareness, individuals' thoughts, feelings, and behaviors change. Further, much work is needed in terms of evaluating the usefulness of the CBF model in treatment and education. For example, outcome studies need to compare the CBFT approach with other approaches and no treatment controls. Work is needed to develop the most effective way to deliver CBFT interventions to individuals with certain characteristics who are part of certain types of family units.

IMPROVING RELATIONS BETWEEN AND AMONG FAMILY RESEARCHERS AND CLINICIANS

Kimble (1984) suggested that there are two separate and not easily reconcilable cultures in psychology—scientific and humanistic. Based on empirical findings, those identifying with the scientific culture, in contrast to those in the humanistic culture, were more likely to: (a) have scientific scholarly values, (b) be determinists, (c) use observation rather than intuition as basic sources of knowledge, (d) search for nomothetic rather than idiographic levels of generalizability, and (e) view the appropriate level of analysis as specific details rather than a holistic approach. Kimble's analysis suggests that the task of improving working relations among individuals interested in the family who come from these two cultures will be a formidable one.

Another issue has been noted by a number of family scholars: Researchers and clinicians often engage in their primary work activities without substantive input from each other (Stith, Rosen, Barasch, & Wilson, 1991; Williams, 1991). According to this perspective, many researchers conduct investigations based exclusively or primarily on the needs identified in the empirical literature. This often leads them to address questions not directly applicable to the needs of clinicians. Clinicians who seek to inform their practice and treatment approaches with input from empirical studies must, therefore, depend exclusively on clinical literature for substantive input. Although such work can be extremely helpful, it has limits related to the fact that clinical populations are being studied. To the extent that this schism exists, our understanding of and our ability to assist families, as a field, is likely to suffer. However, the possibility of synergy exists: Empirical research can be conducted that is useful to clinicians and clinical reports can consider issues in ways that add substantively to our knowledge of families.

An excellent example of an analysis that supports the presence of a schism between family researchers and clinicians was provided by Ganong and Coleman (1987) in the area of the effects of parental remarriage on children. In samples of empirical and clinical works, they found that researchers and clinicians differed substantively in the types of issues addressed, in data-collection procedures, and in interpretation of results/observations.

In the area of child adjustment in stepfamilies, researchers tend to address relationships, behaviors, and attitudes; usually administer on one occasion measures that they use to assess stepchildren from stepfather households; and generally conclude that living in a stepfamily has little effect on child adjustment. By contrast, clinicians tend to examine changes in individual and systemic functioning; assess multiple family members over an extended time period; and, because their samples include families experiencing difficulties, conclude that stepfamilies inherently have problems and difficulties. Ganong and Coleman (1987) recommended that clinicians more systematically evaluate the effectiveness of their interventions and provided a series of clinically relevant questions that researchers could fruitfully examine.

It is important to recognize that, ideally, there are quantitative rather than qualitative differences between researchers and clinicians. Talented researchers often either engage in applied work themselves or are sensitive to the observations of those who do. Likewise, skilled clinicians often maintain a scientific, hypothesis-testing approach to their intervention efforts and keep current by reading relevant research journals.

The CBF framework described in this book may help improve relations between researchers and clinicians in several ways. First, we believe that the framework's language and terms are sufficiently clear that communication should be facilitated between members of the two groups. Concepts such as the family constitution, relationship script, and cost–benefit analysis are relevant and accessible to investigators and clinicians alike.

Second, we believe that the CBF framework may help clinicians and researchers identify possibly maladaptive and irrational cognitions in themselves that contribute to the schism between the two groups. Persons (1989) identified several dysfunctional cognitions held by some cognitive therapists and discussed how these may negatively influence therapeutic work. Some examples of these include: "If the therapy fails, this means I'm an incompetent therapist"; "Failure is unacceptable"; and "If I terminate the treatment, this will mean to the patient that I think he's a hopeless case." The standards, expectations, and assumptions implied in these cognitions are likely to be dysfunctional.

Similarly, we believe that misunderstandings and dysfunctional beliefs may contribute to the lack of interaction between researchers and clinicians. Researchers may hold any or all of the following stereotypes of clinicians: They are only interested in pathology and exaggerate the extent of problems, they do not appreciate the precision necessary for scientific investigation, they do not appreciate the value of empirical findings in influencing therapeutic behavior, and they do not have much to offer researchers because of their lack of interest in conducting research. Whereas these stereotypes may characterize some clinicians, they are also inaccurate for many others. To the extent that researchers adhere to these stereotypes, they are likely to avoid interacting with clinicians.

Clinicians, on the other hand, may hold any or all of the following stereotypes of researchers: They are only interested in publishing basic research and do not care about applications of their work, they study minute details and miss the global perspective, they study such large numbers of individuals that they lose any sense of what any one person individually experiences, and they look down on clinicians because they do not advance science but rather apply it to their work with individuals. Again, whereas there may be some truth to these stereotypes for some researchers, there are many researchers who do appreciate clinical contributions. It may be helpful for both researchers and clinicians to examine the extent to which they maintain these stereotypes and to realize that they may benefit from modifying these beliefs.

In addition, researchers and clinicians may set unrealistic performance standards for those in the other camp. Some researchers may believe that clinicians should systematically evaluate the effectiveness of their interventions and should read most of the relevant journals. Some clinicians, on the other hand, may believe that researchers should study more global facets of family life, should regularly seek input from clinicians to assist in the process of conducting and interpreting empirical results, and should routinely report their findings in applied, rather than technical, journals. To the extent that individuals hold these possibly unrealistic expectations, they are likely to be disappointed with those in the other camp and discount the contributions that have been made.

CONCLUDING COMMENTS

Our journey in this book began as an attempt to further our understanding of families and to use this knowledge to develop ways to assist individuals in bettering their family relationships. We proposed a cognitive-behavioral model of families (CBF)—one that is an integration of family systems theory and cognitive-behavioral models—as a way to gain perspective on the intricacies of family life. The CBF model is certainly not the only useful way to understand families. Rather, we view it as a perspective that is complementary to other approaches (e.g., structural, functional, systems).

We believe that the CBF model can enrich many of the professional activities that family practitioners engage in, including assessment, psychotherapy, education, and research. We hope that readers share our enthusiasm and attempt to integrate pieces of this model into their work. We think that it is quite possible to consolidate the CBF model into those that most family professionals are currently using.

To further develop the CBF model, researchers and clinicians need to explore the viability of its tenets and the usefulness of its possible applications. A concerted effort on the part of scholars and practitioners is necessary to achieve these objectives. We encourage those interested to join us in these endeavors.

REFERENCES

Acitelli, L. (1988). When spouses talk to each other about their relationship. *Journal of Social and Personal Relationships, 5,* 185–199.

Ackerman, N. W. (1966). Family psychotherapy—Theory and practice. *American Journal of Psychotherapy, 20,* 405–414.

Adler, A. (1964a). *Social interest: A challenge to mankind.* New York: Capricorn Books.

Adler, A. (1964b). Typology of meeting life problems. In H. L. Ansbacher & R. R. Ansbacher (Eds.), *Superiority and social interest* (pp. 66–70). Evanston, IL: Northwestern University Press.

Aldous, J., & Dumon, W. (1990). Family policy in the 1980s: Controversy and consensus. *Journal of Marriage and the Family, 52,* 1136–1151.

American Heritage Dictionary, The (2nd College ed.). (1985). Boston: Houghton Mifflin.

American Psychological Association. (1992). Ethical principles of psychologists and code of conduct. *American Psychologist, 47,* 1597–1611.

Antonovsky, A., & Sourani, T. (1988). Family sense of coherence and family adaptation. *Journal of Marriage and the Family, 50,* 79–92.

Arcus, M. (1987). A framework for life-span family life education. *Family Relations, 36,* 5–10.

Arcus, M. (1990). The nature of family life education. In D. C. Cassidy (Ed.), *Family life education curriculum guidelines* (pp. 1–3). Minneapolis: National Council on Family Relations.

Armstrong, D. M. (Ed.). (1965). *Berkeley's philosophical writings.* New York: Macmillan.

Asch, S. E. (1956). Studies of independence and conformity: A minority of one against a unanimous majority. *Psychological Monographs, 70*(9, Whole No. 416).

Ayres, J. (1983). Strategies to maintain relationships: Their identification and perceived usage. *Communication Quarterly, 31,* 62–67.

Bahr, S. J., Chappell, C. B., & Leigh, G. K. (1983). Age at marriage, role enactment, role consensus, and marital satisfaction. *Journal of Marriage and the Family, 45,* 795–803.

Bandura, A. (1969). *Principles of behavior modification.* New York: Holt, Rinehart & Winston.

Barton, C., & Alexander, J. (1981). Functional family therapy. In A. Gurman & D. Kniskern (Eds.), *Handbook of family therapy* (pp. 403–443). New York: Brunner/Mazel.

Bateson, G., Jackson, D., Haley, J., & Weakland, J. (1956). Toward a theory of schizophrenia. *Behavioral Science, 1,* 251–264.

Baucom, D. H. (1987). Attributions in distressed relations: How can we explain them? In S. Duck & D. Perlman (Eds.), *Heterosexual relations, marriage and divorce* (pp. 177–206). London: Sage.

Baucom, D. H., & Epstein, N. (1990). *Cognitive-behavioral marital therapy*. New York: Brunner/Mazel.

Baucom, D. H., Epstein, N., Sayers, S., & Sher, T. (1989). The role of cognitions in marital relationships: Definitional, methodological, and conceptual issues. *Journal of Consulting and Clinical Psychology, 57*, 31–38.

Beavers, W. R., & Hampton, R. B. (1990). *Successful families: Assessment and intervention*. New York: Norton.

Beck, A. T. (1988). *Love is never enough*. New York: Harper & Row.

Beck, A. T., & Emery, G. (1985). *Anxiety disorders and phobias: A cognitive perspective*. New York: Basic.

Beck, A. T., Rush, A. J., Shaw, B. F., & Emery, G. (1979). *Cognitive therapy of depression*. New York: Guilford.

Becvar, D., & Becvar, R. (1988). *Family therapy*. Newton, MA: Allyn & Bacon.

Bell, J. (1962). Recent advances in family group therapy. *Journal of Child Psychology and Psychiatry, 3*, 1–15.

Belsky, J. (1984). The determinants of parenting: A process model. *Child Development, 55*, 83–96.

Bem, D. (1972). Self-perception theory. In L. Berkowitz (Ed.), *Advances in experimental social psychology* (Vol. 6, pp. 2–62). New York: Academic.

Berg, J., & Clark, M. (1986). Differences in social exchange between intimate and other relationships. In V. Derlega & B. A. Winstead (Eds.), *Friendship and social interaction* (pp. 101–128). New York: Springer-Verlag.

Beutler, I. F., Burr, W. R., Bahr, K. S., & Herrin, D. A. (1989). The family realm: Theoretical contributions for understanding its uniqueness. *Journal of Marriage and the Family, 51*, 805–816.

Bourne, L. E. (1992). Cognitive psychology: A brief overview. *Psychological Science Agenda, 5*(5), 20.

Bowen, M. (1961). Family psychotherapy. *American Journal of Orthopsychiatry, 31*, 40–60.

Bowlby, J. (1988). *A secure base: Parent–child attachment and healthy human development*. New York: Basic.

Bradbury, T. N. (1990). *Cognition, emotion, and interaction in distressed and nondistressed couples: Toward an integrative model*. Unpublished manuscript, University of California, Los Angeles.

Bradbury, T. N., & Fincham, F. D. (1988, November). *The impact of attributions in marriage: Attributions and behavior exchange in marital interaction*. Paper presented at the 22nd Annual Convention of the Association for the Advancement of Behavior Therapy, New York.

Bradbury, T. N., & Fincham, F. D. (1990). Attributions in marriage: Review and critique. *Psychological Bulletin, 107*, 3–33.

Braswell, L., & Kendall, P. C. (1988). Cognitive-behavioral methods with children. In K. S. Dobson (Ed.), *Handbook of cognitive-behavioral therapies* (pp. 167–213). New York: Guilford.

Brehm, S., & Cohen, A. R. (1962). *Explorations in cognitive dissonance*. New York: Wiley.

Brock, G. W. (1993). Ethical guidelines for the practice of family life education. *Family Relations, 42*, 124–127.

Buehler, C., Betz, P., Ryan, C. M., Legg, B. H., & Trotter, B. B. (1992). Description and evaluation of the Orientation for Divorcing Parents: Implications for postdivorce prevention programs. *Family Relations, 41*, 154–162.

Burr, W. R. (1971). An expansion and test of a role theory of marital satisfaction. *Journal of Marriage and the Family, 33*, 368–372.

Buss, D. (1985). Human mate selection. *American Scientist, 73*, 47–51.

Carter, E., & McGoldrick, M. (Eds.). (1989). *The family life cycle: A framework for family therapy* (2nd ed.). Needham Heights, MA: Allyn & Bacon.

Chess, S., & Thomas, A. (1987). *Know your child*. New York: Basic.

Constantine, L. (1986). *Family paradigms: The practice of theory in family therapy*. New York: Guilford.

Cutrona, C., & Russell, D. (1990). Type of social support and specific stress: Toward a theory of optimal matching. In B. R. Sarason, I. Sarason, & G. Pierce (Eds.), *Social support: An interactional view* (pp. 319–366). New York: Wiley.

Dattillo, F. M., & Padesky, C. A. (1990). *Cognitive therapy with couples*. Sarasota, FL: Professional Resource Exchange.

Deal, J., Halverson, C., & Wampler, K. (1989). Parental agreement of child-rearing orientations: Relations to parental, marital, family, and child characteristics. *Child Development, 60*, 1025–1034.

DeRubeis, R. J., & Beck, A. T. (1988). Cognitive therapy. In K. S. Dobson (Ed.), *Handbook of cognitive-behavioral therapies* (pp. 273–306). New York: Guilford.

deTurck, H. A., & Miller, G. A. (1986). The effects of husbands' and wives' social cognition on their marital adjustment, conjugal power, and self-esteem. *Journal of Marriage and the Family, 48*, 715–724.

Dindia, K., & Baxter, L. (1987). Maintenance and repair strategies in marital relationships. *Journal of Social and Personal Relationships, 4*, 143–158.

Dobson, K. S., & Block, L. (1988). Historical and philosophical bases of the cognitive-behavioral therapies. In K. S. Dobson (Ed.), *Handbook of cognitive-behavioral therapies* (pp. 3–38). New York: Guilford.

Doherty, W. J. (1981a). Cognitive processes in intimate conflict: 1. Extending attribution theory. *American Journal of Family Therapy, 9*, 3–13.

Doherty, W. J. (1981b). Cognitive processes in intimate conflict: 2. Efficacy and learned helplessness. *American Journal of Family Therapy, 9*, 35–44.

Dryden, W., & Ellis, A. (1988). Rational-emotive therapy. In K. S. Dobson (Ed.), *Handbook of cognitive-behavioral therapies* (pp. 214–272). New York: Guilford.

Duck, S. (1988). *Relating to others*. Chicago: Dorsey.

Duvall, E. (1977). *Marriage and family development* (5th ed.). New York: Lippincott.

D'Zurilla, T. J. (1988). Problem-solving therapies. In K. S. Dobson (Ed.), *Handbook of cognitive-behavioral therapies* (pp. 85–135). New York: Guilford.

Ebbinghaus, H. (1910). *Abriss der Psychologie* [Summary of psychology]. Leipzig: Veit.

Egan, G. (1986). *The skilled helper: A systematic approach to effective helping* (3rd ed.). Monterey, CA: Brooks/Cole.

Eidelson, R. J., & Epstein, N. (1982). Cognitions and relationship maladjustment: Development of a measure of dysfunctional relationship beliefs. *Journal of Consulting and Clinical Psychology, 50*, 715–720.

Ellis, A. (1984). The essence of RET-1984. *Journal of Rational-Emotive Therapy, 2*, 19–25.

Ellis, A. (1986). Rational-emotive therapy. In I. Kutash & A. Wolf (Eds.), *Psychotherapist's casebook* (pp. 277–287). San Francisco: Jossey-Bass

Ellis, A. (1989). Rational-emotive therapy. In R. J. Corsini (Ed.), *Current psychotherapies* (4th ed., pp. 197–238). Itasca, IL: Peacock.

Epstein, N. B., Baldwin, L. M., & Bishop, D. S. (1982). *McMaster Clinical Rating Scale*. Unpublished manuscript, Brown/Butler Family Research Program, Providence, RI.

Epstein, N. B., Baldwin, L. M., & Bishop, D. S. (1983). The McMaster Family Assessment Device. *Journal of Marriage and Family Therapy, 9*, 171–180.

Epstein, N. B., Bishop, D. S., & Baldwin, L. M. (1982). McMaster model of family functioning: A view of the normal family. In F. Walsh (Ed.), *Normal family process* (pp. 115–141). New York: Guilford.

Epstein, N. B., & Eidelson, R. (1981). Unrealistic beliefs of clinical couples: Their relationship to expectations, goals, and satisfaction. *American Journal of Family Therapy, 9*, 13–22.

Epstein, N. B., Schlesinger, S., & Dryden, W. (1988). *Cognitive-behavioral therapy with families*. New York: Brunner/Mazel.

Festinger, L. (1957). *A theory of cognitive dissonance*. Palo Alto, CA: Stanford University Press.

Fichten, C. S. (1984). See it from my point of view: Videotape and attributions in happy and distressed couples. *Journal of Social and Clinical Psychology, 2*, 125–142.

Fincham, F. D. (1985). Attribution processes in distressed and nondistressed couples: 2. Responsibility for marital problems. *Journal of Abnormal Psychology, 94*, 183–190.

Fincham, F. D., Beach, S., & Nelson, G. (1987). Attribution processes in distressed and nondistressed couples: 3. Causal and responsibility attributions for spouse behavior. *Cognitive Therapy and Research, 11*, 71–86.

Fincham, F. D., & Bradbury, T. (1987). Cognitive processes and conflict in close relationships: An attribution-efficacy model. *Journal of Personality and Social Psychology, 53*, 1106–1118.

Fincham, F. D., & Bradbury, T. N. (1988). The impact of attributions in marriage: An experimental analysis. *Journal of Social and Clinical Psychology, 7*, 147–162.

Fincham, F. D., Bradbury, T., & Beach, S. (1990). To arrive where we began: A reappraisal of cognition in marriage and marital therapy. *Journal of Family Psychology, 4*, 167–184.

Fine, M. A. (1992). Families in the United States: Current status and future prospects. *Family Relations, 41*, 430–435.

Fine, M. A., & Kurdek, L. A. (1992). *Parenting Role Perceptions Inventory*. Unpublished instrument available from the first author.

Fish, M., Belsky, J., & Youngblade, L. (1991). Developmental antecedents and measurement of intergenerational boundary violation in a nonclinic sample. *Journal of Family Psychology, 4*, 278–297.

Fletcher, G. J. O., & Fitness, J. (1990). Occurrent social cognition in close relationship interaction: The role of proximal and distal variables. *Journal of Personality and Social Psychology, 59*, 464–474.

Fletcher, G. J. O., & Kininmonth, L. (1991). Interaction in close relationships and social cognition. In G. J. O. Fletcher & F. D. Fincham (Eds.), *Cognition in close relationships* (pp. 235–255). Hillsdale, NJ: Lawrence Erlbaum Associates.

Foa, U. G., & Foa, E. G. (1974). *Societal structures of the mind*. Springfield, IL: Thomas.

Forehand, R. L., & McMahon, R. J. (1981). *Helping the noncompliant child: A clinician's guide to parent training*. New York: Guilford.

Frank, J. D., & Frank, J. B. (1990). *Persuasion and healing: A comparative study of psychotherapy* (3rd ed.). Baltimore: Johns Hopkins University Press.

Gaelick, L., Bodenhausen, G. V., & Wyer, R. S. (1985). Emotional communication in close relationships. *Journal of Personality and Social Psychology, 49*, 1246–1265.

Ganong, L. G., & Coleman, M. (1987). Effects of parental remarriage on children: An updated comparison of theories, methods, and findings from clinical and empirical research. In K. Pasley & M. Ihinger-Tallman (Eds.), *Remarriage and stepparenting: Current research and theory* (pp. 94–140). New York: Guilford.

Gilbert, L. A., & Hanson, G. R. (1983). Perceptions of parental role responsibilities among working people: Development of a comprehensive measure. *Journal of Marriage and the Family, 45*, 203–212.

Glick, P. C. (1984). Marriage, divorce, and living arrangements: Prospective changes. *Journal of Family Issues, 5*, 7–26.

Goldenberg, I., & Goldenberg, H. (1991). *Family therapy* (3rd ed.). Pacific Grove, CA: Brooks/Cole.

Gottlieb, B., & Pancer, S. M. (1987). Social networks and the transition to parenthood. In G. Michaels & W. Goldberg (Eds.), *The transition to parenthood* (pp. 235–269). New York: Cambridge University Press.

Gottman, J., & Levenson, R. (1988). The social psychophysiology of marriage. In P. Noller & M. A. Fitzpatrick (Eds.), *Perspectives on marital interaction* (pp. 182–200). Philadelphia: Multilingual Matters Ltd.

Gottman, J., Notarius, C., Markman, H., Bank, S., Yoppi, B., & Rubin, M. E. (1976). Behavior exchange theory and marital decision making. *Journal of Personality and Social Psychology, 34*, 14–23.

Grotevant, H. D., & Carlson, C. I. (1989). *Family assessment: A guide to methods and measures.* New York: Guilford.

Hahlweg, K., Revenstorf, D., & Schindler, L. (1983). Treatment of marital distress: Comparing formats and modalities. *Advances in Behavior Research and Therapy, 4,* 411–435.

Haley, J. (1973). *Uncommon therapy: The psychiatric techniques of Milton H. Erikson.* New York: Norton.

Haller, E., Child, D., & Walberg, A. (1988). Can comprehension be taught: A quantitative synthesis of "metacognitive" studies. *Educational Researcher, 19,* 5–8.

Hollon, S. D., & Beck, A. T. (1979). Cognitive therapy of depression. In P. Kendall & S. Hollon (Eds.), *Cognitive-behavioral interventions: Theory, research, and procedures* (pp. 153–203). New York: Academic.

Hollon, S. D., & Kendall, P. C. (1980). Cognitive self-statements in depression: Development of an Automatic Thoughts Questionnaire. *Cognitive Therapy and Research, 4,* 383–395.

Holtzworth-Munroe, A., & Jacobson, N. S. (1985). Causal attributions of married couples: When do they search for causes? What do they conclude when they do? *Journal of Personality and Social Psychology, 48,* 1398–1412.

Homans, G. (1961). *Social behavior: Its elementary forms.* London: Routledge & Kegan Paul.

Honeycutt, J. (1986). A model of marital functioning based on an attraction paradigm and social-penetration dimensions. *Journal of Marriage and the Family, 48,* 651–667.

Huntley, D. K., & Konetsky, C. D. (1992). Healthy families with adolescents. *Topics in Family Psychology and Counseling, 1,* 62–71.

Ickes, W., Robertson, E., Tooke, W., & Teng, G. (1986). Naturalistic social cognition: Methodology, assessment, and validation. *Journal of Personality and Social Psychology, 51,* 66–82.

Ivey, A. E., & Authier, G. (1978). *Microcounseling.* Springfield, IL: Thomas.

Ivey, A. E., & Simek-Downing, L. (1980). *Counseling and psychotherapy: Skills, theories, and practice.* Englewood Cliffs, NJ: Prentice-Hall.

Jacobson, N. (1984). A component analysis of behavioral marital therapy: The relative effectiveness of behavior exchange and communication/problem-solving training. *Journal of Consulting and Clinical Psychology, 52,* 295–305.

Jacobson, N. S., & Gurman, A. S. (1986). *Clinical handbook of marital therapy.* New York: Guilford.

Janis, I. (1972). *Victims of groupthink.* Boston: Houghton Mifflin.

Jones, E. (1990). *Interpersonal perception.* New York: Freeman.

Jones, E. E., & Nisbett, R. E. (1971). *The actor and the observer: Divergent perceptions of the causes of behavior.* Morristown, NJ: General Learning Press.

Kanfer, F. H. (1980). Self-management methods. In F. H. Kanfer & A. P. Goldstein (Eds.), *Helping people change* (pp. 334–389). New York: Pergamon.

Kantor, D., & Lehr, W. (1975). *Inside the family: Toward a theory of family process.* San Francisco: Jossey-Bass.

Kaplan, L., & Hennon, C. B. (1992). Remarriage education: The personal reflections program. *Family Relations, 41,* 127–134.

Kelly, G. A. (1955). *The psychology of personal constructs* (Vols. 1–2). New York: Norton.

Kendall, P. C., & Bemis, K. M. (1983). Thought and action in psychotherapy: The cognitive-behavioral approaches. In M. Hersen, A. E. Kazdin, & A. S. Bellack (Eds.), *The clinical psychology handbook* (pp. 565–592). New York: Pergamon.

Kimble, G. A. (1984). Psychology's two cultures. *American Psychologist, 39,* 833–839.

Kleinke, C. (1986). *Meeting and understanding people.* New York: Freeman.

Knaub, P. K., & Hanna, S. L. (1984). Children of remarriage: Perceptions of family strengths. *Journal of Divorce, 7,* 73–90.

Kuiper, N., & MacDonald, M. (1983). Reason, emotion, and cognitive therapy. *Clinical Psychology Review, 3,* 297–316.

Kurdek, L. A. (1992). Assumptions versus standards: The validity of two relationship cognitions in heterosexual and homosexual couples. *Journal of Family Psychology, 6,* 22–35.

Kurdek, L. A., & Berg, B. (1987). Children's Beliefs About Parental Divorce Scale: Psychometric characteristics and concurrent validity. *Journal of Consulting and Clinical Psychology, 55,* 712–718.

Kurdek, L. A., & Fine, M. A. (1991). Cognitive correlates of satisfaction for mothers and step-fathers in stepfather families. *Journal of Marriage and the Family, 53,* 565–572.

Lachman, R., Lachman, J. L., & Butterfield, E. C. (1979). *Cognitive psychology and information processing.* Hillsdale, NJ: Lawrence Erlbaum Associates.

Lakoff, R. (1975). *Language and woman's place.* New York: Harper Colophon.

Larson, J. H. (1988). The marriage quiz: College students' beliefs in selected myths about marriage. *Family Relations, 37,* 3–11.

Lazarus, R. S., & Alfert, E. (1964). Short-circuiting of threat by experimentally altering cognitive appraisal. *Journal of Abnormal and Social Psychology, 69,* 195–205.

Lazarus, R. S., & Folkman, C. (1984). *Stress, appraisal and coping.* New York: Springer.

Lazarus, R. S., Opton, E. M., Jr., Nomikos, M. S., & Rankin, N. O. (1965). The principle of short-circuitry of threat: Further evidence. *Journal of Personality, 33,* 622–635.

Leigh, G. K., Loewen, I. R., & Lester, M. E. (1986). Caveat emptor: Values and ethics in family life education and enrichment. *Family Relations, 35,* 573–580.

Leman, K. (1991). *Were you born for each other?* New York: Delacorte.

Leslie, L. A., & Epstein, N. (1988). Cognitive-behavioral treatment of remarried families. In N. Epstein, S. Schlesinger, & W. Dryden (Eds.), *Cognitive-behavioral therapy with families* (pp. 151–182). New York: Brunner/Mazel.

Levine, M. (1974). Some postulates of community psychology practice. In F. Kaplan & S. Sarason (Eds.), *The psychoeducational clinic papers and research studies* (Vol. 4, pp. 209–224). Boston: Massachusetts Department of Mental Health Monographs.

Lewin, K. (1951). *Field theory in social science.* Chicago: University of Chicago Press.

Lewis, J. (1979). *How's your family?* New York: Brunner/Mazel.

Lewis, M., & Michalson, L. (1983). From emotional state to emotional expression: Emotional development from a person-environment interaction perspective. In D. Magnusson & V. L. Allen (Eds.), *Human development: An interactional perspective* (pp. 261–275). New York: Academic.

Locke, J. (1974). *An essay concerning human understanding* (A. D. Wooley, Ed.). New York: New American Library. (Original work published 1706)

MacDonald, A. P., & Games, R. G. (1972). Ellis' irrational values. *Rational Living, 7,* 25–28.

Mace, D. (1983). *Prevention in family services: Approaches to family wellness.* Beverly Hills, CA: Sage.

Madden, M. E., & Janoff-Bulman, R. (1981). Blame, control, and marital satisfaction: Wives' attributions for conflict in marriage. *Journal of Marriage and the Family, 43,* 663–674.

Marciano, T. D., & Sussman, M. B. (1991). Wider families: An overview. *Marriage and Family Review, 17,* 1–8.

Markman, H. J., Floyd, F., Stanley, S. M., & Storaasli, R. (1988). The prevention of marital distress: A longitudinal investigation. *Journal of Consulting and Clinical Psychology, 56,* 210–217.

Maslow, A. H. (1954). *Motivation and personality.* New York: Harper & Row.

Maslow, A. H. (1970). *Motivation and personality* (2nd ed.). New York: Harper & Row.

Masters, W., & Johnson, V. (1966). *Human sexual response.* Boston: Little, Brown.

McCubbin, M. A., McCubbin, H. I., & Thompson, A. I. (1987). FHI: Family Hardiness Index. In H. I. McCubbin & A. I. Thompson (Eds.), *Family assessment inventories for research and practice* (pp. 125–130). Madison: University of Wisconsin-Madison, Family Stress Coping & Health Project.

Meichenbaum, D. (1977). *Cognitive-behavior modification: An integrative approach.* New York: Plenum.

Meichenbaum, D. (1985). *Stress innoculation training.* New York: Pergamon.

Milgram, S. (1963). Behavioral study of obedience. *Journal of Abnormal and Social Psychology, 67,* 371–378.

Mirvis, P. H., & Marks, M. L. (1992). *Managing the merger: Making it work.* Englewood Cliffs, NJ: Prentice-Hall.

Moore, K. A. (1989). *Facts at a glance 1989.* Washington, DC: Child Trends.

Moos, R. H. (1990). Conceptual and empirical approaches to developing family-based assessment procedures: Resolving the case of the Family Environment Scale. *Family Process, 29,* 199–208.

Moos, R. H., & Moos, B. (1986). *Family Environment Scale manual* (2nd ed.). Palo Alto, CA: Consulting Psychologists Press.

Murdock, G. (1949). *Social structure.* New York: Macmillan.

Murstein, B. (1976). *Who will marry whom?* New York: Springer.

Nelson, G. (1984). The relationship between dimensions of classroom and family environments and the self-concept, satisfaction, and achievement of grade 7 and 8 students. *Journal of Community Psychology, 12,* 276–287.

Nelson-Jones, R. (1990). *Human relationships: A skills approach.* Pacific Grove, CA: Brooks/Cole.

Nichols, M. (1984). *Family therapy.* New York: Gardner Press.

Nisbett, R. E., & Ross, L. (1980). *Human interference: Strategies and shortcomings of social judgement.* Englewood Cliffs, NJ: Prentice-Hall.

Norman, W. H., Miller, I. W., & Dow, M. G. (1988). Characteristics of depressed patients with elevated levels of dysfunctional cognitions. *Cognitive Therapy and Research, 12,* 39–52.

Norton, A., & Moorman, J. (1987). Current trends in marriage and divorce among American women. *Journal of Marriage and the Family, 49,* 3–14.

Nye, F. I., Bahr, H., Bahr, S., Carlson, J., Gecas, V., McLaughlin, S., & Slocum, W. (1976). *Role structure and analysis of the family.* Beverly Hills, CA: Sage.

Olson, D. H. (1991, November). *Three-dimensional (3-D) circumplex model: Theoretical and methodological advances.* Paper presented at the Theory Construction and Research Methodology Workshop at the annual convention of the National Council on Family Relations, Denver.

Olson, D. H., & Killorin, E. (1985). *Clinical rating scale for the circumplex model of marital and family systems.* St. Paul: University of Minnesota, Department of Family Social Science.

Olson, D. H., McCubbin, H. I., Barnes, H., Larsen, A., Muxen, M., & Wilson, M. (1982). *Family inventories: Inventories used in a national survey of families across the family life cycle.* St. Paul: University of Minnesota, Department of Family Social Science.

Olson, D. H., Portner, J., & Lavee, Y. (1985). *FACES–III manual.* St. Paul: University of Minnesota, Department of Family Social Science.

Papernow, P. (1984). The stepfamily cycle: An experiential model of stepfamily development. *Family Relations, 33,* 355–363.

Patterson, G. R. (1982). *A social learning approach: Vol. 3. Coercive family process.* Eugene, OR: Castalia.

Patterson, G. R., Ray, R. S., Shaw, D. A., & Cobb, J. A. (1969). *Manual for coding family interactions.* New York: Microfiche.

Persons, J. B. (1989). *Cognitive therapy in practice: A case formulation approach.* New York: Norton.

Peters, T. J. (1982). *In search of excellence: Lessons from America's best run companies.* New York: Harper & Row.

Peterson, C., Semmel, A., von Baeyer, C., Abramson, L. Y., Metalsky, G. I., & Seligman, M. E. P. (1982). The Attributional Style Questionnaire. *Cognitive Theory and Research, 6,* 287–299.

Piaget, J. (1965). *Judgment and reasoning in the child.* London: Routledge & Kegan Paul.

Piaget, J. (1972). Intellectual evolution from adolescence to adulthood. *Human Development, 15,* 1–12.

Pino, C. J., Simons, N., & Slawinowski, M. J. (1984). The Children's Family Environment Scale. *Family Therapy, 9,* 85–86.

Pretzer, J., Epstein, N., & Fleming, B. (1987). The role of cognitive appraisal in self-reports of marital communication. *Behavior Therapy, 18,* 51–69.

Rayner, E. (1986). *Human development.* London: Allen & Unwin.

Reid, J. B. (Ed.). (1978). *A social learning approach to family intervention: Vol. 2. Observation in home settings.* Eugene, OR: Castalia.

Reiss, D. (1981). *The family's construction of reality.* Cambridge, MA: Harvard University Press.

Renick, M. J., Blumberg, S. L., & Markman, H. J. (1992). The Prevention and Relationship Enhancement Program (PREP): An empirically based preventive intervention program for couples. *Family Relations, 41,* 141–147.

Rickard, K. M., Graziano, W., & Forehand, R. (1984). Parental expectations and childhood deviance in clinic-referred and non-clinic children. *Journal of Clinical Child Psychology, 13,* 179–186.

Riskin, J. (1982). Research on "nonlabeled" families: A longitudinal study. In F. Walsh (Ed.), *Normal family processes* (pp. 67–93). New York: Guilford.

Robin, A., & Fox, M. (1979). *Parent–Adolescent Interaction Coding System: Training and reference manual for coders.* Unpublished manual.

Robin, A. L., Kent, R., O'Leary, K. D., Foster, S., & Prinz, R. (1977). An approach to teaching parents and adolescents problem-solving communication skills: A preliminary report. *Behavior Therapy, 8,* 639–643.

Robin, A. L., & Weiss, J. (1980). Criterion-related validity of behavioral and self-report measures of problem-solving communication skills in distressed and non-distressed parent–adolescent dyads. *Behavioral Assessment, 2,* 339–352.

Roehling, P. V., & Robin, A. L. (1986). Development and validation of the Family Beliefs Inventory: A measure of unrealistic beliefs among parents and adolescents. *Journal of Consulting and Clinical Psychology, 54,* 693–697.

Rogers, C. R. (1970). *On becoming a person: A therapist's view of psychotherapy.* Boston: Houghton Mifflin.

Roosa, M. W., & Beals, J. (1990). Measurement issues in family assessment: The case of the Family Environment Scale. *Family Process, 29,* 191–198.

Rosenthal, R., & Jacobson, L. (1966). Teacher's expectations: Determinants of pupils' IQ gains. *Psychological Reports, 19,* 115–118.

Rusbult, C. E. (1983). A longitudinal test of the investment model: The development (and deterioration) of satisfaction and commitment in heterosexual involvements. *Journal of Personality and Social Psychology, 45,* 101–117.

Rusbult, C. E. (1987). Responses to dissatisfaction in close relationships: The exit-voice-loyalty-neglect model. In D. Perlman & S. Duck (Eds.), *Intimate relationships: Development, dynamics, and deterioration* (pp. 209–237). Beverly Hills, CA: Sage.

Rush, A. J., Beck, A. T., Kovacs, M., & Hollon, S. D. (1977). Comparative efficacy of cognitive therapy and pharmacotherapy in the treatment of depressed outpatients. *Cognitive Therapy and Research, 1,* 17–37.

Sabatelli, R. M. (1984). The marital comparison level index: A measure for assessing outcomes relative to expectations. *Journal of Marriage and the Family, 46,* 651–662.

Sandy, W. (1990). *Forging the productive partnership.* New York: McGraw-Hill.

Sarason, S. (1972). *The creation of settings and the future societies.* San Francisco: Jossey-Bass.

Schwebel, A. I. (1992). The family constitution. *Topics in Family Psychology and Counseling, 1*(1), 27–38.

Schwebel, A. I. (1993). Family defense mechanisms (FDMs): The concept and its utility to family scientists, practitioners and educators. *The Family Journal: Counseling and Therapy for Couples and Families, 1,* 31–41.

Schwebel, A. I., Barocas, H. A., Reichman, W., & Schwebel, M. (1990). *Personal adjustment and growth: A life-span approach* (2nd ed.). Dubuque, IA: Brown.

Schwebel, A. I., & Fine, M. A. (1992). Cognitive-behavioral family therapy. *Journal of Family Psychotherapy, 3,* 73–91.

Schwebel, A. I., Fine, M. A., & Moreland, J. R. (1988). Clinical work with divorced and widowed fathers: The adjusting family model. In P. Bronstein & C. P. Cowan (Eds.), *Fatherhood today: Men's changing role in the family* (pp. 299–319). New York: Wiley.

Schwebel, A. I., Fine, M. A., & Renner, M. A. (1991). An empirical investigation of perceptions of the stepparent role. *Journal of Family Issues, 12,* 43–57.

Schwebel, A. I., Schwebel, B., Schwebel, C., Schwebel, M., & Schwebel, R. (1989). *A guide to a happier family: Overcoming the anger, frustration, and boredom that destroy family life.* Los Angeles: Tarcher/St. Martin's Press.

Schwebel, M., Maher, C., & Fagley, N. (1990). The social role in promoting cognitive growth over the life span. In M. Schwebel, C. Maher, & N. Fagley (Eds.), *Promoting cognitive growth over the life span* (pp. 1–20). Hillsdale, NJ: Lawrence Erlbaum Associates.

Select Committee on Children, Youth, and Families (1987). *Divorce: The impact on children and families.* Washington, DC: U.S. Government Printing Office.

Seligman, M. E. P., Abramson, L. Y., Semmel, A., & von Baeyer, C. (1979). Depressive attributional style. *Journal of Abnormal Psychology, 88,* 242–247.

Selvini Palazzoli, M., Boscolo, L., Cecchin, G., & Prata, G. (1978). *Paradox and counterparadox.* New York: Aronson.

Small, S. A. (1990). Some issues regarding the evaluation of family life education programs. *Family Relations, 39,* 132–135.

Spivack, G., Platt, J., & Shure, M. (1976). *The problem-solving approach to adjustment.* San Francisco: Jossey-Bass.

Spivack, G., & Shure, M. (1974). *Social adjustment of young children.* San Francisco: Jossey-Bass.

Stith, S. M., Rosen, K. H., Barasch, S. G., & Wilson, S. M. (1991). Clinical research as a training opportunity: Bridging the gap between theory and practice. *Journal of Marital and Family Therapy, 17,* 349–353.

Teichman, Y. (1984). Cognitive family therapy. *British Journal of Cognitive Psychotherapy, 2,* 1–10.

Thibaut, J., & Kelley, H. H. (1959). *The social psychology of groups.* New York: Wiley.

Thomas, J., & Arcus, M. (1992). Family life education: An analysis of the concept. *Family Relations, 41,* 3–8.

Thompson, J. S., & Snyder, D. K. (1986). Attributional theory in intimate relationships: A methodological review. *Journal of Family Therapy, 14*(2), 123–138.

Thompson, L., & Walker, A. J. (1989). Women and men in marriage, work, and parenthood. *Journal of Marriage and the Family, 51,* 845–872.

Touliatos, J., Perlmutter, B. F., & Straus, M. A. (Eds.). (1990). *Handbook of family measurement techniques.* Newbury Park, CA: Sage.

Vaillant, G. (1986). *Empirical studies of ego mechanisms of defense.* Washington, DC: American Psychiatric Association.

Vess, J., Moreland, J., & Schwebel, A. (1985). Understanding family role allocation following a death: A theoretical framework. *Omega, 16,* 115–128.

Visher, E., & Visher, J. (1988). *Old loyalties, new ties: Therapeutic strategies with stepfamilies.* New York: Brunner/Mazel.

Von Bertalanffy, L. (1968). *General systems theory.* New York: Braziller.

Vygotsky, L. S. (1978). *Mind in society: The development of higher psychological process.* Cambridge, MA: Harvard University Press.

Watzlawick, P., Beavin, J. H., & Jackson, D. D. (1967). *Pragmatics of human communication.* New York: Norton.

Watzlawick, P., Weakland, J., & Fisch, R. (1974). *Change: Principles of problem formation and problem resolution.* New York: Norton.

Weiner, N. (1954). *The human use of human beings: Cybernetics and society.* New York: Doubleday.

Weiss, J. (1990). Unconscious mental functioning. *Scientific American, 262,* 103–109.

Weissman, A. N. (1980, April). *Assessing depressogenic attitudes: A validation study.* Paper presented at the 51st annual meeting of the Eastern Psychological Association, Hartford, CT.

Wenar, C. (1990). *Psychopathology from infancy through adolescence* (2nd ed.). New York: McGraw-Hill.

Whitaker, C. A., & Keith, D. V. (1981). Symbolic-experiential family therapy. In A. S. Gurman & D. P. Kniskern (Eds.), *Handbook of family therapy* (Vol. 1, pp. 187–225). New York: Brunner/Mazel.

Whiteside, M. (1983). Families of remarriage: The weaving of many life-cycle threads. In H. A. Liddle (Ed.), *The family life cycle: Implications for therapy* (pp. 100–119). Rockville, MD: Aspen Corp.

Williams, L. M. (1991). A blueprint for increasing the relevance of family therapy research. *Journal of Marital and Family Therapy, 17,* 355–362.

Wood, L. F., & Jacobson, N. S. (1985). Marital distress. In D. H. Barlow (Ed.), *Clinical handbook of psychological disorders* (pp. 344–416). New York: Guilford.

Zimbardo, P. G. (1975). On transforming experimental research into advocacy for social change. In M. Deutsch & H. Hornstein (Eds.), *Applying social psychology: Implications for research, practice, and training* (pp. 33–66). Hillsdale, NJ: Lawrence Erlbaum Associates.

AUTHOR INDEX

SUBJECT INDEX